Negative microfilm
received from university   67-2249

HEAD, John Morris, 1935-
A TIME TO REND: THE MEMBERS OF THE
CONTINENTAL CONGRESS AND THE DE-
CISION FOR AMERICAN INDEPENDENCE,
1774-1776.

Brown University, Ph.D., 1966
History, general

University Microfilms, Inc., Ann Arbor, Michigan

A TIME TO REND

The Members of the Continental Congress and

the Decision for American Independence, 1774-1776

By

John Morris Head

A.B., Baylor University, 1957

Thesis

submitted in partial fulfillment of the requirements for the
Degree of Doctor of Philosophy in the Department of History at Brown
University

June, 1966

This thesis by John Morris Head is
accepted in its present form by the
Department of History as satisfying
the thesis requirement for the Degree
of Doctor of Philosophy.

x

Date: *8/5/65* *Forrest McDonald*

Recommended to the Graduate Council

Date: *Aug 27/65* *Jens B. Rys*

Date: *Sept. 14, 1965.* *William A. McLaughlin*

Approved by the Graduate Council

Date: **JUN 1 1966** *R. B. Lindsay*

TABLE OF CONTENTS

"To every thing there is a season,
And a time for every purpose under heaven:
A time to be born,
And a time to die;
A time to kill,
And a time to heal;
A time to laugh,
And a time to mourn;
A time to rend ...."

Ecclesiastes 3: 1-7

I

INTRODUCTION

A generation after the Revolution, old disputes and differences about the decision for American independence lay hidden beneath a cloak of patriotic unanimity. The young United States grew stronger each year, and the first Patriots, with good reason, looked with pride upon the results of their labors to free America from Great Britain. Public acclaim and time had done much to heal the old wounds of disagreement, and new problems kept the old leaders occupied with the present. But some of the Patriots had neither the inclination nor the desire to let all the popular stories about their old doings stand for fact. A few years after the nineteenth century began, two of the most important leaders of the Revolution discussed their part in the rebellion, and dissensions going back thirty years popped into the open. For an instant the benevolent cloak of unanimity slipped from the shoulders of the old guard, and Americans got a brief but informative glimpse of what had happened among the men who led the Revolution.

In 1805 John Adams of Massachusetts was in his seventieth year
and determined to complete his autobiography.[1] Adams was still strong
and alert (he would live twenty-one more years), and as he wrote of
his part in the struggle for American independence, he occasionally
referred to the printed journals of the Continental Congress and to
notes which he had taken some thirty years before. Experience and
accomplishment enabled Adams to trust his memory where a lesser man
might have proceeded more cautiously. After all, he had been a
leading advocate of independence in Massachusetts and in the Continental
Congress. His public career, of course, had not ended in 1776: he
had written important sections of the Massachusetts Constitution, taken
part in the treaty negotiations at the end of the war, and served as
an ambassador under the Congress of the Confederation. His long career
had culminated in two terms as Vice-President and one as President of
the United States. Few men matched Adams in political experience; fewer
still could have questioned his knowledge of what had taken place in
the colonies and in the Continental Congress during the early years of
the Revolution.

Now in retirement, Adams thought it time to take a close look at independence. He felt intensely about that part of American history which he had helped to create. For that reason, he felt no obligation to qualify his views or to assume a false hesitancy about what he wrote, and if he was didactic concerning major episodes and events and in cataloguing men's blunders, stupidity, and ineptitude, it was because he intended to be.

As Adams remembered it, when England moved to take away the rights and liberties of colonial subjects by force, Americans resisted and eventually declared their independence in order to insure their freedom. Adams said that the British Parliament's repeated efforts to tax the colonies during the 1760's and 1770's betrayed its inveterate design to enslave the colonies. Parliament sought to assert power over colonials where it had no right to do so, then showed its true intent by bellicose action against Massachusetts. Adams wrote that by May of 1775 colonials could expect nothing from England save war and enslavement. Colonial petitions for redress of grievances had failed to halt Parliament's infringement of liberty; so too had a mild form of coercion -- refusal

to import English goods and manufactures. In April of that year,

British troops had slain Americans at Lexington and Concord.

Independence was, at this juncture, the only constructive course for

the colonies.

Adams related with more than a hint of pride that he had grasped

the reasonable and inevitable course for America. In the spring of

1775, he stood for a confederation, a strong continental army and navy,

trade with all the world, foreign alliances, and the arrest of every

royal official in the colonies. The matter-of-fact manner in which

Adams expressed his assessment of American destiny in 1775 made opposition

to his measures appear irrational. He believed no less and wished to

convey no more.

Adams might have gone no deeper into the event. He might have let

the single, simple theme of American versus England suffice. But he

did not. He rejected simplicity because he found it superficial, and

turned to a theme of equal importance. Sounding exasperation in every

sentence, Adams wrote that at a time when the most powerful nation in

the world was ready to pounce on America and when union of sentiment

and bold action were indispensable, a group of men in the Continental

Congress, led by John Dickinson of Pennsylvania, flew in the face of

historical decree; they threatened to withdraw their colonies from the

conflict unless Adams and Patriots of like mind gave up their measures

and permitted a second attempt at reconciliation with England by

petitioning the king. Dickinson's group had gone so far, Adams related,

as to wage a personal vendetta against him. "The party made me as

unpopular as they could among all their connections," he said, "but I

regarded none of these things. I knew and lamented that many of these

gentlemen of great property, high in office, and of good accomplishments,

were laying the foundations, not of any injury to me, but of their

own ruin."[2] For a time, Dickinson and his group succeeded, and the

results of their success, Adams wrote, were appalling: Congress remained

weak and ineffective and made only half-hearted gestures at winning

the war. Colonial troops staggered to defeat at Charlestown and Quebec,

and because Congress did little to prepare for war, demoralization

set in among the people.

As Adams wrote, page followed on page of a conflict in the

Continental Congress. He wished Americans to know that he and

other Patriots of like mind finally carried the struggle for independence

against the English without and misguided Patriots within. Dickinson

and his group, he said, did everything in their power to retain the

connection with England and even detested independence once Congress

finally adopted it. Apprehensive that those who read his autobiography

might confuse this group of men with those who supported the English

side early in the war, Adams hastened to make himself understood. He

said: "I mean, not the Tories, for from them I received always more

candor, but a class of people who thought it proper and convenient to

themselves to go along with public opinion in appearance, though in their

hearts they detested [independence]. They secretly regretted the

separation, and above all things the connection with France." [3] In

Adams' estimation, the misguided Patriots had done nearly as much harm

as England. In fact, he said, the Dickinson group had become and

remained his enemies from that time onward. [4] The cloak of Patriot

unanimity fell away.

Adams' account of independence discussed the American arena

on the advent of revolution because to him the early years of the

Revolution were meaningless unless one understood Americans themselves.

He left an ineradicable impression that a large portion of the

history of independence and the young Republic was closely related

to the fact that some Patriots opposed independence in principle, and

that their acquiescence in independence did not change "their hearts"

or make them less destructive in their intrigues. Rather than damn

with faint praise, he loudly indicted part of the old guard and left

to Americans a piercing view of an internal struggle for independence.

John Adams also succeeded in opening old wounds, for two years

later, in 1807, word of Adams' views reached John Dickinson at his

estate in Wilmington, Delaware.⁵ Dickinson was ill; in another year

he would be dead. But his thin blood boiled at the rumors which

hummed in the air about him, and, as far as he was concerned, he had

every right to his anger.

He too had a long list of public services to his credit. In 1765,

he had opposed Parliament's taxation measure, the Stamp Act, and had

served as a Pennsylvania delegate to the Stamp Act Congress. One of

his more outstanding contributions to American liberty had come in

1767 when Parliament enacted the Townshend Acts. Many former opponents

of Parliamentary taxation had paid scant attention to the Acts (Richard

Henry Lee, the Virginian, had **writt**en that the Acts were "not perhaps,

literally, a violation of our rights.") But Dickinson had read the

Townshend Acts carefully, and he had written a series of twelve letters

denouncing Parliament's new legislation. Dickinson's Letters from a

Farmer in Pennsylvania appeared in most major colonial newspapers

and went through seven editions as a pamphlet. R.H. Lee changed his

mind about the legality of the duties and wrote his thanks to Dickinson;

Samuel Adams quoted verbatim from the Letters from a Farmer, and

colonial resistance, strengthened by Dickinson's contribution, moved

from lethargic protest to more determined opposition.[6]

Moreover, Dickinson had worked incessantly for defense of colonial

rights in Pennsylvania and, later, in the Continental Congress. He

had opposed the Tea Act, taken part in extra-legal assemblies at the

time of the Intolerable Acts, and used his influence in the Pennsylvania

Assembly to prevent its splintering the unity of colonial opposition.

He had shared co-authorship with Thomas Jefferson in drafting the

Declaration on the Causes and Necessity for Taking-Up Arms, and made

a hasty but/successful effort to prevent New Jersey from pursuing a

divisive course in late 1775. In these years, Dickinson's reputation

had dwarfed that of John Adams throughout the colonies, just as, in

later years, John Adams' career had dwarfed that of Dickinson. However,

Dickinson did not decline into obscurity. He served in high offices

in both Pennsylvania and Delaware. His thinking influenced the final

form of the Articles of Confederation and the Constitution of 1787, and,

later, he supported the Federalists.

Now, a generation after the event, his early patriotism had been

questioned, and his quiet retirement in Delaware had been rudely

interrupted. Dickinson took neither the accusations nor the interruption

lightly. As was his wont, he calmly but firmly denied the essence of

Adams' account of the events leading to independence. In a letter to

a life-long friend of John Adams', he wrote that his own motives for

supporting the 1775 petition to the king (the "Olive Branch Petition")

had been dual: first, he had hoped that Congress could induce England

to redress colonial grievances and, thereby, prevent a long and bloody

war; and second, he had hoped that the second petition would serve

as a rallying point for colonials themselves. If England rejected

a second attempt at reconciliation, then colonials would have no

alternative but to follow the lead of Congress. In 1775, he was sure

colonials were uncertain of themselves, and he had reasoned that the

Congress must take every precaution to avoid accusations of irresponsibility

and, by doing so, unite the people. The second petition was, he implied,

an astute maneuver which most men in Congress had supported. Furthermore,

his plan had worked. "After the rejection of the second petition," he

said, "not a syllable, to my recollection, was ever uttered in favor

of reconciliation with Great Britain." [7] America rallied to Congress.

Dickinson's feelings were obvious: if Adams' account had not slandered

everyone, it had at least confused everything.

Dickinson went on to say that the patriots in Congress had not

been in perpetual clash about independence or anything else.

As to government, he wrote, everyone had agreed that any new government

would be republican in form. Rather, Congressional debates in early

1776 had turned on two mild questions of strategy: whether the

people were sufficiently advanced in their thinking to accept a

declaration of independence, and what France could be expected to do.

The cloak of Patriot unanimity began to settle back into place.

Dickinson almost succeeded, but he could not manage a task that

had now become impossible. The fact that he answered Adams, though

indirectly, gave Adams' story a respectability beyond that of the

garrulous ramblings of a tired, old ex-President. Dickinson left the

distinct impression that Adams belonged to a fringe group in Congress,

and that these Patriots had not been attentive to, or realistic about,

problems of war. As far as Dickinson was concerned they were still

confused. Dickinson reminded men that the colonial situation in 1775

and 1776 demanded deliberate, even subtle, guidance, and with this, he

adroitly shifted the burden of having blundered and the nomer of "misguided"

to the other side.

By their disputes, the first Patriots bestowed a strange legacy

upon those who came after them. Everyone knew that the Americans had rebelled for the best reason imaginable: to preserve their liberty. Yet, the men who led the rebellion could not agree about what had happened. The revolutionary heritage comes down to Americans as two legacies rather than one. Leading exponents of colonial rights and liberties left differing accounts which often contradicted one another and clouded traditions about American independence. Indeed, the burden of Patriot history of the Revolution hinges on the fact that men like Dickinson and Adams were long after independence was achieved disposed to reject the views of one another, a disposition which they communicated to each generation down to our own time, a disposition which leaves room for doubt that Americans fully understand the decision for independence and, with it, the Revolution.[8]

What had really separated the Patriots on the advent of revolution was more complicated than either Adams or Dickinson admitted or, perhaps, knew. It is certainly true that the Patriots were all subjects of the same king, and as such, lived under the same general system of English laws and jurisprudence. They came from colonies with similar local institutions, and, as men who live in the same era are wont to

do, they made similar assumptions about the world of fact. For
more than a decade they had made common cause against Parliament's
legislative enactments pertaining to the colonies.

But for all that, men in America were still separated by tradition,
time, distance, and circumstance. Although there was a good deal more
communication between Americans than is commonly supposed, Pennsylvanians
knew little about Massachusetts, Marylanders knew little about New
Hampshire, Virginians knew little about Georgia. Educated Americans
in the seaport cities tended to have a broad cosmopolitan outlook, but
most Americans were still an intensely particularistic and provincial
people when their leaders came together in the Continental Congress. [9]
In short, for all their similarities, the first Patriots had grown up
and lived in, and were attached to, different localities, with different
political systems, economic conditions and interests, social climates,
and religious backgrounds. Every man of them was a British North
American ("I am not a Virginian, sir, but an American," Patrick Henry
said), but every one was also a provincial from a particular province
("Virginia, sir, there is my country," said Jefferson).

And therein lay the sources of much of the confusion, then
and later, about what happened at the outset of the Revolution. It
is not that historians have not been industrious and able in gathering
and interpreting various components of the story of the decision of
independence. On the level of particular aspects of colonial government
and society, the monographic studies of a host of historians supply a
great amount of information about the internal politics of each of the
respective colonies, the growth and development of cities, the powers
and activities of governors and assemblies, the role of merchants in
the Revolution, and the relation of religion to Anglo-American clash.
Numerous biographers furnish details about the lives of scores of
Americans. And, on the level of intercolonial history, several historians
have written multi-volume works that bring many of the particular aspects
of independence together in a general survey. Also, historians have
left studies and materials that provide an almost day-by-day account
of the proceedings of the Continental Congress. These studies vary
in quality and scope, but all furnish reliable information, and together

10

they supply a large portion of what is knowable.

On the most general level, that of the Empire and the Imperial system in the years leading up to and during Anglo-American controversy, the work of various scholars has been diligent and much of it has been brilliant. These studies furnish a means of viewing independence from another vantage point, and together with several special studies on the operation of branches of Imperial administration, they provide a fairly comprehensive picture of the Empire as a whole.[11]

Finally, on the matter of the development of American theories of government and of the constitutional nature of the Empire, historians have been thorough, even if their findings have not always been compatible one with the other. Historians have concerned themselves with the general development of both the English and American position, and claims have been made that both sides were sincere and accurate in their constitutional argumentation. These studies have been supplemented by study of the ideas and views of particular Americans and by a monograph which centers on the constitutional statements of colonial assemblies at the time of the Stamp Act Crisis. Other historians have made it their task to investigate American political thinking at the time

of transition from colonies to nation. [12]

The general sequence of events leading to the Revolution, then, have been fairly well worked out, though the story will **doubtless be** filled in and corrected to some extent by future historians.

Nonetheless, much is left to be done from the standpoint of the interaction of Americans in their several capacities as British subjects, continental statesmen, and particularly in their reactions as inhabitants of particular localities. The present study proposes to fill in this gap by attempting to place many of the major Imperial and continental events in their plural local contexts; to determine what local reactions of those events were; to show how men in the Continental Congress reflected those local contexts; and to discuss these three things in so far as they relate directly to the decision for independence within the local setting and in the Congress. Four American leaders--John Adams, John Dickinson, Thomas Jefferson and John Rutledge--illustrate and elucidate the variety of Patriot actions and beliefs on the advent of Revolution. Such a study will, it is hoped, broaden our understanding of the initial years of the Revolution and clarify the sources and nature

of Patriot conflict about the decision for independence.

Before this is undertaken, it will be well to remind the
reader of the general sequence of events in the long Imperial
conflict--the British actions and the American reactions, and vice-versa,
from 1764 to 1775. It is of little consequence, for present purposes,
whether British policy reflected a blundering, if not sinister, design
calculated to subvert the liberties of the Americans, as many colonials
thought, or whether, on the opposite extreme, George III and most
Parliamentary leaders were deeply concerned about American rights
and liberties and actually trying to protect the colonies from what
they thought a disastrous course; or whether, as is more likely,
British actions flowed from vastly deeper and more complex springs.
But is is necessary to have in mind the legislative enactments of
Parliament to which Americans were reacting.

At the end of the French and Indian War in 1763, the colonies
in North America were connected with England by attitude, allegiance,
and a loose framework of Imperial laws. Men in America were proud of

being English subjects. For the most part, colonial assemblies

handled problems of internal government, and England reserved the

right to veto colonial legislation deemed inconsistent with laws of

the realm. Moreover, the colonies were connected with England by

commerce and interest. The Acts of Trade and Navigation required

colonials to observe commercial and industrial regulations which

worked generally on all inhabitants of the Empire. Both England and

America benefited from commercial intercourse, and the union was the

envy of the world; indeed the Seven Years' War (called "The French

and Indian War" in America) was fought to protect and extend the system.

But the victory at arms brought aggravating changes and additional

burdens. At the close of the war, English administration faced

problems created by the acquisition of new domains, notably New France,

and public debts incurred by war. The old problem of how to regulate

and protect trade and territory, and to pay for that protection,

assumed sizably larger proportions.[13]

The task of finding solutions to these problems fell to George

Grenville, new Chancellor of the Exchequer, and what he and others

might propose was bound to touch America. Grenville, like his

predecessors, felt that if the acquisition of New France was a

liability, it could also be made an asset by turning the vast amounts

of unoccupied lands into a perpetual source of revenue for Imperial

administration. In 1763, pending organization of an efficient system

of land sale and distribution, the Crown proclaimed that the land

west of the Allegheny Mountains was closed to colonial settlement.

On receiving word of Indian disturbances in the Ohio region, Grenville

organized the American frontier into two military departments. To pay

for this, and to cover some of the costs of Imperial administration,

Grenville sent a bill to Parliament which increased standing duties

on colonial imports of foreign manufactured products, including

molasses, reduced duties on English molasses, and strengthened the

customs service in order to insure that customs violators were

prosecuted once they were caught. Grenville's so-called "Sugar Act"

became a law in 1764. That same year Parliament passed another bill

designed to meet a financial problem in relation to the **colonies.**

Colonial legislatures had emitted large sums of paper currency during

the war and made the currency legal tender in payment of all debts,

public and private. The privilege of issuing such currency was being

abused by some colonies, particularly Virginia, and Grenville sought

to remove the abuse by removing the privilege. The Currency Act of

1764 enjoined the colonies to retire their war currency and prohibited

further paper emissions to pass as legal tender in payment of debts.

These three actions--the Proclamation of 1763, the Sugar Act and the

Currency Act--reached America in rapid succession.

Colonials protested them all--the Sugar Act most strongly--and

taken **together** the laws stirred up a hornets' nest in North America.

But no great crisis ensued, and a year later Grenville proceeded

with his plans to require Americans to bear a portion of the costs

of managing and **protecting** the Empire. He designed another bill for

the colonies, based on an old **form** of English taxation. For some

time in England, men had been accustomed to paying indirect taxes

by way of small fees for stamps required on public transactions such

as deeds, wills, property transfers, and other legal documents; the

tax had also been extended to newspapers. What was new about Grenville's

Stamp Act and what earned him enduring infamy was that he proposed to

extend this tax to America. Moreover, the Stamp Act fell equally

on all the colonies and gave colonials a common ground for protest.

Colonial assemblies and pamphleteers protested the tax even

before the bill became law. By this time, prosecutions in the

courts of admiralty for customs violations and more rigid enforcement

of customs had alerted colonials to shift in Imperial policy. Englishmen

in America inclined an ear to regulatory legislation, and when the

Stamp Act arrived, men questioned the constitutionality of Parliamentary

taxation. Within the space of a few months, most colonial assemblies

had petitoned Parliament for repeal. Ministry and Parliament did not

budge as America moved from economic arguments to arguments based upon

their rights and former traditions of taxation. In 1765 and 1766,

colonials denied Parliament's right to tax and insisted that only

their respective assemblies could pass taxation bills. Faced with

the charge of irresponsibility toward support of the Empire, they

said that they preferred the old method of raising such funds, namely,

that their assemblies continue to render "free gifts" to the Crown

when requested to do so. When Americans saw that the act might

actually be enforced, violence erupted. Groups called the "Sons of

Liberty" led riots against stamp distributors and royal officials who

sympathized with the act. For a year the colonies remained in a state

of agitation as colonials put up stiff resistance; they held extra-legal

meetings, met in a general congress, and refused to import English

goods. In the end colonial appeals to liberty gained them a friend in

William Pitt, and economic coercion induced English merchants to support

repeal of the tax. Parliament repealed the Stamp Act and scaled down

the duties on foreign molasses imposed by the Sugar Act.[14]

The Stamp Act crisis also shaped the pattern of American opposition

to Parliament. Colonials' refusal to import English goods demonstrated

that they could be harsh and stubborn, and in some instances they even

resorted to violence. Yet, when charged with sedition and designs

on independence, they flatly denied both. They resisted the Stamp Act,

they said, because their liberties as Englishmen were jeopardized by it. Colonial Whigs said that Parliament could not tax them; that privilege belonged to their respective legislatures by law, charters, and tradition. Furthermore, they did not like to be prosecuted for criminal offenses in courts of admiralty without juries. That too impinged upon the rights of Englishmen in the Empire. The colonies resisted, Americans said, to defend their rights within the Empire. And they won.

Colonial optimism was in for a rude awakening, for although colonials seemed to have won a clear victory, the question of their rights had just begun. Problems of Imperial administration still remained. Consequently, even before Parliament retreated, it passed the Quartering Act, and as it retreated, it passed the Declaratory Act. The Quartering Act required the colonial assemblies to vote funds for support of royal troops stationed in the respective provinces. And members of Parliament, disturbed by colonial assertions as to what Parliament could or could not do, made their own position clear. The Declaratory Act said, simply, that Parliament had the right to

legislate for the colonies in "all cases whatsoever."

In the meantime, from 1764 to 1767, colonials paid the duties under the Sugar Act. That fact, together with the fact that people in England and America had disagreed in their definitions of the powers of Parliament and the rights of colonials, laid the ground for further conflict. The Sugar Act provided that money derived from customs duties would go for the support of Imperial government. Justifiably, Englishmen were confused by colonial arguments. Many thought that Americans objected to "internal taxes," (witness their hostility to the stamp tax which would have operated within each colony), and not "external taxes, " (witness their payment of customs duties which operated on trade and commerce, or activity on the high seas). Benjamin Franklin, a colonial agent from Pennsylvania, had said as much when he was examined before Parliament in 1766.[15] Charles Townshend, the new Chancellor of the Exchequer, put all these bits and pieces together. He asked Parliament to lay duties on American imports of paper, glass, lead, paints, and tea. Moreover, his bill specified that funds from these duties would go for support of Imperial government.

In another bill, Parliament suspended the New York Assembly for

non-compliance with the Quartering Act. These two bills, and a third

establishing a continental Customs Commission at Boston, reached

the colonies as the "Townshend Acts" in November, 1767.

Colonials chewed on the Acts for awhile; some merchants paid

the duties charged on the goods. Then, under the leadership of

Massachusetts, Americans rejected part of the new legislation. They

were less vitriolic and less united in their opposition than they had

been in 1765-66, but no less emphatic about their rights in the Empire

and the powers of Parliament. Colonial pamphleteers and Assembly

petitions reiterated the claims which they had made at the time of

the Stamp Act, and with that, Americans moved into a stance of

traditional opposition. Colonials Whigs once again denied the right

of Parliament to tax America. Their objection, they said, was the

same objection which they had made in 1765: duties levied on imports

for purposes of revenue were taxes. As before, the colonies denied

charges that they sought independence, and pointed out that Parliament

might certainly regulate trade and commerce and levy duties for the

purpose of regulation of trade. As before, colonials refused to import

English goods and manufactures and resorted to economic coercion.

Opposition crystallized: colonials would resist any attempts to tax ,

they would contend for their rights within the Empire, and they would

use coercive measures if need be, but they would not fall prey to

sedition, and they certainly had no intention to separate from the

Empire.

For a second time, Parliament retreated; but it did not lift

the duty on tea, and thereby protected itself against the charge that

repeal meant agreement with colonial constitutional arguments.

From 1770 to 1773, disputes shifted to a series of clashes between

royal administration and individual colonies. New York settled her

dispute over the Quartering Act. In Massachusetts things did not go

as well and in 1770 royal troops shot and killed Bostonians. Boston

seethed; men did not forget. In 1772, Rhode Islanders burned a customs

ship, and royal officials swarmed into the colony. That encounter

engendered more ill will. Men on each side of the water grew more

suspicious of the motives of those on the other. For their part,

Americans said that if Parliament might legislate for the colonies

in all cases whatsoever, that power destroyed their rights and liberties.

They had their own legislatures which were vested with specific, unalterable

powers, taxation of inhabitants being the most important. Englishmen

maintained that colonials denial of Parliament's supremacy was evidence

that colonials wished to become independent and was a ruse to hide

colonial irresponsibility. Nevertheless, the Empire had not seffered

irreparable damage, though each side grew increasingly impatient with

the other.

The decision of George III and Lord North to give the East India

Company what amounted to a virtual monopoly on the sale of tea in

the Empire again united the colonials around a common issue. For a

tax was still attached to tea, and if Americans purchased tea from

English merchants only, then they would, they said, be doing what

they maintained that they would never do: pay taxes levied by

Parliament. In November and December of 1773, colonials moved to

prevent purchase of English tea and to insure that merchants did not receive it. In Boston, Americans and royal officials reached an impasse, and more zealous defenders of American liberty dumped tea consignments into the harbor. The actions of the Bostonians were alarming, but colonials had destroyed property before without serious consequence. All along the Atlantic seaboard colonials made their position perfectly clear: they would not be tricked into buying tea which had a tax attached to it.

As 1773 passed into 1774, most colonials fully expected that next spring would bring news that the home government had retreated or, at the worst, that the home government was still undecided about how best to deal with the stand of the colonies. Whatever the situation might afford, most colonials believed that economic boycott would suffice to bring the crisis to end in their favor. Their expectations rested firmly on eight years of experience and a crass but accurate notion of their economic importance and the motivation of the English. But with spring came the unexpected. Word arrived that Parliament had

refused to be cowed and that it fully intended to enforce its assertion of the right to legislate for the colonies in all cases. Parliament singled out Massachusetts to show how it could deal with riots and destruction of property. The Boston Port Bill closed the harbor to commerce. Colonials heard of the law in May, 1774. England made her stand as painfully clear as the Americans had made their own. Crown, Lords, and Commons would stand firm at this juncture of the Imperial crisis.[16]

Americans were baffled and enraged; none more so than the inhabitants of Massachusetts. Caught in the center of a maelstrom, colonials felt their optimism and confidence melt away. Then, other acts of Parliament hit home: the government and judiciary of Massachusetts were reorganized. Troops were dispatched to maintain order in the colony. From June through July of 1774, the colonies were in turmoil, and the depth of their shock registered in their lack of agreement concerning what ought to be done. Provincial committees declared that the cause of Boston was the cause of all, but when Samuel Adams sent out a letter calling for an immediate non-importation

agreement, Patriots balked. [17] What seemed a natural thing in the

light of past opposition and success did not now appear at all desirable.

On the other hand, local committees and groups went their own ways: some

immediately stopped English imports, others stopped exports to England

as well, and still others sounded a louder note by calling for militia

organizations and training. [18] Patriots divided in their opinions of

what to do about Boston. From Philadelphia, New York, and Portsmouth

came recommendations that Boston pay for the tea which the Sons of

Liberty had destroyed and thereby remove the stated grounds of

Parliament's action; others said that to pay for the tea subverted

the cause of liberty. [19] By argument and counter-argument, colonials

were made to face the fact that previous unanimity of action had been

dependent upon the good humor of the mother country.

Though Patriots indulged in fantasies of removing thousands

further west and establishing semi-military republics, and shouts

went up to march on the royal army at Boston, the crisis had a deeper

impact. [20] It acted as a purgative and cleared men's minds. In the

midst of confusion, Americans decided that local, provincial action

was sufficient to meet the situation and move the colonies along

a sane and able course. Beginning in May, 1774, colonials called for

a general congress to discover grounds of agreement and to present

a united front against England.[21]

The efficacy of the traditional means of opposition to England

was in doubt as the first Congress convened in September, 1774.

Parliament had used unusual procedures against as American colony,

and the high-handed way it had disposed of a governmental charter

frightened many American leaders. Despite that, colonials in Congress

stuck to their claims, and acted in such the same manner as they had

before. American opposition had a definite character about it. Once

again, for the fourth time in decade, Americans petitioned for a redress

of their grievances and sought to use their economic power to force

repeal of unjust laws. The Congress sent a petition to the Crown

stating each grievance and by this time, the list was long, but

colonial grievance was still based upon the demand for colonial

rights within the Empire and forswore any intention of separation.

The First Congress did, however, alter the traditional Whig position

with respect to the powers of their colonial assemblies. Heretofore,

colonials had argued mainly on the basis of the right to tax

themselves, but in the Declaration of Rights and Grievances, they

argued for the right of their assemblies to exclusive powers over

"internal legislation." At the same time, Congress recommended that

each colony support resistance by support of the Continental

Association-- an agreement not to purchase or consume English manufactures

or goods. Among other things, Congress explained its actions by

published addresses to the inhabitants of North America, Quebec, and

England. It also approved the resolves of Suffolk County, Massachusetts,

which flatly stated that if royal troops in Massachusetts tried to force

colonials to observe unconstitutional legislation, then Americans

had the right to meet force with force. [22] The men of the First Congress

took their stand with resistance to unjust laws of Parliament within

the Empire; they provided for another Congress should their attempts

at redress go unanswered, and they went home. No one knew what

would happen. The outcome appeared to rest with Great Britain.

33

Again British statesmen would not be cowed by colonials. George III

and Lord North directed colonial governors, and especially General

Thomas Gage in Boston, to hold firm; the Intolerable Acts would remain

in force. Colonials waited for repeal and no repeal came. In April, 1775,

General Gage moved to seize Patriot military stores at Concord,

Massachusetts, and militiamen moved to stop him.[23] British troops

and Americans killed one another. Although Americans and Englishmen

did battle, and the Empire was shaken, there were colonials who believed

that the damage was not irreparable.

34

II

THE MIDDLE COLONIES: LIBERTY AND EMPIRE

When the Imperial crisis erupted, the people of the Middle
Colonies held firm to the position they had maintained for ten years:
demanding their rights and liberties but insisting on the preservation
of their connection with the Empire. Though they had been quarrelsome,
riotous, and vitriolic in opposing Parliament, they had categorically
denied that they sought independence or even contemplated sedition.
Indeed, when English troops occupied Massachusetts in 1774, most people
in the Middle Colonies sympathized with the plight of their fellow
Americans, but thought that petitions and provisions not bullets,
were the appropirate remedy. On hearing of the Battle of Lexington and
Concord some prepared for war, yet even as late as July of 1776 most
still hoped to remain British subjects.

If anything, people in the Middle Colonies supported the American
cause with only half their hearts. Those few Patriots who espoused
independence-- mechanics and artisans in New York and Philadelphia,
farmers in eastern New Jersey and northern Delaware,

and the frontiersmen of central Pennsylvania -- were surrounded

by traditional Whigs who contended for their rights within the

Empire. And by no means did all inhabitants of the Middle Colonies

embrace Patriotism of either variety --advocacy of independence or

the traditional Whig position. Along the far frontiers of Pennsylvania

and New York, most men sided with Great Britain.[1] Quakers in eastern

Pennsylvania and western New Jersey defied the Continental Congress'

admonitions and disowned those Friends who proved overly zealous.[2] In

and around New York City, most non-English-speaking Americans stayed away

from extra-legal meetings and militia exercises, and upriver, many

tenant farmers refused to follow the lead of their Patriot landlords.[3]

In Delaware, two-thirds of the people actively sided with England or

were neutral, and even among the twelve thousand or so who supported

the Congress, a majority opposed independence.[4] In New York, Whig

leaders only belatedly supported the First Continental Congress'

recommendation for a non-importation Association, and the House of

Assembly refused to approve either this or any of its other recommendations

and actions. Instead, on its own, the Assembly petitioned the Crown

for redress of grievances, a divisive action that ran counter to

the wishes of Congress. The assemblies of Pennsylvania, Delaware, and

New Jersey approved the work of the First Congress, but New Jersey

sent a separate petition to the king, and thereby weakened Patriot

unity.[5]

The delegates to Congress from the Middle Colonies reflected

these divergent responses to the Imperial crisis, though not in detail;

and they rallied to the common ground of the traditional Whig position.

Of the thirty-six men who attended Congress from New York, New Jersey,

Pennsylvania, and Delaware before July 1, 1776, twenty-eight were

anti-independence Whigs who consistently sought redress and reconciliation.

Their beliefs and actions varied considerably, but on this central issue

they formed a solid body of sentiment in and out of Congress.[6]

Delegates from New York and New Jersey opposed separation until

it had become a fact , and some were never reconciled to it. John

Alsop, for example, a New York merchant and delegate to the Congress

from April of 1774 until August of 1776, consistently opposed Great

Britain but, when the New York Provincial Congress approved independence,

37

Alsop demanded to be recalled and eventually became a Loyalist.[7]

On the other hand, Philip Schuyler of Albany County, who fought for

approval of Congress' recommendations in the New York House of Assembly,

toyed with the idea of independence early in 1776 but did not exert

himself in favor of it, and hoped for reconciliation even as late as

1778; yet when the war came he accepted command of Patriot troops in

New York and Canada.[8] William Livingston of New York and New Jersey

opposed independence but, when it came, stayed with the American cause

and became the first governor of New Jersey.[9] John De Hart, a lawyer

and farmer from New Jersey, resigned his place in the Continental

Congress in the winter of 1775 on the ground that he could not fulfill

his instructions to gain a reconciliation with Great Britain. He

did not become a Loyalist, but he refused to serve in the new

government formed in New Jersey in 1776.[10]

Pennsylvania and Delaware Whigs followed similar courses. Even

James Wilson, the most fiery of the colony's delegates, equivocated.

In 1774, he published a ringing indictment of English tyranny, but

instead of following his own ideas to their logical conclusion, he

followed John Dickinson and helped engineer opposition to independence

in Congress. Wilson opposed the Declaration until July 2, then

finally voted in favor on that day.[11]   Two other members of the anti-

independence group hedged: the merchant partners Thomas Willing and

Robert Morris maintained that the summer of 1776 was not the time

for formal separation from England. Willing voted against the Declaration.

Morris refused to vote, absented himself, and then, a month after the

Declaration of Independence, finally signed the document.[12]   George

Read of Delaware voted against independence, then took a course of

action similar to that of Morris.[13]

Socially and economically these eight men represented a cross-section

of Patriot leadership in the Middle Colonies. Six were members of

popular branches of the legislatures, three held colonial appointive

offices, and one held an elective local office (dual office-holding

was common in colonial America). Three (Alsop, Willing, and Morris)

were international merchants and shipowners who exported wheat and

imported, largely for sale to retail suppliers, wares from all over

the Atlantic world; like most such men, they also had investments

in a variety of ventures not related to commerce. Five were lawyers:

Wilson's income was derived almost exclusively from his practice,

De Hart supplemented his legal fees by operating a farm, Read more than

matched his professional income by the return on assorted investments,

Livingston had retired from practice and was living on the income from

his £21,000 inheritance, and Schuyler held large (but hardly vast) tracts

of land along the Hudson, some of which he farmed with hired labor; he

grew wheat for export, participated in the river trade, and occasionally

ventured into fur trading and other side activities. Together, the eight men

represented all the major geographical sections of Patriot strength in

the Middle Colonies, and they represented each of the dominant religions

in the area except the Quaker (four were Anglican, two Presbyterian,

two Dutch Reformed). Their social standings ranged from that of Livingston,

high to the ranks of the New York aristocracy, to that of Wilson, once

an impecunious immigrant. The experience of most of them bred an

international viewpoint: five of the eight were born or educated

or spent their entire adult lives engaged in international trade.[14]

40

But the position taken by the Middle Colonies at the climax

of Imperial crisis was rooted far deeper than in the biographies

of a handful of leaders. These colonies were populated by an explosive

mixture of cultural groups which had managed to live in some semblance of

harmony largely, if not only, because they had plenty of room. In the

1760's a concatenation of pressures from the outside-- from Indians,

from New England, and from Britain -- suddenly jeopardized their safety

valve. For this reason, people in the Middle Colonies were prepared to

resist and did resist what was happening in the broad theatre of empire:

they sought redress of grievances. Yet, the politics of turmoil in the

Middle Colonies unfolded in an incongruent context, for men were

thriving in their day to day economic affairs, and the Empire

treated them well. For this reason (as well as the fact that part

of the threat to them came from independence-minded New Englanders),

they sought reconciliation.

English settlers along the Delaware and the Hudson had been

preceded by Indians, Dutch, Walloons, Swedes, Finns, Norwegians, and

Germans. After the English established their political supremacy, only

the Indians were forced to leave, and other non-English-- French

Huguenots in trickles and Germans in waves -- continued to pour into the

area.[15] By the middle of the eighteenth century the area was teeming

with only partially compatible Christian sects and cultural groups.

Dutch Reformed, French Huguenots, Swedish and German Lutherans,

Scotch-Irish Presbyterians, and English Quakers, Anglicans, Baptists

and a host of lesser groups preserved their religions, their

languages, and their cultures.

In New York, Anglicans dominated the government but enjoyed

an establishment of their religion only in the lower counties around

the city. The Dutch Reformed retained their communities in Kings County

and on Long Island. On the middle and upper Hudson, Presbyterians and

Dutch Reformed were strong enough to prevent an Anglican establishment,

as were the New England Presbyterians who abounded on the eastern

end of Long Island.[16]

In northeastern New Jersey Dutch Reformed churchmen were

concentrated in Bergen County (nearest New York City), and large

numbers of Presbyterians occupied Essex, the next county down.[17]

42

Anglicans and Presbyterians lived in Middlesex County, in and around

Perth Amboy. In the southwestern half of the colony large numbers of

Quakers kept, for the most part, quietly to themselves, separate and

aloof from a concentration of Presbyterians around Trenton. Eastward

and southward on Cape May, Presbyterians mixed with Anglicans.[18]

In Delaware the sectarian pattern was different in each of the

three counties. In the northernmost county of New Castle two out of

every three church members were Presbyterians. In Sussex County two

out of three were Anglicans, and in Kent just over half were Anglicans.

Scattered throughout the colony were a handful of Quakers and Baptists.[19]

In Pennsylvania, religious toleration was the rule in principle,

but that did not mean sectarians respected one another's views. In

Philadelphia Quakers and Anglicans contended for domination, Scotch-

Irish Presbyterians challenged both, and a conglomerate of lesser

groups went their several ways. In the nearby counties the same

groups, being less close together, engaged in fewer disputes. In the

back country the most numerous groups, the Presbyterians and the various

German sects, avoided friction only by avoiding one another.[20]

43

These divergent groups remembered only dimly the two centuries

of bitter European religious conflict that had gone before, but

the years had not totally erased memory -- neither of murder and

imprisonment and war in Europe nor of hanging and enslavement of

Quakers in New England. And as if the proliferation of historically

hostile sects were insufficient to appease the spirits of Luther, Calvin,

and Knox, the evangelist George Whitefield came in the 1740's and set

church against church for thirty-five more years. Protestants sects

of all varieties, including the Quakers, experienced a renewal of

religious ferror.[21]

Even among more enlightened members of New York society -- and men

on the Governor's Council were enlightened for the most part -- religious

suspicion cropped up from time to time. Once the Dutch Reformed Church

at Schenectady sent a petition to the Council asking for leave to issue

a £1,000 revenue measure for their church. William Smith, a Presbyterian,

supported the petition before the governor and pointed out that the small

congregation of Anglicans in Albany was permitted a £5,000 revenue each

year. Oliver De Lancey, an Anglican and devout foe of all who professed

otherwise, immediately objected on the ground that the Anglicans

in Schenectady were permitted the funds "because they were Christians."

Smith rejoined: "What, are not the Dutch of Schenectady, Christians?"

DeLancey said, "Not such Christians." "How do you mean,"Smith inquired,

"not Episcopalian? Do you mean that?" "Aye," said DeLancey.[22]

That episode was trivial but it was symptomatic of something far

from trivial: distrust and animosity smouldered just beneath the

surface. And other differences compounded basic ones: the land

systems in New York, Pennsylvania, and New Jersey were all jumbled

and mixed. Cliques of families which owned or hoped to own large

tracts fought continuously about who should and did own what, and

especially about titles to manorial lands on the Hudson and the

proprietary lands in Pennsylvania and New Jersey, and they were in

regular conflict with yeoman farmers, who believed in fee-simple

landholding.[23]

Two things, one a physical fact and the other an attitude, prevented

the explosive mixture from bursting into flames. The fact was that

there was plenty of room in the Middle Colonies, more than enough land

to go around. The attitude was that the obstacles to settlement of the land -- merely being hostile human beings -- would disappear when the time came to settle it. That had always happened in the past. In the meantime, people in the Middle Colonies could make do on four to six million acres that were unoccupied and immediately habitable.[24]

But then, in the early and middle sixties, external pressures hit from three directions in rapid succession, and internal pressures mounted space. The defeat of the French in North America had just confirmed the attitude that the obstacles to settlement were bound to fall, when the home government imposed a new barrier to expansion by proclaiming that Anglo-Americans would have to wait to occupy land west of the Alleghenies -- which happened to be just at the edge of existing Pennsylvania settlement. Simultaneously, various Indian tribes, under the leadership of the Ottawa chief, Pontiac, began a series of frontier raids that lasted fully twenty-four months. And then came an invasion by what Philip Livingston called the Goths and Vandals: hordes of land hungry New Englanders.[25]

The demand for land hardened old antagonisms and created new ones.

46

In New Jersey, where two groups of proprietors (of East Jersey and West Jersey) held large tracts under separate grants, a conflict developed; the outcome was that little land changed hands but each set of proprietors faced the hostility of the other and of an anti-proprietary faction in its own domain.[26] In Pennsylvania a long, sporadic, and vague attack on the proprietors came to focus in a major though futile effort to overthrow them entirely and take their lands.[27] In New York an old rivalry between the DeLancey and Livingston families and their connections hardened into permanent hostility: the DeLanceys, temporarily ascendent, arranged for the granting of well over two million acres, of which the Livingstons only got a fraction.[28]

The Indian scare turned frontiersmen against city dwellers and tenant farmers against landlords. In Pennsylvania the notorious Paxton Boys led several hundred frontiersmen in a massacre of a peaceful Indian tribe, then turned and marched on Philadelphia. Benjamin Franklin met them before they reached the city and dissuaded them from further action, but the episode left scars, and incidentally sharpened the conflict between the proprietary and anti-proprietary factions.[29] In New York

tenant farmers in the upper Hudson Valley rioted against their landlords

in a frantic demand for protection, then went south on river boats and

rioted against the landlords of others; and then the germ of riot spread

further south, where tenants used violence as a means of complaining about

rents, taxes, and assorted other things having nothing to do with

Indians.[30]

The Yankee invaders seemed to pour in everywhere. They appropriated

a section of the upper Delaware River region and squatted in droves

upon land in the jurisdiction of New York. Their most audacious move

was the planting of a sizable colony squarely in the interior of

Pennsylvania, a colony which the Connecticut Assembly solemnly annexed

as a voting township of Connecticut, then promised to defend with

militiamen. A decade of such doings left such deep scars of mistrust

and suspicion that, when the need arose for joining New England in

common cause, many men in the Middle Colonies simply could not bring

themselves to do it, and believed that if England abandoned the colonies

they would go to war among themselves.[31]

The legislative enactments of the British Parliament, and

especially Parliament's decision to tax the colonies, reduced diffuse patterns of frustration into a single, highly focused policy of resistance. During all this Parliament told colonists that they should help pay for the cost of defense against external danger -- a directive that Englishmen thought as just as it was sensible. To many inhabitants of the Middle Colonies it was as pernicious as it was absurd, for it came when, for the first time, external dangers were an immediate and constant threat. Accordingly, they launched a crusade for defense of American rights against British tyranny and sought to protect their powers of taxation in the bargain. Such a course had little more relation to the solution of all problems of the people of the Middle Colonies than did, say, rioting on the Hudson; but it had far more significance.

All these things unfolded in an incongruous context: a decade of boom and almost uninterrupted prosperity. True, the Middle Colonies were struck by a severe depression at the end of the war, but it passed quickly and then prosperous times came to stay. New York City and Philadelphia prospered most, for the orbits of their economic influence

were vast. New York serviced all the Hudson Valley, the farming areas

south and west of it, and much of western Connecticut as well; and

Philadelphia's markets and sources of exports were even greater.[32]

The dynamic ingredient of economic expansion was wheat, the area's

principal agricultural staple: for a decade after 1764, wheat production

steadily increased and wheat prices steadily rose. The wheat belt, an

area extending down the Hudson from Albany to New York, across to the

Delaware and down it beyond Philadelphia into northern Maryland, yielded

tons upon tons of grain and flour products which the city merchants

shipped to insatiable markets in the West Indies, parts of Europe, and

the New England and Southern colonies. As early as 1755 Philadelphia

had advanced so far in the production of flour that one observer

believed that it alone exported enough grain to feed 100,000 people, and

in any event, by 1774 Philadelphia was exporting 350,000 barrels of

flour a year.[33] Wheat prices increased both absolutely and relatively to

other staples. Over the decade, the Middle Colonies' first staple rose

and, with minor fluctuations, continued to rise above depression-year

prices; by contrast, beef, one of the two most important agricultural

staples of New England, stayed below depression-year prices and the
other, corn, fluctuated but hit the second lowest price of the
decade in 1774.[34]

A second basic industry in the Middle Colonies -- iron manufacturing --
grew by leaps and bounds in New York and Pennsylvania and northern
New Jersey, far outstripping local demand. Exporters of raw iron from
Pennsylvania and New York were resilient, as their action during the British
credit crisis in 1772 demonstrated. The Bank of England tightened credit
and loans to its subsidiaries and, along with other restrictive measures,
blocked the efforts of English finishing manufacturers to obtain raw
iron. Pennsylvania and New York merchants might have suffered considerably,
for they held large stores of iron, but instead they profited by
quickly diverting the iron to the New England ports.[35]

The flour and iron industries led the commercial community of
the Middle Colonies out of the depression which followed the French and
Indian War. Economic growth continued to 1768, when both New York
and Philadelphia experienced brief recessions, but in neither place
did prices drop below the depression level of 1764-1765, and prices

soon resumed their upward march. Furthermore, the value of goods
shipped from the two ports rose more rapidly than did population, even
though the population of the Middle Colonies increased at a prodigious
rate. By contrast, in New England the expansion of production did not
keep pace with population increase, even though the growth of population
there was somewhat slower.[36]

The Middle Colonies managed their fiscal affairs in a way that
facilitated economic growth. The legislatures of New York, New Jersey,
and Pennsylvania avoided the consequences of rapid deflation by leaving
in circulation some of the paper currency they had issued to help pay
for the war[37] and Pennsylvania and New York subsequently took the
further step to increase the currency supply as the economy expanded,
Pennsylvania through new "loan emissions" of ₤300,000 and New York
through a similar loan of ₤120,000. Moreover, just to the south,
Marylanders had issued more than ₤200,000 and part of that currency
flowed into Delaware and Pennsylvania. By contrast, New England had
scarcely ₤75,000 outstanding for a population approximately as large
as that of the Middle Colonies.[38]

52

Prosperity and economic growth, though the norm in the Middle Colonies, did not extend to every community. Philadelphia and New York ports as centers of trade were centers of prosperity, and merchants there fared better than merchants in the smaller ports in New Jersey and Delaware. Wheat farmers in the Hudson Valley and on the western tip of Long Island reaped greater benefits from the soil than did farmers west of the Hudson and on eastern Long Island. The agricultural communities in eastern Pennsylvania and western New Jersey were--on the whole--better off than farmers in the western part of Pennsylvania and in northern and southern New Jersey. Northern Delaware farmers were less fortunate than southern Delaware farmers. And, in various places in New York, New Jersey, and Pennsylvania, iron masters were more prosperous than their neighbors.

But in general, the farming, manufacturing, and commercial communities of the Middle Colonies moved forward on the tide of expansion, and the exploits of the local merchants showed the results of it. New Yorkers stole the Mediterranean trade from Boston shippers and moved retail outlets right into Connecticut, and what they had to trade or

sell was steadily increasing. Both Pennsylvanians and New Yorkers,

on one occasion, actually more than doubled the value of their season's

exports through shrewd marketing.[39] That they did such things was

important, but it was vastly more important that the doings of the

merchants were based in a wholesome, expanding economy, for the health

of the economy was one of the essential components of broad context in

which people in the Middle Colonies reacted to the rush of events.

Just as essential were the internal politics of the colonies in the

area, which sometimes did and sometimes did not reflect events in the

outside world. There was, however, a general pattern: intra-colony

politics, while continuing to be driven in part--as politics always

are--by an inner logic and that had little to do with the outer context,

increasingly mirrored external events, until external and internal

had become nearly indistinguishable.

In New York two fractional groups had long contended for control

of the Assembly and Council and for the favor of the governors. The

DeLancey-Livingston feud had originated in rivalry over the fur trade,

differences in enterprise (the Livingstons were large landholders,

the DeLanceys were merchants), and differences in religion (the Livingstons

were Presbyterians, the DeLanceys Anglicans). The original differences

had ceased to be strong motives for action, and the rivalry continued

only out of habit; but it was habit with a meaning, for control of

the government of New York could be the means to preferment and

wealth.[40]

In the mid-sixties the DeLanceys came to power through their

stand on the Imperial question: at the time of the Stamp Act crisis

they opposed the tax more vociferously than did the Livingstons, and

that won them a slight majority in the Assembly. Subsequently they

increased their popularity by firmly resisting other Parliamentary

encroachments--until the opportunity arose to strike a bargain with

Parliament, involving mutual conciliation. Meanwhile, they consolidated

their power, increasing their popular majority and gaining more favors

from the governors. By 1770 they held every seat on the Council save

two or three and had comparable strength in the Assembly.[41] The few

Livingstonians who managed to get into office--the senior R.R. Livingston,

Lewis Morris, and a Livingston supporter from Orange county--were removed

after DeLancey men charged them, falsely, with fraud and conflicts of

interest. In the counties, DeLancey men replaced Livingstonians in

sheriff's offices on two occasions, and when R.R. Livingston, Jr., and

John Jay, seeking to prosecute squatters on Livingston's estates,

appealed to the Council to reform the judiciary in Dutchess County,

DeLancey men wheedled a refusal from the governor.[42] And all this

political hammering yielded abundant rewards: the lion's share of more

than two million acres of land grants.[43]

As the storm clouds gathered in 1773-1774, the DeLanceys had a

firm grasp on the reins of power, but when the storm broke they lost

it, through the same mechanism by which they had won it earlier.

This time they totally misjudged the force of the local response to

Imperial events. When the call came to choose delegates to the

First Continental Congress, DeLancey men outside New York City, perhaps

blinded by overconfidence, refused to take part in the extra-legal

meetings that made the choice and Livingstonians--John Haring and

Henry Wisner from Orange County, and Philip Schuyler of Albany--won three

of four seats, and Livingston men continued to hold them despite the

increasing radicalism that ensued in those counties during the next
two years. [44] Inside the city DeLancey men did choose to do battle,
but they could do no better than hold their own: the city's delegates
included two DeLancey men, James Duane and John Alsop, two Livingstonians,
Philip Livingston and John Jay, and a fifth delegate, Isaac Low, who
held a large personal following in the city. [45]

The Livingstonians, thus assured of a majority in Congress in
1774, followed with another victory. When the colony called a Provincial
Convention in the spring of 1775, they won a clear majority, and thereafter
they dominated the Convention as well as New York's delegation to
Congress. Furthermore, even as they fended off DeLanceyites on the
one side, Livingstonians checked or controlled the doings of the
independence-minded Whigs on the other. Although the favorites of the
Mechanics Association in the city and the more forward Whigs in Long
Island gained a few seats in the Convention, the mechanics' delegates
attended only irregularly and those who did attend usually followed
the lead of Livingstonians. Even Alexander McDougall, the "John Wilkes"
of America and long-standing favorite of the Sons of Liberty, was

against independence and sided with the Livingstons.[46]

However, when the Livingstons gained control, their victory
proved to be a barren one. Once in power, they were eager to do just
what the DeLanceys had done earlier, namely, smooth out the principal
differences with Britain as quickly as possible, so as to get on with
the business of exploiting control of government for their own profit.
This was New York's version of the traditional Whig position, and the
Livingstons were disposed toward it out of sentiment as well as
interest. But the Imperial crisis impeded settlement of the differences,
and as the crisis deepened the Livingstonians became increasingly
frustrated and increasingly fixed in their determination to settle
them. And even had the crisis as a general phenomenon not elicited that
response, various details of the crisis, as they affected New York, would
have: Isaac Sears led a band of Connecticut militiamen and enthusiasts
for independence in a foray into New York City and destroyed a Tory
printing press; Charles Lee, a general by Congressional appointment,
appeared with a sizable body of New England militia and threatened
the colony; and rumors were rife that the British were organizing the

58

Indians to the west and a full-scale naval attack from the sea. To

the Livingstonians, redress and reconciliation grew progressively

more desirable and progressively less obtainable.

It also grew progressively more difficult for their delegates

to keep pace with the rapid developments in Congress. For one thing,

they reacted slowly to changes in the situation; for example, as

late as 1775 the elder R.R. Livingston was still advising his son, a

delegate, to hold fast to the position, long since rendered obsolete

by events, that Parliament had a right to levy external taxes but not

internal taxes.[47] For another thing, some of the Livingstonians in

Congress, while prepared to protest that England was acting tyrannically,

became frightened as soon as it appeared that Congress was likely to

go a good deal further, and they promptly vacated their seats and some

forswore active attachment to the Congress or the Patriot cause. Most of

the Livingston men who served in Congress between 1774 and 1776--including

John Jay, R.R. Livingston, Jr., Philip Livingston, John Haring, Philip

Schuyler, Lewis Morris, Francis Lewis, and Henry Wisner--were willing

to go along (however reluctantly) with all measures of resistance

up to and including taking up arms, but drew the line just short of independence.[48] Only two of them, George Clinton and William Floyd, favored crossing that line, and neither of them was prepared openly to advocate independence, and neither, on July 2, 1776, was willing to go against the remainder of New Yorkers and cast his vote for independence.[49]

The course of events in New Jersey, while springing from different internal conditions, led Congressional delegates from New Jersey in the same direction as those from New York. Politically--and socially and economically as well--New Jersey was split into two distinct parts. The division originated in early grants of land to two sets of proprietors, the Council of Proprietors of West Jersey and the Board of Proprietors of East Jersey. The western section was an economic dependency of Philadelphia, the eastern of New York; the west had a large Quaker population, the east was culturally and religiously more diverse. In colonial politics the two sections differed sharply.

The shares of the proprietorship in West Jersey had very early been divided into minute fractions, and that fact, together with Quakerism, bred a generally harmonious kind of political life in

the area. Western representatives in the colonial Assembly could

usually be counted on to support the royal governor, William Franklin.

When the imperial crisis arose in 1774 they agreed to the decision

to send delegates to Congress (at the time that was consistent with

continuing to support the governor), but the delegates from West

New Jersey were extremely moderate. There were three, one of

whom (John Cooper) never attended, one of whom (James Kinsey) resigned

in November of 1775 and refused any further part in the matter, and

one of whom (Richard Smith) went along with the New Yorkers who were

willing to take up arms but not declare independence.[50]

East Jersey was a much more volatile place. Distribution there

of ownership of the proprietary shares was extremely narrow, and a

small clique of men, in close alliance with the royal governor,

dominated the distribution of land and the control of lucrative offices,

thereby engendering bitter resentment among the people at large.

In recent years there had evolved a loosely organized but powerful

anti-proprietary political faction, based largely in Essex County.

Men there headed opposition in New Jersey to the Stamp Act and the

61

Townshend duties, and they were the most vigorous and vocal opponents

of the Intolerable Acts in 1774. The three delegates from East Jersey

to the First Congress—William Livingston, John De Hart, and Stephen

Crane—were representative of the best of the area's opposition to the

governor and the oppressive measures of Parliament. All three

adopted the traditional Whig position of seeking liberty within the

Empire; De Hart dropped out in 1775 but the other two were among those

who advocated every measure of opposition short of independence.[51] All

three stood, however, on treacherous footing, for the general populace in

the area was considerably less restrained than they were, and by the

winter of 1775-1776 a number of independent-minded men were aspiring,

with a good deal of popular backing, especially from the local Scotch-Irish,

to overthrow their leadership.

Delaware proved to be the weakest link in an otherwise solid

chain of traditional Whiggism in the Middle Colonies. As in New Jersey,

the area settled and inhabited by Scotch-Irish (New Castle County

and the upper part of Kent) took the lead in opposition to Great

Britain from 1765 onward. Three principal leaders emerged—George Read

and Thomas McKean from New Castle County, and Caesar Rodney from

Kent--and they were the delegates to Congress from Delaware from

the beginning until after independence was declared. McKean and

Rodney openly favored independence by early 1776.[52] Read joined those

Congressmen who were willing to resort to arms, but for a number

of personal and political reasons he refused to go further. He was a

leading member of the so-called Court Party in Delaware, which remained

antipathetic to separation and which was supported by a minority of

the people in New Castle County, perhaps half or more of those in

Kent, and the overwhelming majority of those in Sussex.[53]

Pennsylvania appeared, in general matters of Empire, to be much

like the other Middle Colonies. Throughout the decade of Imperial

controversy, most of its inhabitants, like those in the other Middle

Colonies, were firm and often militant in their insistence on the

sanctity of American rights, and equally firm in their insistence

that the Empire be preserved. They took that stand for the same

broad cultural, economic, social, and political reasons that the

others did. As in New York and New Jersey, the game of politics was

played in Pennsylvania as a means of contending for preferment and

wealth, principally in the form of land, and had, at first, little

or no direct connection with political developments in the broader

theater of Empire. As in the others, too, internal and external politics

increasingly impenged upon one another until at last they had become

inseparable.

But there was a vital difference in Pennsylvania. It was the

largest and most populous of the Middle Colonies, and in it the social

matrix of politics was most complex; and for those reasons, as well as

certain accidents of history, the course of politics was both intricate

and unique. Whereas in New York, New Jersey and Delaware the lines

of political development were fairly straight, the procession of events

fairly logical, and the personnel of factions relatively stable, in

Pennsylvania it was the opposite; events unfolded erratically and turned

on bizarre pivots, and the membership and positions of factions were

confused, irregular, and shifting.

Prior to the French and Indian War, politics in Pennsylvania

had centered in a conflict between Proprietary and Anti-Proprietary

factions. Powerful and numerous Quakers led repeated attempts to wrest

control of the colony from the governors and their allies, and disputes

of that nature lent regularity to the political arena. War and issues

engendered by war disrupted the system and the factions fell apart.

Two men, neither of whom was a Quaker, Benjamin Franklin and Joseph

Galloway, rose to power by capitalizing on popular hostility toward

the Penns and fashioning various remnants of the old Anti-Proprietary

faction into a new faction; however, the new factions never polarized into

permanent groups, largely because efforts to pursue local ends in local

politics were disrupted by a succession of problems arising from

the intrusion of external forces--the outbreak of a serious Indian

problem, the invasion of the colony by large numbers of new immigrants,

and above all the conflict between Parliament and the colonies.

The attitude of the Galloway-Franklin Anti-Proprietary faction toward

most matters of Imperial controversy was largely one of vacillation,

except that its leaders were usually eager to settle such matters, one

way or the other, so that they might be about the execution of a grandiose

scheme they had devised. Their opponents, the Proprietary faction, was not

really a faction at all but a loose coalition of occasional friends

or allies of the Penns, together with various personal enemies

of Galloway and Franklin and, for reasons that had to do more with

external rather than with internal affairs, John Dickinson. Governor

John Penn was generally disposed to side with Parliament in its disputes

with the colonies; Dickinson was the "William Pitt of America," the

firmest, most articulate, and most respected leader of those who sought

a redress of grievances within the framework of Empire. When the last

Imperial crisis came, the leaders of the Anti-Proprietary faction made a

desperate effort to seize control of the resistance movement, failed,

and fell apart; Galloway took one extreme position, becoming a Loyalist,

Franklin took the other, emerging as an outspoken champion of

independence, and their erstwhile followers went in all directions.

In gross, that was what happened in Pennsylvania. But the colony

and its leaders, especially Dickinson, require a much closer examination,

partly because the details of the interplay between political leaders

in Pennsylvania had a great deal to do with determining the outcome of

the Imperial contest, and especially because Dickinson both epitomized

the stand taken by Patriot leaders in all four of the Middle Colonies

and played a central role as a leader in the Continental Congress.

67

III

JOHN DICKINSON

Of all colonial leaders of resistance to Parliament, John Dickinson was the most firm and influential exponent of the policy of seeking redress of colonial grievances within the Empire. He helped create this traditional Whig position, and he defended and sustained it for a full decade. From the beginning of the dispute, Dickinson asserted that colonials had rights and liberties, notably the right to tax themselves, which they were obligated to defend, and he emphatically denied that such resistance was a covert effort to gain independence or that independence was a practical solution to Americans' problems. Even during the final Imperial crisis, and in the face of riots, insurrection, war, and threats to his person, Dickinson remained firm; he modified his position only to accomodate events, and he abandoned traditional opposition to Great Britain only after the Declaration of Independence made his position meaningless.

Dickinson's stand, and his adamant defense of it, arose in large measure from his background and experience. Dickinson was by birth

68

A Quaker and a native of the Delaware Valley. Born in 1732, he grew to

maturity in an atmosphere that inspired confidence in members of the

Quaker community. Quakers dominated life in the Valley at its center,

Philadelphia, and Dickinson was one of many young men who reaped

the benefits of the strength and solidarity of the Quakers. His father,

a gentlemen farmer of Dover, Delaware, gave Dickinson a good education,

encouraged him in the practice of law in Philadelphia, and in 1753 sent

him to England for study at the Inns of Court. And, Dickinson made the

best of the opportunities presented him. He studied diligently, profited

by his experience abroad, moved freely in the upper strata of Philadelphia

society, and later married into one of the most wealthy Quaker families in

Pennsylvania. Dickinson's background and intimate familial experience

bred a sense of confidence in his place as a gentlemen farmer and leader.[1]

Dickinson's Quaker heritage meant something more than place,

preferment, and wealth, for by the time Dickinson reached his twenties

Quakerism offered clear alternatives in beliefs and practices. The

first immigrants of the Quaker persuasion had been puritanical in habit

and evangelical in outlook. They had had a strong sense of divine

mission and a strong belief that they might build a holy community

of brotherly love and material disinterestedness, but two generations

of profitable struggle in the wilderness had left its mark. A significant

number of Quakers had lost their fervor at time they made striking

gains in farming and commerce. Men learned to balance piety and prosperity.

By the 1750's, it was apparent that many members of the Society of

Friends had comprised the virtues of their fathers with material success.

When repudiation of the past became painfully conspicuous, the more

strict members of the sect reacted by calling for abandonment of

"this worldliness." Sectarian evangelicalism waxed strong, but Dickinson

eventually resisted the renewal of religious enthusiasm, and stood with

the more secular Quakers.[2]

That did not mean that either Dickinson, or men who took the same

position as he, rejected Quakerism. They rejected the renewal of

religious fervor, but they retained many of the traditions of the faith.

Quakers, unlike most protestant sects, emphasized the power of the

"inner light" in revealing the will of God, knowledge of right and

wrong, and right action to the individual Christian. Every man , Quakers

taught, had within him this spark of divinity. Quakers, unlike other

protestant sects, de-emphasized holy scripture as a source of authority

and, as a result, were less restrained by outward law than by inner

conscience. They did not, however, press the doctrine to extremes--

that would have brought them to the brink of religious anarchy--rather,

the Society of Friends substituted consensus of the majority of their

sect as the final authority on points of dispute.[3] Hence, in Dickinson's

religious tradition, the community of believers had a large share in

deciding right and wrong, and Dickinson's religious experiences

contributed to his habits of life and mind. He retained his attachments

to some Quaker social values, shunning overly conspicuous displays

of wealth, yet taking advantage of the comforts wealth always affords--

a middle way. More revealing was his suspicion of religious enthusiasm,

which, in combination with his retention of the faith on his own terms,

indicated a disposition toward caution and deliberation. Dickinson

was rarely impulsive--though he could be obstinate and vitriolic--

and strongly urged moderation and reflection.[4]

71

Last of all, Dickinson's study abroad was directly connected

with his place in Quaker society, and with the cultural ties between

Philadelphia and England. From 1753 to 1757, his study at the Inns

of Court broadened his experience and outlook. He observed

the Empire at its center, and he read not only in law, history,

and political theory, but also in the commercial authors of the day.[5]

He knew a good deal about English institutions and imperial commerce,

about the general flow of trade, the theories behind regulatory

legislation, and the Imperial view of the American colonies. In 1757,

at the age of twenty-five, Dickinson returned to Pennsylvania extremely

well-informed, and, as events would soon reveal, a young man of

cultivated talent and political acumen.

The Pennsylvania to which Dickinson returned was decidely

different from the Pennsylvania which he had left. A series of

events which had begun in 1755 and which would extend to 1763 had

changed and would change further the world Dickinson had known. The

advent of war had brought a serious conflict between the Quaker-dominated

Assembly and the governor. The Quakers had been severely beaten, and

their power broken. By 1757, new leaders (who were not Quakers at all) assumed leadership of the anti-proprietary forces and the political arena was the scene of widespread alteration. This change and others to come brought uncertainty.[6] Nonetheless, Dickinson threw himself into law practice and into politics, and in 1762 he was elected to the Pennsylvania Assembly by the voters of Philadelphia.

One year later, in his first major political showing, Dickinson found himself in head-on opposition to a proposal instituted by a powerful and popular group headed by Galloway, Franklin, and many influential members of the Society of Friends. In 1763, the French and Indian War had officially ended and Pennsylvania settlements had just begun to resume their westward expansion, only to be abruptly halted. Settlement beyond the Appalachians was legally prohibited by royal proclamation, and at the same time Indians began a vicious and effective struggle to keep settlers out of the trans-Allegheny region. The hapless inhabitants of the frontier, convinced by the inaction of the Assembly that the east was dedicated to their destruction, gathered a small army and marched on Philadelphia. In these developments

73

Franklin, Galloway, and their ally Samuel Wharton saw opportunity.

Franklin personally went out to meet and turn back the frontiersmen,

returned to Philadelphia as the hero of the hour, and led a chorus

of cries that the Proprietary government had failed. The three men,

playing on the Quakers' long-standing animosity to the Proprietary,

called for revocation of the colonial Charter and reorganization of

Pennsylvania as a royal colony; and by these and similar means they

gained control of the Assembly. They had distinct plans for exploiting

their newly won power: a plan to induce the Crown to revoke the

charter, confiscate the Penns' lands, and (perhaps by way of gratitude)

give them a grant of some ten million acres in Ohio. In 1764 they

launched their attack: Galloway and Franklin introduced a bill in

the Assembly recommending a change to a royal charter, and later,

Franklin left for England to let everyone there know that the Penns

were ruining America and to press the request for the land grant.[7]

Dickinson vehemently opposed the maneuver; in the Assembly he

assumed leadership of those who sought to protect the Charter, and

outside the Assembly he exchanged hotly worded pamphlets with

74

Anti-Proprietary men. Dickinson did not pretend that the existing system was perfect--indeed, he pointedly specified a number of the evils of the Proprietors as well as of the system--but he was certain that greater evil would result if the Charter were revoked. If Pennsylvania became a royal colony, he said, its inhabitants might expect an established church, a standing army, and diminution of the powers of the Assembly.[8]

Certainly Dickinson's stand was not that of a temperamental aristocrat bent on supporting the existing system because that system was autocratic.[9] Under the Charter of Liberties of 1701, the Pennsylvania Assembly enjoyed powers similar to those of the assemblies of Connecticut and Rhode Island. It had full power over legislation, appointment of judges, and elections to its body (which were annual), and it had shown an ability to increase the scope of its powers when, in 1755, it forced the Penns to agree to the taxation of their estates. The Charter guaranteed religious toleration by its eighth article; "Liberty of Conscience," it read, "shall be kept and remain, without any alteration, inviolably forever."

75

Probably most men were qualified to vote; statutory law enfranchised adult males of twenty-one who professed a belief in Jesus as the son of God and who held fifty acres of land, twelve of them cleared, or held a £50 rateable estate.[10]

In his fight to retain the Charter, Dickinson was supported by those men who had consistently supported the proprietors and now stood to gain by it in a colony suddenly grown smaller in amount of available land, along with most of the frontier communities; the outspoken and powerful Quaker Israel Pemberton, the Anglican merchant Thomas Willing , the Anglican ministerial lights William Smith and Jacob Duché, the Allen family, and Francis Alison, Dickinson's former tutor and so-called "Presbyterian Pope." Thus old, well-established powers and new, aggressive frontier farmers joined with Anglicans, Quakers, Presbyterians, merchants, large landowners, and artisans in the belief that the existing system best served their interests and that change might prove ruinous. They eventually won.[11]

76

All this made one thing clear: Pennsylvania was devoid of internal consistency. No single, simple majority ruled the colony. The political sentiment of the various cultural groups was unpredictable, and often economic interests and personal preferences divided the groups against themselves. Quaker merchant and Quaker farmer were often on different sides on domestic policies, and Presbyterian artisans and Presbyterian frontiersmen supported different factions in the crisis of 1763-1764. Anglicans often opposed the Proprietary party, but could not be depended upon to support a change to royal government.

Such an unsettled and confused state of affairs ran against Dickinson's grain. He longed for a politics of consensus where none was to be found, and through most of his life he was torn between his instincts and experience. Long before he entered the debating arena of the Continental Congress, he took a middle way that bridged his hopes and the realities of politics in Pennsylvania.

77

The first major Imperial crisis arose just as Dickinson was
ending his fight to keep the Charter. Word arrived that Parliament
had received a bill proposing a stamp tax for America, and Dickinson
saw the consequences of submission. Harassed by the movement for
change from within, he nonetheless turned to face the challenge from
without. In a brief pamphlet entitled The Late Regulations Respecting
the British Colonies, he reviewed the Currency Act, the Sugar Act, and
prohibitions on trade with the Spanish West Indies. He declared that
the laws were economically ruinous to the colonies and partially to
blame for the state of affairs in Pennsylvania (the short-lived, as
it turned out, post war depression). The currency supply in the
colony, he said, was already low; the Sugar Act drew hard money to
England; Pennsylvania merchants were cut off from the Spanish islands,
formerly a good source of specie; and now England had proposed a
tax that would draw more money from the colonies. Dickinson protested
that the colony could not bear the additional load, and, at the end
of the pamphlet, hinted also that the tax would crush the powers of
colonial assemblies.[12]

78

There was little reason to expect that the caldron of

Pennsylvania politics would bubble up any appreciable support for

Dickinson. None of the members of the powerful Franklin-Galloway

clique saw anything to recommend a stamp tax, but when it passed

they accepted the fact. In England, Franklin took steps to put one of

his supporters in the office of stamp collector, and at home, Joseph

Galloway prepared to support Parliament.[13] But even as they did so,

pamphleteers and colonial assemblies rose up to denounce the Act,

and in 1765, colonials everywhere convinced one another that Parliament

had no power to tax them and that the Act should not go into force.[14]

In Pennsylvania, the unpredictable happened: Galloway and Franklin

had to beat a hasty retreat , for when the news arrived that the

Stamp Act had indeed become law, the whole colony fell into a state

of agitation, and Pennsylvanians forgot their local factional attachments

and moved in concert against the Act.

The colony trembled dangerously close to the brink of violence.

City dwellers--merchants and artisans -- took the lead in creating

non-importation agreements, and sporadic riots broke out. Dickinson

did not back down. He opposed enforcement of the Act and favored

refusing to import English goods. His earlier stand against a royal

charter for the colony and against the Stamp Act now stood him in

good stead. The Assembly sent him, along with George Bryan, John

Morton, and Joseph Fox, to a general meeting of colonial delegates

in New York. There Dickinson assumed the role of the penman of the

Congress, and as such he formulated many of the broad statements

of colonial opposition to Parliamentary taxation. 15

In the Stamp Act Resolves, Dickinson defined colonial attitudes

as to where colonials stood in the Empire. He first stated that all

colonials were faithfully allegiant to the crown. He next affirmed

that colonials owned "all due subordination to that august body -- the

Parliament of Great Britain." But then, in three articles, he specified

what was not included, from the colonial view, in "due subordination."

He maintained that colonials were entitled to all the inherent rights

and liberties of natural-born subjects of the realm; that taxation

by their own representatives was one of these rights; that colonials

could never be represented in Parliament; and that, therefore, only

colonial assemblies could levy tax bills. The Resolutions were as ingenious in what they did not admit as they were in what they admitted, in what they affirmed as in what they did not affirm.[16]

In early 1766, Dickinson took and further helped create the position taken by all well-informed Whigs. "Kings and Parliament," he wrote in an attach on statements in a petition to England from Barbados, "could not give the rights essential to happiness as you confess those invaded by the Stamp Act to be. We claim them from a higher source -- from the King of kings, and Lord of all the earth." Rights, he continued, were born in men, created in men, and existed with men, and one of those rights was "to be taxed by those I trust."[17] It was a Stuart error, he said, to think that charters granted liberties. Dickinson anticipated the Declaratory Act when he inquired rhetorically: did Barbadians suppose that, since Parliament legally made some laws to bind colonials, it could make any laws to bind colonials? Resistance to such stupidity, he said, was not rebellion but good sense. He closed the article by reiterating the essence of the Stamp Act Resolves, and by saying that colonial action in 1765 had constituted neither

rebellion nor a desire for colonial independence, but merely a
refusal to admit that Parliament had the right to tax the colonials.[18]

Pennsylvania remained in a state of excitement until news of
repeal came in early 1766. Dickinson drew one important inference from
the events. For the first time in nearly eight years, Pennsylvania
had united as one man, and Dickinson openly warned England that the
only way to unify colonials was to continue to threaten their rights
and pass legislation which worked economic hardships upon them.[19]
On word of the repeal of the stamp tax, politics in Pennsylvania resumed
their normal, bitterly divisive course. Dickinson was made painfully
aware of that, because city voters had earlier turned him out of office
despite his leadership of the opposition to Parliament.[20] Dickinson
did not , however, dwell on the crisis overly long; as far as he was
concerned riots, suspensions of courts, and the general congress had
passed into history. He moved into the countryside near Philadelphia
and, surrounded by Quaker farmers who resented his previous support of
the Proprietary faction, he was left out of the Assembly for five
years. Even so, though he did not know it, his labor for American

rights in the Empire had just begun.

The quiet that repeal of the Stamp Act brought to Pennsylvania was short-lived. Word filtered into the province that the New York Assembly was having difficulty with Parliament over the provisions of the Quartering Act of March, 1765. Then in September, 1767, Pennsylvanians learned of the Townshend Acts. But again most Pennsylvania leaders held back, and did not join the resistance until large numbers of Pennsylvanians, after learning that Massachusetts and Virginia were opposing the Townshend Acts., also began to oppose the Acts. Again too, Dickinson took an early, strong and widely influential stand.

The provisions of the Townshend Acts were published in Philadelphia newspapers in October, 1767. Dickinson read the three bills carefully, then took up his pen and began to draft what turned out to be a series of classic letters. In December, the first of his twelve Letters from a Farmer in Pennsylvania appeared; the last was published in mid-February, 1768.[21] Dickinson had a double purpose: he aimed at stirring Pennsylvanians out of their lethargy and at making known the unconstitutionality of the Acts. His sequence of attack was important.

83

He first remonstrated against the act that suspended the legislature

of New York; next, he turned on the act levying duties on certain

exports to the colonies; then, he laid down means of opposition. Not

until the fourth letter did he feel bound to go into intricate detail

on the vexing question of the distinction between "internal" and "external"

taxation--which, he maintained, was a nonsensical distinction and one

that neither the Stamp Act Congress nor any responsible American

leader had ever made.

Parliament, Dickinson wrote, followed unconstitutional procedures

when it tried to force the New York Assembly to follow its directive

under the Quartering Act, and went far beyond its legal powers when

it suspended the New York Assembly for refusing to comply. The

Imperial framework provided legitimate channels, he said, for supplying

of troops: the Crown could and should have requested that New York

supply the troops, and the Assembly would have been bound to comply.

Had New York refused, the Crown could have legitimately punished New

York. Parliament's action under the Quartering Act, he said, was in

fact a subterfuge. "It is a parliamentary assertion of the supreme authority

of the British legislature over these colonies, in the point of taxation,

and it is intended to COMPEL New York into a submission to that

authority." [22]

In the second letter he amplified his position. "The parliament,"

Dickinson said, "unquestionably possesses the legal authority to

regulate the trade of Great Britain, and all her colonies." It did this

in legitimate fashion until it passed the Stamp Act, he continued, for

though Parliament "imposed duties on trade, yet those duties were always

imposed with design to restrain the commerce of one part, that was

injurious to another, and thus to promote the general welfare."

Colonists were legally bound to pay such general duties, but not to pay

any special duties levied for the purpose of raising a revenue. The

colonies had resisted the Stamp Tax as legislation for revenue purposes,

and they won their point. The issue now was the same, Dickinson said,

for though the Townshend duties were offered in the guise of trade

regulation they were in fact revenue measures. He thundered at colonials

in an ominous tone: "If you ONCE admit, that Great Britain may lay duties

upon her exportations to us, for the purpose of levying money on us only,

she will then have nothing to do, but lay duties on the articles

she prohibits us to manufacture -- and the tragedy of American liberty

is finished." [23]

The third letter rounded out his theme and discussed the suitable

forms of resistance. Some few persons, he said, counselled Americans

not to resist at all, lest they provoke a powerful Britain into even

greater oppression, and instead to leave themselves "at the mercy of

chance, time, ministers." Foolish counsel, said Dickinson, for

"usurpations, which might have been successfully opposed at first,

acquire strength by continuance, and thus become irrestable." Dickinson

outlined what ought to be done to oppose usurpation of rights: first,

petition; second, prevent unconstitutional legislation from being

enforced, by economic coercion if need be; last, "if at length

it becomes UNDOUBTED, that the inveterate resolution is formed to

annihilate the liberties of the governed, the English history affords

frequent examples of resistance by force." But, Dickinson warned,

colonials must exercise caution at every point, lest their firmness

degenerate into anger and lead them to forget their loyalty to king

and mother country. That would be the worst of calamities, he

said: "Torn from the body, to which we are united by religion, liberty,

laws, affections, relation, language and commerce, we must bleed at

every vein." [24]

Dickinson's first Letters from a Farmer had greater impact outside

Pennsylvania than inside. As his statements attracted a wider following,

Dickinson gathered momentum. In succeeding letters he indicated the

instrumental changes in the relationships between colonials and

Parliament made by the Townshend duties. He deplored the insidiousness

of dressing taxation and money bills in the guise of unrelated legislation.

He summarized the "general history of oppression" since 1765 and declared

that Parliament's pretended right to legislate for the colonies in

all cases was at the root of English policies. He asserted that the

Townshend Acts were leveled at the continental colonies only and not

at the other colonies of the Empire, and that the Townshend Acts, if

enforced, would destroy the balance of legislative powers in the

Empire. And in the last letter Dickinson reiterated his challenge

to the colonial assemblies that they adopt resolutions against the new tax. [25]

87

By mid-February, 1768, Massachusetts representatives had done just that. The Representatives remonstrated against the duties by issuing the "Circular Letter," wherein they rebuked Parliament's imposition of trade duties on the people of Massachusetts "with the sole and express purpose of raising a revenue."[26] Governor Bernard asked the Massachusetts representatives to rescind the letter. They refused by a majority of ninety-two to seventeen, whereupon Bernard dissolved the General Court. Bostonians stepped-up their cry for economic retaliation.[27]

At a large meeting of Philadelphians held a month later, Dickinson was defeated when he proposed that Philadelphia join Boston in calling for a non-importation agreement, and add a plan for a non-exportation agreement as well.[28] Faction and interest combined successfully against him: the Anti-Proprietary leadership, abetted by various merchants who feared the monetary losses implicit in an interruption of commerce, raised a cry against "illegal combinations," riots, and anarchy. It was another year before Philadelphia merchants, as a group, agreed not to import English manufactures, and they never adopted the non-exportation plan.[29]

88

And that was not the worst of it. As the Townshend Act crisis
abated, factiousness in Pennsylvania politics increased. The non-
importation agreement among the merchants and inhabitants of Pennsylvania
continued as a source of friction during most of 1769 and 1770. Furthermore,
the artisans and mechanics in Philadelphia began to crystallize as a
separate faction with its own leadership. Non-importation, by cutting
the flow of British goods, increased the demand for home manufactures.
Accordingly, the artisans stopped supporting the Anti-Proprietary faction
and joined those who favored tighter enforcement of non-importation.
Two men emerged as their principal leaders: Charles Thomson, an immigrant
who had steadily moved up the ladder of success, and Thomas Mifflin,
a retail merchant and lawyer. In 1769, when Parliament repealed all the
Townshend duties save that on tea, Thomson and Mifflin headed a movement
to keep the non-importation agreement intact. But in the committee that
had been chosen to police non-importation, Philadelphia merchants
insisted that Marylanders, who were not pledged to non-importation, were
stealing their customers, and the committee rejected Thomson's and

89

Mifflin's proposal. They resigned from the committee and, under

their leadership, their faction temporarily turned its attention

to domestic politics--particularly, agitation for extension of the

franchise, increased representation in the Assembly for the city,

and equitable representation in the colony. So solid was the group

that Joseph Galloway could no longer hold an Assembly seat from the

city; he was, however, able to retain a seat by being elected as a

representative of Bucks County.[30] In Philadelphia County, the

Anti-Proprietary faction continued to be dominant, though in 1770

the county returned Dickinson to the Assembly, largely because of

the great intercolonial and even international prestige he had

won as author of the Letters from a Farmer.

For three years, 1770 to 1773, internal political alignments

in Pennsylvania continued to shift, never quite polarizing but nonetheless

following a pattern. Despite its losses, the Anti-Proprietary faction

retained its control of the Assembly and in 1771 Galloway was re-elected

Speaker for the sixth consecutive year. Quakers, in general, continued

to support the Anti-Proprietary faction and continued to hold the balance

of power in domestic politics, but they were less cohesive than

they had been, and they no longer had unchallenged control of the

city. Ranged against the Anti-Proprietary faction were, first, the

Proprietary governor and those who supported him for personal and

internal reasons, and second, several groups which opposed the Franklin-

Galloway clique because of its indecisive and opportunistic stand on

Imperial issues but, at the same time, harbored a variety of attitudes

toward the Proprietary, extending from open hostility to indifference

to warm support. Thomson and Mifflin, despite their flirtation with

domestic issues, were primarily concerned with Imperial issues, and so

were their followers. On matters of Empire they were allied with a

number of merchants in the city, including Thomas Willing and Robert

Morris, though the merchants were devout supporters and the mechanics

devout enemies of the Proprietary. Outside the city these groups

were supported by Dickinson in the county, William Allen representative

for western Northampton, and a newcomer and acquaintance of Dickinson's,

James Wilson, in Carlisle and Reading. [31]

91

In 1773, news of the Tea Act reinjected Imperial issues into Pennsylvania politics. Thomson and Mifflin immediately set the artisans in motion, formed a "new Patriot" organization, and in December of 1773 turned back the tea ship Polly.[32] Opposition to Great Britain reached riotous proportions again, and Dickinson himself was little short of inflammatory. Under another self-effacing pseudonym, "Rusticus," he penned a series of letters to the Pennsylvania Journal that were far more vitriolic than those of the "Pennsylvania Farmer." He attacked the East India Tea Company as a "pillaging horde, " and charged that the Act itself was designed to establish a monopoly for a private company without an iota of moral fiber. "I have no doubt, " he said, that "this company, hackneyed as they are in murders, rapine and cruelty, would sacrifice the lives of thousands to preserve their trash, and enforce their measures. "[33] But Pennsylvanians again refused to unite. The meetings held in Philadelphia to discuss a new non-importation agreement were tempestuous. Anti-Proprietary leaders denounced as licentious the destruction of property by the Bostonians; Thomson and Mifflin defended the Bostonians; the violence and talk of violence alienated a number of

92

Quakers who had previously supported economic coercion of England.

By early 1774 disagreement was everywhere.[24]

It was into this volatile situation that the news of the Boston

Port Bill burst. The bill was designed to crush all resistance in all

colonies by totally crushing a single colony, but what it did was

create general pandemonium. In the face of the bill the colonists

everywhere could and did take a wide range of positions. On one extreme, they

could take up arms and march to Boston, an attitude shared by a few men,

but only a few; on the other, they could abandon Boston to its fate and

forswear resistance altogether, an attitude shared by a goodly number

of men. Another position on further resistance was to give Massachusetts

moral support with resolutions of sympathy and tangible support with

gifts of food and provisions, to adopt immediate and total policies

of non-importation and non-exportation, and to organize standing

conventions in each colony to stand by to take more drastic measures.

The more moderate and more widespread position on capitulation was to

disregard Boston or do nothing more about it than adopt resolutions

of sympathy, but to sooth the general agitation by some conciliatory

action, such as adopting mildly worded petitions and sending them

to London. And out of both wings of both camps began to come support

for a congress of delegates from all the colonies, which could in

solemn deliberation determine what was the best course for colonials

to take.[35]

In Pennsylvania the news of the bill evoked pretty much the

same reactions and left the inhabitants with pretty much the same range of

choices, though no one seriously proposed taking up arms. Specifically,

Thomson and Mifflin demanded the immediate adoption of non-importation

and non-exportation agreements, and not only agitated to bring this about

in Philadelphia, but went out into the back country and began trying

to organize support, county by county, for the establishment of

an extralegal colonywide convention. The friends of the Proprietary governor

and a considerable number of Philadelphia Quakers demanded total

capitulation and the immediate cessation of further resistance. That

polarization threw Galloway into a difficult and potentially fatal

situation: if Thomson and Mifflin succeeded they would overthrow

the authority of the Assembly and Galloway's power with it; if he took

any stand advocating firm resistance he would lose the support

of his Quaker friends in and around Philadelphia; if he took a

position that was even remotely like that of the governor and his

supporters, he was politically undone. Then the suggestions for

a continental congress began to be heard, and though he did not like

the idea it did offer Galloway a possibility however slim, of

saving himself; to endorse a Congress was to repudiate the radically

activist position of Thomson and Mifflin, and it also afforded a means

whereby Galloway could appear as both a friend of American liberty

and a confirmed moderate.[36]

Dickinson too was in a dilemma. He could destory Galloway's

political power by throwing his entire support to Mifflin and

Thomson, but the thought that if he did so, he would sacrifice

the possibility of unity against England. Earlier, in the Letters

from a Farmer, he had cautioned against an angry course. Anger

produces anger, he had said, and then a blind fury governs all. And

so he tried to strike a middle course by discussing economic coercion

as a good policy, but recommending, for the time being, moderation

and petition for redress of grievances. Also, Dickinson asked

the people to allow a general congress to direct American action.[37]

Dickinson also strove to work out a basis of Imperial

reconciliation in an essay entitled A New Essay on the Constitutional

power of The British Parliament. Here Dickinson proposed that

Parliament stop its aggression against Massachusetts, repeal its

assertion of the right to legislate for the colonies in all cases

and that henceforth, each respective colonial assembly should confirm

Parliamentary legislation touching on each respective colony. In

fine, Dickinson ceased to argue on the basis of the right to tax

and enlarged his views to include legislative procedures.[38]

Galloway managed to hold on to his power-temporarily. Philadelphia

refused to adopt a new non-importation agreement and the colony agreed

to call a convention in June to nominate delegates to a general congress.

Furthermore, though the June convention nominated Dickinson as a

delegate, Galloway was able to see to it that the Assembly excluded

him. Galloway was also able to rewrite the instructions for the

Pennsylvania delegation and to attend the Congress himself. Then

the wheel turned: in June Galloway's faction controlled the Assembly

and the Thomson-Mifflin-Dickinson group dominated the various extra-

legal meetings, but in the October elections the latter won control of

the Assembly. Philadelphia County elected Dickinson and the city re-elected

Mifflin, and the Assembly soon sent Dickinson to Congress.[39] John

Adams wrote that Pennsylvanians had struck a blow for liberty.[40]

In September and early October, before Dickinson arrived in Congress,

colonial delegates had debated what they ought to do and say about the

Coercive Acts. Every colony had some grievance to register, and every

colonial thought he knew how best to state the rights, liberties, and

beliefs of Englishmen in America. They all agreed that the Coercive

Acts were detestable, tyrannical, and oppressive. Even men whom others

called Tories agreed to that.[41] Americans might have been another

fifty years doing what they did, had not the British lion roared so

loudly at their door. The delegates clamped a lid of secrecy on the

proceedings. The clerk, Charles Thomson, recorded only what Congress

did, not what it debated, and he recorded in a purposely skimpy manner.[42]

97

Congress could not have created a more conspiratorial atmosphere had it tried. What the delegates did not realize was that their fears of disunity were more than justified, and to close the doors to the public worked directly in favor of their opponents.

By the time Dickinson took his seat most of the immediate issues had been decided. The Congress had agreed upon a petition of rights and grievances that called for a return to the state of affairs which had existed between the colonies and Great Britain prior to 1763. The fourth article of the petition of rights asserted the right of colonial legislatures to exclusive power over internal legislation, but left to Parliament the right to regulate trade. In other articles Congress protested against the Coercive Acts, the admiralty courts, the manner of prosecution for treason, and the appointment of men to the upper houses of some colonial legislatures "during pleasure of the Crown;" and, once again it flatly denied Parliament's right to tax. In addition, Congress urged colonials to establish local committees to set up non-importation agreements(the"Continental Association"), and simultaneously warned Britain that if colonial grievances were not redressed within

the year, then exports from the colonies, expecting rice to Europe, would also cease. Furthermore, Congress published addresses to the inhabitants of America, Great Britain, and Quebec, explaining American action and asking for support. Finally, Congress endorsed the Suffolk County, Massachusetts, resolves of September 9, declaring that force should and would be met with force.[43] Subsequently, when R. H. Lee submitted his petition to the king, Congress rejected it and requested that John Dickinson write another.[44] Once more colonials called for redress and reconciliation, this time systematically.

For all the calm and sane proposals of Congress, Pennsylvania political leaders broke completely, first on the Coercive Acts, then on the resolves of the Continental Congress. Joseph Galloway was defeated at every turn in the Congress, and when he requested that Congress enter his dissent, it refused.[45] In a last-ditch effort to hold on to power in Pennsylvania, Galloway attempted a series of maneuvers aimed at getting the Assembly to repudiate the Congress--either directly or by sending a separate petition to the Crown--and he almost succeeded.[46] Dickinson worked furiously to defeat Galloway, and in the end, as one

observer said, his activities turned the day.[47] Then Galloway

petulantly did what he had wanted to do all along: he published a

tract denouncing Congress as a seditious body whose members were bent

on obtaining independence.[48] In January of 1775, the Quakers in

Pennsylvania and New Jersey adopted resolutions condemning Congress'

actions, and thereby a large and powerful segment of Pennsylvania

moved to hostile opposition to the cause of America.[49] On the other

hand, the frontiersmen of central Pennsylvania made a move for more

power, and so did the artisans in the city. Thomson, Mifflin, George

Bryan, and George Ross of Lancaster encouraged and supported both.[50]

Dickinson played a cautious role, electing to respond to

developments rather than to direct them. Thus when Galloway attacked

the First Congress, Dickinson immediately wrote in full support of

Congress's measures; again, he did not personally take part in the

enforcement of the non-importation agreement, but when a rumor spread

that he was against the Association he put in an appearance at a

non-importation committee meeting. He refused to participate in efforts

to obtain armaments and begin militia training, though he was prepared

to fight if fighting became necessary. [51] This kind of conduct

fostered rumors of Dickinson's timidity. One Tory was pleased to

report that the Pennsylvania Farmer seldom, if ever, attended meetings

of the non-importation committee and in general had become "silent upon

the head of politics." [52] Dickinson, in other words, acted as he had

cautioned all to act at the Provincial Congress back in June of 1774,

when he had warned Pennsylvania to beware of excess in adopting

coercive measures and to stand by what Congress decided. He fully

appreciated the explosiveness of the situation during the months of

waiting for England's response to Congress' petition. He wrote to

Arthur Lee in London that if Parliament did not retreat as it had before,

then it would involve itself in a civil war that would make that of

the seventeenth century pale by comparison. [53] He hoped, anxiously, for

dislocation of the Ministry in England, for repeal and reconciliation.

Nearly a year passed and none came.

But word did come of a battle between Massachusetts militiamen and

royal troops at Lexington and Concord. A great wave of hostility to

England swept the people. Militia bands formed and trained for

war, and newspapers carried open statements that Americans were prepared
to fight. Then, sullen dissatisfaction set in, and Pennsylvanians
drew back. Though strong movements for war continued among men in the
city and in the central Pennsylvania frontier region, Pennsylvanians in
general grew hesitant. Even as late as 1776, only about eleven per cent
of the adult males in Pennsylvania were in arms, only a little
over ten thousand men out of a total of nearly a hundred thousand. [54]
Later, General Charles Lee would observe that Pennsylvania had been
a "quaking nag" that should have been kicked and whipped into support
of America. [55] Pennsylvanians were in fact not disloyal, but neither
were they particularly enthusiastic about defending American liberty
except with words.

During the tense weeks after Lexington and Concord, Pennsylvania's
leaders again followed different paths. Mifflin, Thomson, and Byran
agitated and worked for increased militia training. Dickinson accepted
command of a battalion of Pennsylvania militia, moved to a position
of leadership in the Assembly, and represented Pennsylvania in the
Second Continental Congress. The old Anti-Proprietary faction fell

apart. Galloway, after one defeat, abandoned politics. Franklin returned from his sojourn in England thoroughly disenchanted with Parliament and the Crown, and without the land grant he had gone to get. [56] Philadelphia elected him to the Assembly, and the Assembly elected him to Congress.

When the Second Congress opened in May, 1775, Dickinson stood pat on redress and reconciliation and fought against every proposal that breached the limits of traditional opposition. He wanted Congress to defend colonial rights and liberties, but not to abandon the Empire; he wanted Congress to lead America in the war that loomed on the horizon, but not to forswear allegiance to the Crown; he wanted Congress to adopt a policy that would allow most men to follow its lead, and thereby present England with a united front. He sought a flexible approach to the crisis that would leave the colonies uncommitted, and he looked askance at irrevocable action of any kind. That meant standing on what America had decided at the First Congress and going no further. "Our rights have already been stated," he said, "war is actually begun . . . . If Administration be desirous of stopping the effusion of British blood,

the opportunity is now offered to them." [57]

In May, Dickinson insisted upon a second petition to the Crown. New Englanders in Congress scoffed and disputed the value of the proposal. Massachusetts, they said, needed more than words. During the debates, Dickinson caught John Adams in the foyer of Congress and dressed him down. He told Adams that he would withdraw from Congress, and so would most other delegates from the Middle Colonies, if Adams persisted in his assaults upon petition and redress. [58] Dickinson told Congress that if England dared reject a second petition, "the more humble it is, the more such treatment will confirm the minds of our countrymen to endure all the misfortunes that may attend the contest." [59] In June and July, Dickinson agreed to the creation of a Continental Army. On the other hand, he found wide support in Congress and blocked a proposal that a formal confederation be established, and blocked another calling for abandonment of the Association in favor of opening trade with foreign nations and establishing an American navy. And, Dickinson drove John Adams, among others, to distraction. Adams wrote a personal attack on Dickinson which was intercepted by the British and published. The

two Patriots fell out: thereafter, Dickinson acted as if John Adams did not exist. [60]

Events moved more rapidly after that. Americans won in Quebec, and held Gage to a stalemate in Boston. In Pennsylvania, Patriot leaders stood supreme, and they forced through a tax on those men who refused to train for war. The Crown of Great Britain continued to follow a policy of divide and conquer. In October, 1775, word arrived that George III had issued a Proclamation of Rebellion. [61] America flared with hostility once more, and once again some men refused to support America any further. Two months after the Proclamation of Rebellion arrived, word came that the New Jersey Assembly was on the verge of petitioning the Crown separately, and Dickinson hastened to New Jersey to persuade the Assembly not to do so. [62] He told the Assembly that the Congress had made a decent and firm application for redress of grievances, and, when war began, did so again; any separate action hurt the cause of liberty and peace. [63] By the end of 1775, Dickinson was the leader of a loosely-knit group which urged that the First Congress had

sufficiently stated the aims of war.[64]

Dickinson could never have managed alone. Between 1774 and July, 1776, large numbers of Pennsylvanians remained firm in support of American liberty but equally firm in opposition to independence--despite the beginning of war, the creation of a Continental Army, a proclamation by their king declaring that the colonies were in rebellion, Parliamentary prohibition of colonial trade, and the pursuasive logic of Thomas Paine's Common Sense. Over these same months, their Assembly continually appointed delegates to the Congress who regularly maintained that independence was neither a constructive nor a desirable course for the colonies. In 1774 the delegation included Galloway, Samuel Rhoads, Charles Humphreys and Edward Biddle, all of whom opposed anything but petitioning the home government. The other two delegates, John Morton and George Ross, favored the Association. Dickinson bridged those two groups. Only Thomas Mifflin thought that armaments were necessary. The second delegation to Congress included Galloway and Rhoads, but they declined to serve; even so, most members of the delegation were against a formal declaration of separation. Biddle, Morton and Humphreys accepted

re-appointments, and other delegates--John Dickinson, Thomas Willing,

and James Wilson--stood against separation. Thomas Mifflin and

Benjamin Franklin were the only delegates who thought a second petition

to the Crown would be entirely ineffective and who favored opening

trade to foreign shipping and establishing a navy and a confederation.

In 1776, the Pennsylvania delegation to Congress included a larger

majority of opponents to independence than it had in 1775. Dickinson,

Wilson, Humphreys, Morton, and Willing returned to Congress, and two

new delegates, Robert Morris and Andrew Allen, supported them. Franklin

was the only delegate firmly committed to independence.[65]

In December, 1775, New Englanders made another attempt to force

a confederation and in early January threatened to confederate separately.[66]

But at the same time, Congress received the Maryland Resolves which

expressly stated that their delegates were to concur in no measures

that even implied separation from Great Britain. "The Farmer," one

Marylander wrote, "and some others to whom in confidence [the resolves]

were shown say they brethe [sic] that spirit, which ought to govern

all public bodies, firmness tempered with moderation."[67]

107

For the first few months of 1776 Dickinson and like-minded men in Congress prevailed, though neither they nor the advocates of independence were strong enough to move Congress very far in any direction. An exchange that took place in mid-January illustrates the delicacy of the balance of power. On January 15 Dickinson induced James Wilson to read a long speech introducing a motion calling for Congress to repeat its disavowal of aims at independence. Samuel Adams invoked the right of the colony to defer consideration. The next day Adams re-introduced the proposal that a committee be appointed to establish a confederation, and the traditional Whigs returned the favor of the day before and blocked the motion.[68]

The deadlock was broken in May. As the conflict wore on-- and no news arrived from England other than vague rumors of a peace mission--it became increasingly difficult in several colonies to preserve order, and Congress encourged such colonies to establish governments "under the present emergency." Late in April Congress began to consider making a general recommendation that all the colonies establish their provincial conventions as temporary governments, and on May 10

it adopted a resolution to that effect, apparently with general

agreement. Five days later John Adams executed a surprise maneuver,

one he had conceived a few months before as part of a "scheme," as

he called it, to press the rebellion to its logical conclusion. [69]

He introduced a carefully worded preamble to the resolution of May 10,

declaring that "the exercise of every kind of authority under the

said Crown should be totally suppressed." [70] The timing of the motion

was propitious: Dickinson was absent, and so was the entire Maryland

delegation. It passed, and the backbone of traditional Whig opposition

was broken.

Men who favored independence pressed their advantage in Congress.

Word came that Rhode Island and Virginia had severed their allegiance.

On June 7, R. H. Lee introduced the Resolution for Independence. [71]

Delegates from the Middle Colonies delegates blocked it, and in mid-June,

some of the delegates met at the home of Robert Morris and decided to

hold firm to the policy of redress and reconciliation, but to concede

that a confederation was necessary. [72] In June and July, Dickinson,

though not an instigator, argued a position which sought to mediate

between those who called for separation and those who were on the verge

of complete retreat.

When Dickinson rose to speak on the Resolution for Independence

on July 1, 1776, British troops had regained Quebec, but had been unable

to take advantage of their success. England's first campaign against

the colonies was a failure. In fact, British troops occupied not a

foot of American soil. There was a hope that treaty commissioners

were on their way to sue for peace and that reconciliation lay but months

away. 73 Dickinson seized on that hope.

Dickinson asked Congress to wait, to deliberate and not to take

an irrevocable step that might bring disaster. From the start, he put

the advocates of independence on the defensive. "My conduct this day,"

he began, "I expect will give the finishing blow to my once great, and,

my integrity considered, now too-diminished popularity." But, "I must

speak though I should lose my life, though I should lose the affections

of my country." This reminder that it was the great Farmer who spoke,

and that his defeat meant defeat of a man long known as a leading Patriot

of America, registered Dickinson's self-importance and feeling of betrayal, and lent weight to the attack. He continued: independence was a measure for impassioned men; no advantages to the colonies could arise from it. A declaration, he said, was not necessary for animating the people -- they were already animated. A declaration would not procure alliances with France and Spain. "May they not say to us," he said, "Gentlemen, you falsely pretended to consult us, and disrespectfully proceeded without waiting our resolution. You must abide the consequences. We are not ready for a rupture. Yours is the most rash and contemptible senate that ever existed on earth!"

Throughout most of his speech Dickinson stressed the necessity of obtaining alliances before declaring independence, lest the colonies should find themselves at the mercy of wolves. "When we have bound ourselves to a stern quarrel with Great Britain by a declaration of independence," he said, "France has nothing to do but hold back and intimidate Great Britain till Canada is put in her hands, then to intimidate us into a most disadvantageous grant of our trade."

a declaration premature. "First," he said, "we ought to establish our

governments and take the regular form of a state." He reminded the

members of the Congress of the disputes and dissention among them and

of the disagreements over confederation. Dickinson chided a Congress

that contemplated an act that would make the colonies a nation while

that same Congress could not agree upon a single article of confederation.

"Not only treaties with foreign powers, " he said, "but among ourselves

should precede this declaration. We should know on what grounds we stand

with regard to one another."

Furthermore, Dickinson said, no rationality lay in a measure which

would antagonize and invigorate Great Britain all the more. If the

colonies announced an official declaration of separation, then Great

Britain would increase her war effort; the people of the colonies would

suffer from a conflict become more cruel. Dickinson reduced his plea

to the most elementary level: "It is to our interest, "he said, "to keep

Great Britain in the opinion that we mean reconciliation as long as

possible."

Dickinson prepared his audience well. He dangled independence before

them. He spoke of it as a distinct possibility at some future date but impractical for the war effort and stupid at that juncture in foreign and domestic relations. It appeared that he had come over to the view that independence was inevitable and that the Congress need only wait a more propitious moment. Yet, each time, Dickinson subtly turned his argument and independence became more vague and less necessary. First of all, Dickinson said, the colonies by circumstance and habit must look to a strong nation for protection of their commerce, and in this sense, for protection of their very existence. Once the Congress cut the bonds with the mother country, only France would be powerful enough to act as guardian. Dickinson pointed out that from France must come inestimable danger. France was ambitious and insatiable, and an independent British America would endanger its own colonial holdings here. Her religion conflicts with America's. France, he said, waited only the opportunity to rise on the ruins of a defeated Britain. On the other hand, he said should the colonies be victorious without having severed ties with the mother country, then colonials would reap the rewards of resistance. "Great Britain," he said, "after one or more

unsuccessful campaigns may be induced to offer us such a share of

commerce as would satisfy us, to appoint councillors during good

behavior, to withdraw her armies, to protect our commerce, to establish

our militias-- in short to redress all the grievances complained of

in our first petition." Dickinson stood firm in the tradition of which

he was the grandest examplar: independence was dubious and debatable, but

at the moment reconciliation with the mother country should certainly

be retained as part of congressional policy.

With grave incisiveness, he presented the Congress with the disjunction

between traditional claims and present action. "I am alarmed at this

declaration being so vehemently presented," he said. "A worthy gentlemen

told us that people in this house have had different views for more than

twelve months. This is amazing after what they have so repeatedly declared,

that they meant only reconciliation." Dickinson's meaning was clear.

Advocates of independence sought to alter the policy of Congress, and,

in so doing, make a farce of the traditional claims of the colonies.

From the time of the Stamp Act the mother country had accused the colonies

of aiming at independence, and at each crisis the colonials had denied

that accusation and protested that the home government misunderstood

them. From its first session, the Continental Congress had announced

that its only motive for action was accommodation with Great Britain

on a constitutional foundation.

Dickinson charged that certain men in Congress were seeking to

draw all into the vortex of their ill-conveived designs. The delegates

from the middle and southern colonies, he said, must certainly know

that they were being led to take a step directly contrary to their

original purposes and future interests. "I should be glad to know,"

Dickinson said, "whether in twenty or thirty years this commonwealth

of colonies may not be thought too unwieldy, and Hudson's River be a

proper boundary for a separate commonwealth to the northward. I have

a strong impression in my mind that this will take place." [74]

Dickinson concluded on the note of New England conspiracy. He

had conceded all that he was prepared to concede at the moment. The

colonies were not a nation and ought not to take the step of trying to

become a nation until men were certain that they could live in harmony.

The fact that he used the word "treaties among ourselves" was revealing.

115

His attitude about the colonies as commercially dependent was basic.

His concern over the intentions of New England threw the independence

faction in a critical light, and, at last, Dickinson came to grips with

what was bothering him all the time. He distrusted other colonials,

and life under the old Empire was more attractive than union with

New England on unknown terms. John Dickinson, the grand exponent of

consensus and unity, saw none in either his native Pennsylvania or

in Congress. As to who would support him now, Dickinson was uncertain.

If one or two wavering colonies should rally, he might win again.[75] No

one was surprised, Dickinson least of all, when a New Englander stood

to ask the Congress to reject Dickinson's proposals.

116

IV

THE NEW ENGLAND COLONIES: LIBERTY AND INDEPENDENCE

When the Imperial crisis struck, New Englanders hesitated briefly, then broke beyond the bounds of traditional opposition. Like other colonials, New Englanders had claimed that they sought only their just rights within the Empire, but their loyalty to England disintegrated with the Battle of Lexington and Concord. The men of New Hampshire, Massachusetts, Rhode Island, and Connecticut were the earliest to arm and the most reliable in their support of Congress, and the first two were the most anxious to establish new governments. In fact, Congress moved too slowly for some New Englanders, and in early 1776, a rumor spread that more zealous of them intended to march on Philadelphia, disperse Congress, and erect an independent, popular power.[1] By the winter of 1775 or early 1776, a majority of patriots in New England favored separation from the Empire.

In this environment the position of traditional Whigs, Tories and neutralists was scarcely enviable. In New Hampshire, independence-minded Patriots drove Tories from Portsmouth or bargained them into

silence.[2] As early as December, 1775, New Hampshirites erected a

new, popular government that they felt could never be taken away.[3]

Quakers in New Hampshire agreed to aid the war effort with their

property and moral support, and two small pockets of Tory dissatisfaction

(at Hollis in the south and Cheshire in the west) remained isolated.[4]

In Massachusetts, the presence of royal troops in Boston allowed Tories

to go about their business in comparative safety. For a time, they

were mocking and bold, then came the reckoning. In Western Massachusetts

the supporters of the Crown were intimidated into silence or flight,[5] and

in the east even good Patriots who opposed independence were charged

with being enemies of the state and removed from office.[6] When General

Gage evacuated Boston during March and April of 1776, the last hopes of

Massachusetts men who favored liberty within the Empire left with him.

In Rhode Island, Governor Joseph Wanton, popularly elected to his

office, tried to prevent the legislature from creating an army, whereupon

he was unceremoniously removed from his office. In early May, 1776, Rhode

Island became the first colony to renounce its allegiance to the Crown.[7]

In Connecticut, Tories and traditional Whigs fared little better. In

early 1775 the Governor sent a small militia force to silence westerners

who announced a separate course from that laid down by the First Congress,

and after war began, Patriots made life in the Connecticut Valley

miserable for those who supported Great Britain.[8] Connecticut militiamen

even descended into the city of New York and destroyed a Tory printing

press.[9] Patriotism occasionally wore a bit thin: Massachusetts farmers

charged the Continental Army too much for provisions, New England militiamen

grumbled at having to serve too long and deserted, and some independence-

minded Whigs feared being too open about their views. But on the whole,

New Englanders were swift and sure in their renunciation of allegiance to

the Empire.[10]

To a remarkable extent, New England's delegates to the Continental

Congress reflected the forward disposition of their region. Of the

nineteen New Englanders who attended Congress, all but four favored

separation in 1775, and by early 1776 three of those four had come to

advocate independence. On most issues debated in Congress New England

delegates were aggressive, militant, and unified; they never faltered in

their pursuit of independence, and when the question came to a vote,

119

New Englanders in Congress favored it to a man.[11]

Nonetheless, New England delegates did not act or think identically.

Josiah Bartlett of New Hampshire favored a formal American confederation

in 1775, and when his colony set up a new government, he believed that

no power on earth could force New Hampshire back to the old way. He

sought to make independence a fact in New Hampshire, but was willing

to bide his time about an open declaration by Congress and was not

outspoken about the matter.[12] On the other hand, John Sullivan of the

same colony was open and vociferous. In 1774, when certain timid Patriots

accused Sullivan of forcing the illegal resolutions of an illegal Congress

upon New Hampshire, Sullivan retorted that everything the colonies

did was illegal. In December of 1775. he attacked the British

Constitution as a "folly and a danger," and declared "that what is

called the prerogative of the Crown, or checks upon the licenticusness

of the people, are only the children of designing and ambitious men, no

such thing being necessary."[13] Samuel Adams of Massachusetts was,

of course, one of the most important advocates of independence in

America. A tireless and shrewd organizer, Adams led Massachusetts to

separation and only waited for other men to catch up to his conviction

that independence was the only course for America.[14] John Hancock

of the same colony acted less directly and at first sided with traditional

Whigs. He hedged on the question of separation until early in 1776, then

declared for it. Later, Hancock learned that his hesitation was known

to the people of his colony and that they refused to elect him to any

office in the new government.[15] Stephen Hopkins of Rhode Island

maintained an ambiguous position until late 1775, but had firmly decided

for independence by early 1776.[16] William Ellery of Newport, Rhode

Island, supported independence in his colony and in Congress, denounced

supporters of Great Britain as enemies of the state long before the

Coercive Acts, and proved to be a leader for separation.[17] Connecticut

delegates were little different from other New Englanders: Roger

Sherman rarely voted against the majority of New England men, and he had

no misgivings when he voted for and signed the Declaration of Independence.[18]

Samuel Huntington came to Congress late; he received a seat precisely

because he favored independence and could be counted upon to support

independence in Congress.[19]

121

These eight delegates represent a broad sampling of New England

Patriots in geographical location, governmental offices, and religious

attachments. Between them, the delegates comprised a group drawn from

the Piscataqua region of New Hampshire, an old agricultural region of

the same colony, the cities of Boston, Providence, and New Haven,

the farming and commercial area of southeastern Rhode Island, and

the agricultural and small-city area of eastern Connecticut. [20] One of

the delegates was a former governor, two were members of supreme courts,

two were in the upper houses, and four held assembly seats, and various

of them were justices of the peace, city assessors and collectors,

and militia officers. [21] Most were of Calvinist heritage (as, indeed,

were sixteen or seventeen of the nineteen New England delegates),

though their religious attachments ranged from the rigidity of a

man like Roger Sherman, to the rather mildly sceptical views of the

amateur scientist, Josiah Bartlett. [22] Hopkins had been a member of the

Society of Friends until 1773. [23] Others were either Presbyterians

or Congregationalists.

122

Furthermore, like their counterparts from the Middle Colonies

the New England delegates engaged in a representative range of economic

endeavors and professional pursuits. But unlike the delegates from the

Middle Colonies, the New England men did poorly or only moderately well

after the French and Indian War, and in this, they reflected what was

happening in their region. Of the eight delegates, three were primarily

engaged in mercantile enterprises. Hancock lost, in international

commercial ventures, approximately half of his fortune of eighty to

a hundred thousand pounds.[24] Sherman, a retail merchant, found business

so poor that he closed down operations.[25] Hopkins neither suffered

appreciable loss nor made significant gains in the decade prior to

rebellion.[26] A fourth delegate, Ellery, failed as a merchant.[27] Several

of the remaining delegates were trained in law, one was a doctor,

and one a professional politician. Of these, only Sullivan managed

to accumulate anything resembling a fortune, and he did it by close-fisted

ways that almost cost him his life on two different occasions.[28] The

remainder were scarcely impoverished, but neither were they wealthy;

they managed on incomes from public salaries, farms, and professional

earnings. They also engaged in a variety of other economic endeavors, from ship building and land speculation to grinding corn for market; the returns were low, and they discovered so new, highly profitable investments after the French and Indian War.

But mere facts about particular New Englanders and the contrast they provided to people in the Middle Colonies touches only on surface reasons for their behavior. In the 1760 and early 1770's, New England society entered a troubled period. In a community of farmers, the land rendered less and less subsistence to a people still convinced of their chosen place in western history. When England aggravated the situation by attempting to reorganize the Empire, economic decline, Calvinist religiosity, and Imperial crisis came together in New England and produced a strong and active movement for defense of liberty. The movement carried all before it: yeoman farmers and merchants, preachers and sceptics, the politically powerless and the politically strong, easterners and, later, westerners. New England leaders led the people beyond resistance within the Empire to a revolution for independence

and the restoration of liberty in America.

By the early 1760's, New Englanders had been building a culturally homogeneous society for a hundred and thirty years. Three of the colonies had a common theological heritage and all four had similar landed institutions, educational facilities, churches, and governments. Internal improvements brought New Englanders into close contact with one another, and though local jealousies remained to plague men, those jealousies were muted by common beliefs, similar experiences, and a common sense of destiny.

In New Hampshire, Massachusetts, and Connecticut, Congregationalism was the official state religion, and in all three colonies most men favored that sect. Most of those who were not of Congregational persuasion were Presbyterians or Baptists. No love was lost between the three Calvinist groups, but Congregationalism was so strong that its adherents no longer feared the other two enough to proscribe those faiths or persecute their adherents. By the late eighteenth century, Congregationalist majorities enforced laws of establishment in a loose manner in all three colonies.[29] In New Hampshire, large numbers of Scotch-Irish

125

Presbyterians and Congregationalists lived side by side in Portsmouth,

Exeter, Durham, and the Merrimack Valley. An increase in the number

of Anglicans in Portsmouth and in the Connecticut Valley County of

Cheshire caused a stir among the dominant sects; the more so since the

Governor and the Council invariably supported Anglican power.[30] In

Massachusetts, the Congregational power was stronger than in any colony

in America and that power was often made known. Other sects in

Massachusetts, for example, paid a fee in support of the Congregational

establishment.[31] Anglicans were a distinct minority group, many of

whom had settled under land grants for the Society for the Propagation of

the Gospel, which evoked resentment among Massachusetts Congregationalists.[32]

The people of Massachusetts - Quakers, Presbyterians, and Baptists

as well as Congregationalists- also resented the fact that in Massachusetts,

as in New Hampshire, high governmental offices often went to Church of

England men. In Connecticut, Congregationalism was not as prevalent

as in Massachusetts. Anglicans constituted a larger proportion of the

population and were in a majority in some areas in the western part of

the colony.[33] The Great Awakening made itself felt in provincial politics

when the "New Lights" sided with the Anglicans against the "Old Lights"

in a number of elections in the late 1750's and early 1760's. However,

by 1765 the movement had spent itself and the Congregational church had

healed most of its wounds. As religious factionalism eased in Connecticut,

expansion by means of the Susquehannah Company became the pivotal feature

of local politics.[34]

The most diverse sectarian situation in New England existed in

Rhode Island, where toleration produced diffuse religious patterns.

Baptists--of several varities-- were influential and numerous in the

colony and concentrated in Newport and Providence. Anglicans constituted

a large portion of the population in and around Newport. Many of

the leading families of the colony were Quakers, and Congregationalists

and Presbyterians were scattered throughout the colony. By the mid-

eighteenth century, men of different religious denominations shared

power in the colony. The Anglicans in Newport tended to form closed

circles, but they were not strong enough - nor was any other single

group - to obtain power without the support of men of other sects.

127

By the 1750's, Rhode Island politics was characterized by practical, unholy alliances.[35]

New Englanders were a prolific people, and population expansion came from within and not from large heterogeneous immigrations. The first Puritans occupied the major rivers and natural harbors, and when those were taken up, they built roads. Men occupied the land along the roads, and New Englanders pushed farther inward and outward in the colonies.[36] New Hampshire was the only colony that experienced an exceptionally large migration of Scotch-Irish, and none of the four experienced an influx of non-English-speaking groups. By the 1760's, hundreds of towns which were organized in a similar manner were connected by a network of waterways, several major roads, and many smaller farm-to-market roads.

128

For all that, New England would not have been unified had the
Yankees, when they moved, not taken habits with them and held
tenaciously to them. They retained their Calvinism, their custom of
gathering in town meetings, and their practice of building schools where
their children could be indoctrinated in their common heritage as well as
made literate; and as a result new communities invariably became much
like the old ones left behind. When a new town was founded original
proprietors held the largest parcels of land a large share of political
power. As the population grew, proprietors sold, granted, or bequeathed
their land. After them, their sons did the same, and after them,
so did their sons, until the process minimized differences in land
holding and with that, the differences between men.[37] Often, laws
governing the right to vote in the townships were laxly enforced. When
proprietors were over-bearing, their power was usually broken. New
Englanders, untouched by an influx of diverse people and tenacious about
their traditions, built a veritable northern civilization.

By the 1760's, another habit bred unity among New Englanders. For a
long time past, New Englanders had developed a readiness to fight. First

they had fought the Indians, then the French, then the French and Indians, and they had always fought hard as only men with a vision can fight. If Calvinists did not like Anglicans, they dreaded the heathen Indians as much or more, and words could not express what they felt for French Catholics. In fact, in the eighteenth century, New Englanders recalled that several of the early colonies had united in a general confederation for defense; only Rhode Island had been excluded.[38] New Englanders had common enemies; the New England yeoman farmers fought under common commanders, and they fought in a similar manner. During the French and Indian War, the New England militias fought again; they fought in large numbers, and they won a final victory.[39] By the 1770's, New England had a long tradition of preparedness for war which no other region could equal. They still trained, though infrequently, and they knew that they had had a great deal to do with the defeat of the French in North America.

Until the early 1760's, New England took part in the general economic expansion of the American colonies. Lacking a large agricultural

hinterland, Massachusetts and Rhode Island became commercial civilizations

to a marked extent and to a lesser extent so did New Hampshire and

Connecticut. Yankees drew products from the sea, and they had learned

to convert staples of other English colonies into articles of profitable

trade. In 1764, the fishing industry employed three thousand men and

forty-five thousand tons of shipping.[40] By importing molasses and

distilling it into rum, industrialists manufactured a readily

marketable product.[41] Whale products and some finished iron products

supplemented the list of articles which Yankee merchants in Rhode Island

and Massachusetts used to build two thriving commercial provinces.[42]

New Hampshire and Connecticut took part in these endeavors on a smaller

scale: merchants in Portsmouth engaged in pursuits similar to those of

Boston merchants, and Connecticut confined itself to trade with the West

Indies to which its small fleet took horses, cattle and cattle products.

Climate and soil had always limited farm production in New England.

As early as the 1740's, most farmers save those in the Connecticut Valley

stopped growing wheat, and New Englanders found themselves milling and

marketing wheat imported from other colonies. In the early 1750's,

manufacture of flour proved unprofitable. New England farmers learned to

depend primarily on corn, sheep, horses, dairy farming, lumbering, and

naval stores.[43]

Agriculture and commerce joined, however, to produce even economic

growth, and though the Yankee had to be thrifty, thrift paid off. For

some, it paid handsomely. New England kept pace with the other

continental colonies, and, in fact, until the end of the French and

Indian War New England commerce was anything but destitute. The war

stimulated the New England economy and it expanded on every front: in

sugar trade and rum manufacturing, in ship building and naval stores

and even in the marketing of food products. Merchants did not resist the

temptation to trade with the French. All New **England's** major cities grew

in size, and Boston was easily one of the largest cities in America. When

the fighting ceased in 1761, New England rode the crest of economic boom.[44]

But after the war reversals came in unceasing array, and the section

entered a long, agonizing period of decline, the major problem lay with

the land in relation to the people: the quantity of arable land was

fixed -- if not, as a result of crude agricultural techniques, actually

decreasing -- and the population was rapidly and steadily increasing.

As early as the 1750's R.R. Livingston, Sr., of New York pointed out

one aspect of New England's problems.[45]   In Connecticut, Livingston wrote,

"They never grant land but when a number of people engage to settle, and

then the portion of each is much limited."[46]   Livingston listed the evils

attendant upon such a system: the land was continually subdivided and

its productivity ever poorer; Connecticut obtained little trade since

the farmer did not grow for market; specie went out of the colony. The

land, Livingston said, became scarcely worth defending.[47]   And, if

land holdings were small enough to cause concern in the 1750's, by

the 1760's and 1770's the situation had become critical. Certainly by

1760, most good land that provided an easy access to market was settled

or purchased. And population continued to expand. Massachusetts'

population grew only twelve per cent between 1760 and 1774, but the shortage

of good farming land in that colony pushed Massachusetts farmers into New

Hampshire, helping to swell its population by seventy-four per cent in

the same years, from fifty thousand to nearly ninety thousand.[48]   Rhode

Island's good farm land had long been occupied and the large land

holdings of the Narragansett planters broken into smaller holdings.

Changes in franchise requirements in Rhode Island reflected the absence of good land.[49]   Yet the population of even that small colony increased

by thirteen per cent in the decade prior to the Revolution. Between

1761 and 1774 Connecticut grew thirty-one per cent in spite of migrations

up the Connecticut River and out of the colony.[50]   The Delaware and

Susquehannah land companies' land speculation ventures in the face of

land hunger, were symptomatic of the problem. Land speculators like

Eliphalet Dyer of Windham County and the Huntingtons of Norwich and

New London had a ready surplus population -- if they could find land.

Silas Deane of Wethersfield on the Connecticut River wrote that "not

more than twelve acres to a person" were available to men in the Valley.[51]

Doubtless the situation in Connecticut was more desperate than in

the remainder of New England, but the details of land distribution there

illustrate, even if they exaggerate, the problem that all of New England

faced or soon would face. Windham County in eastern Connecticut

contained 312,000 improved acres, but only 29,000 acres were plow land,

and by the 1770's this gave the adult males in the county an average of

only six arable acres apiece. Meadows, brush, and pasture took up

80,000 acres; only 16,000 acres of the unimproved land was classified as

improvable, and probably little of that was plow land. In New London

County, eighty per cent of the available land (240,000 acres) was

improved but only 28,000 acres was arable, and in 1774 the county had

a population of 27,000. Only 4,000 unimproved acres were first-class

lands. Property holdings declined unevenly as population increased;

large numbers of men with large families were driven to marginal and sub-

marginal farming. In central Connecticut, in Hartford County, where the

land was the most fertile, a population of 50,148 existed on 205,000

acres of improved land, of which only 26,000 was plow land. The land

holdings of a single family in New York, the Beekmans, were larger than

the improved land held by all the farmers in Hartford County; the county

contained between three to four acres of plow land per adult male.

To the west there was a little more land per person, but there was still

not much: in New Haven County about seven arable acres per adult male,

in Litchfield County eight, and in Fairfield County nine. [52]

In the late 1760's Eliphalet Dyer forcast a doleful future for New

135

England if massive migration were not soon forthcoming. "Let us

suppose that no emigrations are to happen," he said, "our wealthiest

farmers engrossing all the lands, the poor lying in the streets,

starving for want of employment; lordships, tenants and slaves...!

What a figure must our towns and societies make, when instead of containing

fields for grazing, there should not only be house joined to house, but one

house erected upon the top of another, and all filled with inhabitants, till

the upper lofts tumble down and dash them to pieces, and the lower buried in

the ruins."[53]

New Englanders had faced the scarcity of good land before and conquered

the problem. In the 1760's and 1770's they did not; the adversity of

external circumstances proved to be too much for them. For one thing,

whereas producers elsewhere in the colonies found ready markets and

increased prices for their staples--rice from South Carolina and Georgia

and wheat from the Middle Colonies--New England farmers did not. For

another, farmers could not supply their cities or themselves with

preferred bread grains; Plymouth, Salem, Boston, Newport, Providence,

New London, Hartford, and New Haven imported wheat. For yet another,

the prices of corn and beef, the New England farmers' prime exports,

declined; both fluctuated erratically in the decade after the postwar

depression of 1765; beef prices never rose as high as they had been in

the heart of the depression and corn fell to its second lowest price of

the decade in 1774.[54]   Furthermore, the decline in prices was far from

offset by increased production; indeed, farm production scarcely

increased as fast as the population did,[55] and such increase as there

was proved to be insufficient to meet the needs of the commercial community

in the West Indies trade. To be sure, the general situation found uneven

expression: that part of western Connecticut which fell in the wheat

belt was much better off than eastern Connecticut, the Connecticut Valley

was better off than the Norwich-New London area, and similar variations were

to be seen in Massachusetts, Rhode Island, and New Hampshire. But on the

whole, New England farmers were in distressed circumstances and things were

growing worse.

Commerce likewise suffered. Massachusetts, for example, had a

favorable balance of trade with the West Indies in only one of the twelve

years after 1763; between 1768 and 1772 the value of goods exported from

137

Massachusetts to the West Indies increased only twenty per cent, while the value of imports from the islands increased fifty per cent. [56] In 1769, Connecticut had a favorable balance of trade with its principal market, the West Indies, amounting to L25,000 sterling. That "profit" represented the combined efforts of 180,000 people; [57] six years later, the lawyer and planter John Rutledge of South Carolina made L9,000 sterling in one year. [58] Nor were New England merchants, as a whole, able to compensate for these unfavorable balances by shrewd trading. Yankee ingenuity hit one of its least imaginative periods at this time-- Bostonians lost the Mediterranean trade, for example, and merchants on the Connecticut River in New London could not compete with New York retailers -- and this happened just when various shifts in costs and prices were necessitating maximum ingenuity. Worse, the profit margin in dealing with molasses and rum, previously the most lucrative of New England mercantile ventures, shrank throughout the postwar decade. In 1763 there was a substantial gap between the prices of molasses and rum; in 1765 that gap was cut in half, and though the ratio between the two commodities fluctuated during the next ten years, the gap was never again as large as

it had been in 1763.[59] Too, the operation of the Sugar Act was
detrimental to the rum and molasses trade; the act accounted for a
total sterling revenue of ₤300,000 between 1764 and 1774, the greater
part of which fell on Rhode Island and Massachusetts.[60] Nor did trade
with England offset the decline created by decreasing per capita
production, falling prices, and other adverse conditions. The value
of goods exported from New England to England moved irregularly downward
in the decade after 1764 and, relative to population, were lower than they
had been during the war years.[61]

To compound matters, the monetary situation in New England was
unfavorable. New England, perhaps even more than the other colonies,
suffered a chronic shortage of hard money, gold and silver, and could
lubricate the engines of commerce only through supplementary issues
of paper currency. J each of the four colonies the paper currency
supply was inadequate during the years after 1763. In New Hampshire
the situation was so desparate that from 1765 onward the colonial
government allowed the inhabitants to pay their taxes in kind.
That brought some relief, but in 1768 the Assembly retired what remained

of outstanding war emissions. In 1771, Governor John Wentworth tried

to launch a plan of recovery. "The commerce of this province declines,

insomuch that it is complained detrimental to those whose former

connections compel them in any degree to continue it," Wentworth said.

"Money is not among us in any proportion to the circulation adequate to

our numbers." Wentworth proposed, among other things, the building

of roads into the interior to rectify a commercial situation wherein

New Hampshire's "laboring inhabitants [are] unemployed and consequently

distressed, and fertile lands lay waste and uncultivated."[62] In 1772,

Parliamentary reimbursement for war debts injected ₤5,500 sterling

into New Hampshire's economy; no taxes were levied that year. For a

population of around 87,000, total currency declined to a dangerous

low.[63] In Massachusetts the currency problem was roughly the same. The

legislature emitted no paper currency between 1764 and 1774. "In this

Colony", James Bowdoin wrote in 1769, "the Parliamentary reimbursement

for the taking of Cape Britain in 1745 enabled us, with the taxes

that were laid, to cancel all our paper currency, and to substitute

real money in its stead,"[64] but the "real money" soon flowed out.

140

Boston merchants mitigated the currency shortage by importing

Spanish coins at a loss. [65] The governments of Rhode Island and

Connecticut took steps to solve their decreasing currency supplies.

Connecticut currency stood around £308,000 in 1763 and at only

£18,000 in 1770. [66] Recognizing the stringency, Connecticut legislators

issued bills bearing interest, as required by law, and, at the same

time, laid taxes equal in amount and provided for retirement. By 1773,

all but a few thousands had been redeemed. [67] In 1770, the colony of

Rhode Island had £45,000 outstanding compared to around £350,000 during

the war. In 1770, 1771, and 1772 the legislature laid £12,000 in

taxes--£2,000 for support of government and £10,000 for retirement.

In 1773 the Assembly called in all "lawful money bills, emitted

by this colony, or treasurers notes given for such." [68] As in the other

New England colonies, some currency continued outstanding, but the

money supply was grossly inadequate to meet the needs of population

of 54,000 souls.

141

All in all, economic contraction resulted in a reduction of the New England economy to payment in kind or in hard specie. The latter resort forced constriction of capital reserves. New England declined in per capita accumulation.

Among the leading New England Patriots who were engaged in mercantile pursuits, there were several who suffered failures, losses, and bad times. In New Hampshire, Nathaniel Folsom, later a delegate to the Continental Congress, began a partnership venture in the middle sixties which closed after two years.[69] In the same colony William Whipple, later a delegate, stopped making full-scale investments, and ventured only small sums.[70] In Massachusetts John Hancock contemplated closing down in the late sixties, and probably should have. Hancock lost nearly ℔ 25,000 in the 1770's alone.[71] Another Boston merchant, Thomas Cusing, "retired" as a merchant after several years of earning poor returns compared to those he had made during the French and Indian War.[72] Elbridge Gerry of Marblehead found his trade in decline. All three were later delegates to the Continental Congress.[73] In Rhode Island William Ellery, also to be a delegate, began a mercantile firm which failed after two years; in 1774, Ellery still had debts outstanding to English creditors.[74] In Connecticut Roger Sherman, still another

delegate, had closed three retail outlets in the early 1770's.[75] The

Governor of Connecticut, Josiah Trumbull, declared bankruptcy in the

late 1760's; his debts were greater than his ₤12,000 estate.[76] In the

same years, another small retail merchant, Benedict Arnold, also went

bankrupt.[77]

Professional men, investors, and speculators among the Patriots fared

little better. John Adams was perpetually disgruntled with the returns

from his law practice. Another lawyer and a man much like Adams, R.T.

Paine, fared no better than Adams did.[78] Both were delegates to the

Continental Congress from Massachusetts. In Rhode Island Samuel Ward,

a man who invested in an assortment of petty ventures but was primarily

a farmer, and a good one, also suffered; he invested considerable sums

in notes and bonds, the largest of which went uncollected for a decade.[79]

In Connecticut, both Eliphalet Dyer and Samuel Huntington had a stake in

the outcome of their investments in the Susquehannah Company, and year

after year went by and that venture yielded small returns.[80] Later, Ward,

Dyer, and Huntington were delegates to Congress.

But what happened to the great majority of men was more important. The

contraction of currency was painful and came on top of decline in prices of farm staples. Starting around 1763, the New England farmer got less for what he grew, and then he got less and still less. Many farmers, those who owned or lived near large stands of timber, tried to escape their plight by engaging in lumbering for market, but this consumed their time in the spring, when the streams and rivers provided ways to get the lumber out, and forced them to leave their crops unplanted and their farms untended. Harsh winters prevented farmers from diversifying to supplement their incomes. And, as population grew, land prices rose. To the average farmer, and to most men, the situation simply did not make sense: money was scarce, good land prices were high, and crop prices were low.

Hemmed in at every turn ordinary New Englanders in great numbers began to migrate --only to encounter serious conflict everywhere they went. Those who moved up the Connecticut River Valley and westward into the Vermont and New Hampshire grants encountered New Yorkers who claimed the land from the Crown, and who charged them quit rents for the privilege of settlement. New Englanders armed, put themselves under the leadership of Ethan Allen and threatened to fight.[81] Other migrants to the north

met the king's representative, Governor John Wentworth, of New Hampshire.

Wentworth intended to enforce the laws pertaining to wood rights in royal

lands, and even prosecuted those who violated wood-cutting laws.[82]

Wentworth also charged quit rents for the privilege of settlement in New

Hampshire, and the thousands of Massachusetts farmers who migrated to New

Hampshire found a scarcity of good land that was accessible to markets.

When Wentworth took office in the late 1760's, he fell agent to about a

million acres, the better portion of it already granted and occupied.

Wentworth carefully watched over what was left.[83]   Other New Englanders

simply moved into the colony of New York and squatted on the estates of

the Hudson River landlords. Others migrated all the way to North Carolina

and Georgia. And still others, under the protection of the government

of Connecticut, expropriated land in Pennsylvania.[84]   The fact that the

New London and Susquehannah land companies originated in eastern Connecticut

was not coincidence, and Connecticut pressed its claims under the

Connecticut Charter to all land from the eastern boundary of Rhode Island

to the "South Sea," or the Pacific Ocean. That included , they said,

northern Pennsylvania, and they not only said it, they settled it; first

along the tributaries of the Deleware and then on the Susquehannah.

Connecticut's leaders violated Orders-in-Council, tried to bribe officials

in England and could not, and ended by encouraging a military force to

hold the land. Later, the legislature of Connecticut annexed the

Susquehannah settlement and gave it full rights as a voting township.[85]

For a decade, then, New England's economic problems bred disgruntlement

and discontent, and New Englanders got into trouble when they tried to

solve their problems. John Langdon, William Whipple, John Hancock, Thomas

Cushing, merchants, all had trouble with customs. Dyer, Huntington, and

Sherman, land speculators, encountered Orders-in-Council and the power

of the Penns. Lawyers like John Sullivan were in constant conflict with

their clients; fifteen armed men tried to shoot and kill him and his

brother and over a hundred people signed a petition asking the legislature

of New Hampshire to stop Sullivan's means of collecting fees.[86] The

people in general were dissatisfied and pessimistic, whether they were

engaged in farming, commerce, or professional careers.

And so the local context, social and economic, in which the drama

of Imperial conflict unfolded was, in New England, radically different from

what it was in the neighboring colonies to the south and west. In the

Middle Colonies, society was marked by cultural diversity, friction, and

general disharmony, and the economy was booming. In New England, society

was homogeneous and essentially harmonious, and the economy was in dire

straits.

Massachusetts was one of the earliest scenes of conflict between

the Imperial administration and the people of the colonies, and

Massachusetts remained at the center of conflict from the 1760's onward.

As early as 1761 the question of the legitimate legislative powers of

Parliament entered disputes in Massachusetts; the colony was one of the

first to protest the Sugar Act; its men resorted to violence in

repudiation of the Stamp Act, the Townshend duties, and the Tea Act. It

was in Boston that, in 1770, British troops first shot and killed colonials.

In 1774 the English government picked Massachusetts as the target of

punitive measures. War first broke out in Massachusetts.

Massachusetts' Charter laid the basis for conflict. When the colony

was reorganized in the 1690's, royal government was superimposed upon

institutions evolved over the course of sixty years of colonial history.

The Crown appointed the governors, and the governors appointed judges to

the Supreme Court. But the lower house of the Massachusetts General Court

remained powerful. The people elected the Representatives and the

Representatives elected members of the Council, though the governors

had the right to disapprove elections to the Council. The General Court

controlled taxation and expenditures, and township government in

Massachusetts relieved the executive branch of local administrative

functions.[87] Of considerable consequence was the fact that the Rep-

resentatives shared with the governor control over the granting of land.

Lacking this instrument of gaining factional support in the legislature,

the executive authority in Massachusetts was doomed to a subordinate role

in governmental affairs.

When the Stamp Act crisis put the system to the test, the actions of

the people in Massachusetts further reduced the power of the "court party."

In 1766, the Council of Massachusetts abandoned the Governor to his own

devices and gravitated toward unreserved support of the popular party.[88]

Thereafter, the governors had no reliable supporters except those to whom

they tendered offices and a few western oligarchs; 89 the struggle

between the court party and the popular party was no struggle at all.

The House of Representatives won, and it always had a majority of the

people on its side.

Thomas Hutchinson, Massachusetts born and bred, Lieutenant Governor

and then Governor of Massachusetts, gave a graphic description of

Massachusetts politics. People in Massachusetts, Hutchinson noted

disapprovingly, divided into political parties "on points of a speculative

nature alone." 90 That was true and, though perhaps Hutchinson himself

did not understand it, it was also quite understandable: the economic

and social conditions that bred factional disputes elsewhere were simply

not operative in Massachusetts. But the people there were interested in

questions of their rights, the powers of their Assembly, and the powers

of Parliament in America. Accordingly, such leaders of the popular party

as Speaker of the House Thomas Cushing, James Otis, James Warren and his

brother Joseph, Samuel and John Adams, James Bowdoin, and a host of

others were all concerned about "speculative points" of government. All

of these men were well-educated, articulate, audacious, and favorites

among the people; they had the support of the Congregational clergy,
the popular press, Harvard professors, and their own wives. During the
decade of crisis few dared to oppose them on important issues, and those
who did had little support.[91]

But the governors, first Francis Bernard then Hutchinson, did oppose
them in a series of desperate efforts to protect and, hopefully, to
increase the power of the executive branch in the colony. During the
French and Indian War, when the courts of admiralty attempted to crack
down on customs violations, Bernard supported the courts in the hope
that doing so would enhance his personal power and the power of his office;
and later, at least in part for the same reasons, he supported the Sugar
Act and the Stamp Act. Bostonians retaliated against all three stands
during the Stamp Act riots. They hanged the stamp collector, Andrew
Oliver, in effigy, looted his house, looted Hutchinson's house, and
published vitriolic articles in newspapers and pamphlets attacking
Parliament and all who supported it.[92] In the midst of all this Samuel
Adams and Thomas Cushing wrote, privately, that though the people of
Massachusetts, above all others, had reasons for maintaining that they

were completely independent of Parliament, they made no such claim, and

asserted only that Parliament could not tax them.[93]

By 1770 the royal faction, completely isolated in the power structure

of the colony, was frantically looking to the outside for ways to

strengthen itself. The governor and his allies supported the customs

service and hoped to attract merchants to their side by favoritism or by

discouraging support of the popular party through insidious means of law

enforcement. They approached popular leaders and tendered them offices

in executive government. Nothing seemed to work. A few merchants with-

held support of the non-importation agreement, but most did not.[94]

Then, late in 1771 and early in 1772, the economic clouds over

Massachusetts lifted. The causes were international. In late 1771,

financial institutions in England tightened credit because of fears of

over-extension and because war with France threatened once more.[95]

Thereupon, most merchants and manufacturers in the British Isles re-

trenched, and many English mercantile houses, to prevent failure, dumped

their goods, with the result that prices fell precipitiously. New England

merchants raced to England to buy goods, on the assumption that they could

purchase vast quantities cheap and sell them dear, particularly if war
did break out.[96]   Before they were done, the New England merchants, and
particularly Bostonians, had bought more English goods than they had
at any time in a decade.[97]   Too, upon learning that the Bank of England
had impeded the sources of supply for British iron manufacturers, Yankee
merchants bought up iron from the Middle Colonies at two and three times
the usual quantities, hoping to sell it at a profit in England.[98]

This flurry of commercial activity brought eastern Massachusetts a year
of prosperity. During that year the Patriot organization softened, and the
royal faction seized the moment to renew its attempts to get free of the
Representatives. Samuel Adams' popular vote in Boston faltered, and he
lost the election for collector in Suffolk County.[99]   Various of the Patriot
leaders pulled back; John Hancock, for example, abandoned politics and
resolved to get involved no further. So did John Adams. Hutchinson
announced that he would take his salary from the home government,
and at least one judge of the Supreme Court concurred.[100]   Samuel Adams, not
to give up so easily, began a systematic organization of the eastern
Massachusetts townships. He wrote to every single individual of note in

152

Massachusetts, and to some outside.[101] The Patriots began to regroup.

Two things worked in Adams' favor. First, before the year 1772 was out, and as 1773 began, reality replaced fantasy in Massachusetts economic life. In 1772 England bought less goods from New England than it had in any of the previous seven years, and in the next year it bought even less.[102] Sales of Massachusetts commodities in the West Indies were not enough to take up the slack, and the New England commercial community found itself crushed under a burden of new debts.[103] Second, Hutchinson pressed his plan to take his salary from England, and also locked in debate with the Representatives over the powers of Parliament, thereby stimulating the Patriots to regroup. In a series of interchanges between the Governor and the House of Representatives, John Adams denied the legislative power of Parliament over Massachusetts, and remarked that the Acts of Trade and Navigation were laws only to the extent that the people had "cheerfully" consented to their operation. Hutchinson countered with the accusation that the Representatives were seeking independence. John Adams denied the charge, professing dependence upon and allegiance to the Crown.[104]

News that Parliament had passed the Tea Monopoly Act arrived in

153

Massachusetts a few months later. Hutchinson, frustrated and perhaps over-wrought, asserted that he would protect the first tea ship that came, and see to it that the tea came ashore. The Sons of Liberty saw to it that Hutchinson did no such thing, and destroyed the tea consignments when they arrived. Massachusetts would not be taxed by Parliament, nor would the Patriots stand idly by and watch Hutchinson and his supporters alter the structure of charter government. The Sons of Liberty were, they said, defending the just rights and liberties of Massachusetts against the pernicuous innovations of their Governor and Parliament. Samuel Adams enjoined men to make a distinction between mobs and reasonable destruction of property, between violence for the defense of liberty and violence without purpose.[105] Someone would have to back down. No one did.

When news of the Boston Port Bill spread through Massachusetts, and Bostonians learned they would not be allowed to engage in trade, Patriots immediately perceived the implications of the action. It meant that the Charter was in danger. It meant unusual Parliamentary action against a standing government. It meant infringement of rights. It meant that Boston would fall into stagnation, and with that it meant destruction of

merchants, lawyers, shipbuilders, carpenters -- everyone save those

protected by royal power. Then, Massachusetts learned that its Charter

was indeed suspended, that miliatry rule was scheduled for the colony,

and that its courts were re-organized, and later, that their old enemies

the French had been given leave to establish the Catholic religion in

Quebec. The Patriots, pleading with good reason that resistance was

imperative, established a tentative extra-legal government of their own

and sent Samuel Adams, John Adams, Thomas Cushing and Robert T. Paine to

Congress.[106] The people of Massachusetts, firmly behind the Patriots,

armed themselves and waited. In September, 1774, Suffolk County warned

that any attempt to use force to enforce the Coercive Acts would be met

with force.[107] A few people became Tories and hid behind the power of

General Gage, but the vast majority held firm, and the Tories faced a

hostile citizenry.

In New Hampshire the conflict proceeded more slowly and with less

severity. There, the Wentworth family governed from a stronger basis of

power. First Benning Wentworth and later his nephew John controlled the

executive and judicial offices of the colony, the distribution of over a

million acres of land, and appointments to the upper house of the

legislature. When John Wentworth took office, he let all know his power

and settled family disputes about land by a simple maneuver; he recalled

all land grants his uncle had made, then reissued them to everyone who had

fulfilled the terms of the land patents. When Wentworth's power stood

assured, he proceeded about the business of governor in a systematic

manner; he knew his prerogatives and he was imaginative in his use of them.

He gave new Council posts to friends and family, thereby assuring control

of the courts. He traveled west to let it be known that he would enforce

the laws of the king's woods and that men who settled his lands would pay

a fee for it.[108] And, he drew the commercial community in Portsmouth to

him with recommendations to extend internal improvements westward and turn

the flow of goods down the Merrimack away from Boston to Portsmouth.[109]

By 1770, Wentworth had a large, dedicated following in Portsmouth and in the

lower house of the legislature.

When word came of the Boston Port Bill, Portsmouth first refused to aid

Boston, then on reconsideration, agreed. The voting in the town meeting

was close on both occasions. When the lower house considered establishing

a committee of correspondence the decision to do so passed by only one vote,

and Wentworth dissolved the Representatives before they had time to do any further damage.[110] The people of New Hampshire reacted by setting up an extra-legal assembly. In Provincial Convention, they chose two Congressional delegates: John Sullivan, a lawyer, and Nathanial Folsom, a former colonel of militia. Neither was from Portsmouth. The Merrimack Valley, dependent on the port of Boston for its continued existence in commercial farming, began to train for war. In Portsmouth itself, William Whipple and John Langdon, both middling merchants who had run afoul of customs collectors, worked to bolster resistance at its weakest point.[111] The Patriots would take other measures later.

In Connecticut there was never any doubt about what course the people would take. The issue of local power and Parliament's power had long been decided. Back in 1765, Thomas Fitch and several Assistants, all opponents of the Susquehannah Land Company, made the fatal mistake of swearing an oath to uphold the Stamp Act. Other members of the Council, including Dyer, President of the Susquehannah Company, refused. Thenceforth, the Fitch faction was never in power again, as William Pitkin, Josiah Trumbull, Sherman, Dyer, the Huntingtons in New London, and, for a

time, the Anglican politician, William Samuel Johnson, formed a loose

coalition that defeated Fitch in every election. By the late 1760's

Johnson and his Anglicans were no longer needed as Trumbull and the question

of Connecticut expansion carried all before them. Connecticut voters

usually turned out in the neighborhood of seven to eight thousand voters.

The Susquehannah Land Company numbered between twelve and eighteen

hundred shareholders, and though many of these were from neighboring

Rhode Island, the voter strength proved sufficient to carry election after

election. By 1770, the Susquehannah settlement in northern Pennsylvania was

closely intertwined with the issue of popular rights and the conflict with

England. [112]

Connecticut's leaders were unapproachable on the question of ex-

pansion. Roger Sherman threw his full support behind Connecticut's

claims to land in the Susquehannah, and what R.R. Livingston abhorred,

Sherman relished. "I know some gentlemen," he said, "who love to

monopolize wealth and power, think it best for lands to be in a few hands,

and that common people should be their tenants." Sherman encouraged all

Connecticut to unify behind the annexation of Westmoreland in Pennsylvania.

158

His argument was grounded on the greater freedom that farmers gain from owning their own property.[113]   Eliphalet Dyer was stronger in his proposals than Sherman. Dyer had gone to England and tried to get administrative approval of land claims by distributing land shares among influential men. Failing in that, he returned to Connecticut, advocated violation of Orders-in-Council, and led the movement to annex the Westmoreland settlement.[114]   When the Imperial crisis produced confusion in America, expansionist politics continued to carry the day in the legislature of the colony. The representatives annexed the settlement, the Trumbull faction gained five hundred more votes, and Connecticut sent three exponents of expansion -- Dyer, Sherman, and Silas Deane -- to the Continental Congress.[115]   The New England way was for export.

Rhode Island sent the most indecisive of the New England delegations to Congress: its delegates, like those of Delaware, were often split, and that, by the rules of Congress, nullified the vote of the colony. Like Delaware, Rhode Island had certain features which made it the exception in its region, and these were expressed in a strikingly direct manner by its delegates. Providence, the home of one of the two delegates,

was the most aggressive and the most thriving port in New England. The

inhabitants of the town and its environs, farmers and artisans and

professional men as well as merchants, diversified their activities and

their investments so as to obtain more to trade; and then they went out

and exchanged their wares with others -- almost always at a profit. By

such means Providence was rapidly overtaking its rival, Newport, and would

soon pass it. The delegate from Providence to Congress was partially

responsible for that success. Stephen Hopkins had all the makings of the

traditional Whig. He had fought and broken the power of the old

proprietors in Providence and forced commercial property out of their

hands. He wanted commerce to come to Providence, and he worked for that

end for twenty-five long years. Though he never became extremely wealthy,

he was always on the side of commercial expansion, and personally held his

own.[116] In the 1760's he and his followers had, after a long see-saw

struggle, triumphed over Samuel Ward and his faction, only to find their

victory jeopardized by the deepening of the Imperial conflict. The

factions were tenuous at best, and one wing of Hopkins' party rested on

the Anglicans in Newport, whose sentiments were generally with Parliament.

In 1774 Samuel Ward, former governor, Baptist, and angry, came bouncing

back to colonial power by taking, with the support of William Ellery, a
more aggressive stand of resistance to Britain than the Hopkins men did. [117]
For a time Hopkins held his ground; a member of the Society of Friends until
1773, Hopkins reflected the religious diversity and commercial prosperity
of his constituency, and he significantly affected the voting in Congress.
Between 1774 and 1776, the division of Rhode Island delegates worked in
combination with the division of the Delaware delegates, and left the voting
strength of New England and the Middle Colonies evenly balanced. [118]
Ultimately Hopkins would succumb to local pressures and join the advocates
of independence.

On the whole, the New England delegates to the Congress provided
a striking contrast to the delegates from the Middle Colonies. New Englanders
represented a more aggressive population: men armed and trained upon first
hearing word of the Boston Port Bill, and in September, 1774, when a false
rumor spread that fighting had broken out in Boston, a militia force estimated at twenty to thirty thousand men marched toward Boston. [119] The
Calvinist ministers supported resistance and repeatedly remained men of their
God-given right to resist force with force and oppose tyranny to last extremity. [120] Moreover, the New England delegates had a long tradition of
constitutional radicalism. Whereas denial of

161

Parliament's right to legislate for the colonies was a relatively new

position for the delegates from the Middle Colonies -- and a position that

few of them advocated with any great force -- many New Englanders had

taken that position long before 1774. Samuel and John Adams, Thomas

Cushing, Roger Sherman, Samuel Ward, and Stephen Hopkins had all denied

121

Parliament's right to legislate before the furor over the Tea Act,

and when the First Continental Congress convened they urged Congress

to make that position an integral part of the Declaration of Rights and

Grievances.

Just as important was the fact that New Englanders in Congress were

overtly unionist, and early advocated some kind of formal confederation.

Silas Deane of Connecticut spent countless hours after February 1774,

poring over the seventeenth-century records of his colony, and in January

of 1775, he wrote an excited letter to Patrick Henry of Virginia. "The

confederation or agreement of the people first settling this colony in

1638,"he said, "under which they subsisted, until the granting of the

charter in 1661, is without a single reference to, or notice taken of

King, Lords, Commons, or any other power on earth, save that of the

162

United Colonies." Those articles of confederation, Deane said, might have remained in force; and certainly they pre-dated the pretended rights of the present King and Parliament of Great Britain. If such a colonial union were now formed, it would be advantageous even if a reconciliation with Great Britain took place, and "if no reconciliation is to be ad," Deane added, "without a confederation we are ruined."[122] In the Second Congress, Deane and a majority of New England delegates pressed for a union which would have helped to protect their region from British armies and, at the same time, would have constituted an implicit renunciation of allegiance to the Crown.[123]

Although New England leadership was affected by a variety of factors, differences in motives and actions did not prevent them from standing on the common ground of advocacy of independence. The career of one leading exponent of separation, John Adams of Massachusetts, reflects both the multipicity of factors contributing to the independence movement and the reasoning behind New Englanders' final justification for rebellion.

163

V

John Adams

By May, 1775, John Adams had made up his mind that the colonies should separate from Great Britain, and nothing short of the gallows was likely to change his thinking. He lamented his lost allegiance, and the thought of war with England displeased him, but the fear that America might fall prey to the designs of despotism commanded all his thoughts and deeds. Adams was convinced that a malignant germ of tyranny infected the king, his ministers, both houses of Parliament, and even the electorate in England. If the colonies were to escape infection themselves, then they had no alternative course. "The cancer," Adams said, "is too deeply rooted and too far spread to be cured by anything short of cutting it out entire."[1]

Adams never retreated. Of all the Patriots who made the decision to bring about a "full revolution," as they called it, he was the most unswerving, the most ingenious, and the most able. Adams did not relish civil war, but neither did he fear it. He did not like inconoclasts, but

when the necessity arose he was willing to destory the idols of English

power in America. Adams was militant, and he justified his militancy

as a means of preserving the sanctity of a cause higher than mortal

man; one which imposed obligations from which no man could in good

conscience retreat. For that reason, Adams was prepared to cut the

arteries of royal authority and let the blood flow to the last drop.

That May in 1775, when Adams entered the Second Continental Congress,

he was forty years of age, and short, plump, and rosy-cheeked.[2] Despite

minor physical ailments, he looked the picture of health. During the

last two decades or more, he had indulged himself in his favorite

addictions, books and tobacco, and he had spent countless hours with both in

any form that came to hand. He was one of the most learned men in

America. Though he had learned to love the solitude of his study, he

also liked dinner parties and enjoyed considering himself the delight

of good company in Braintree and Boston. And Adams had a stubborn will

about things small and large alike, as when he learned to sit a horse in

defiance of nature, and when he said and meant that he would rather die

than agree to the unlimited power of Parliament over America. More

important, Adams had become an excellent lawyer and the theoretician of
the popular faction and Patriot movement in Massachusetts. Over the
last four years, Patriot leaders had repeatedly requested that Adams
squelch the opposition. He had excelled at the effort; in fact, he had
become the backbone of Patriot constitutional argumentation and one
of the most popular men in eastern Massachusetts. When he arrived in
Philadelphia for the Second Continental Congress, he was experienced,
able, and dedicated, and he knew both what America should do and why
America should do it.

John Adams' journey to rebellion began long before he was quite
aware of it. It had to do with his loyalty to Massachusetts and
Massachusetts history, with his attachment to the eighteenth century
Puritan attitudes and habits, and with his studies at Harvard and as a
professional lawyer, and it had to do with the fact that Adams was a
struggling lawyer who found himself in conflict with standing governmental
power in Massachusetts. The turbulence of Anglo-American conflict disrupted the life of a man with a highly developed sense of American

separateness and destiny.

Deacon John Adams, John Adams' father, had lived the usual life of a Massachusetts farmer. He was a Congregationalist, and his faith promised that life would be difficult. For most people who first settled Massachusetts and for most who came after them, that promise was fulfilled, and the Puritan virtues of hard work, frugality, and thrift became second nature to them. Men learned not to expect much and to give thanks for precious little in Massachusetts. Not that a yeoman farmer could not get by in eighteenth century Massachusetts. Deacon Adams proved that he could; it was just that little was left over from a life of "getting by." Deacon Adams bore his circumstances with a conviction that his faith demanded, and careful Puritan abstinence rendered the success that was promised to the faithful. He sent John Adams to Harvard by selling part of his farm. He remained staunch in his beliefs in the face of heresy. He built a ₤1,300 estate, and died.[3]

The two bequests of a Harvard education and orthodoxy in theology did not sit well with young John Adams; they made his adjustment to his lot at once more difficult and more demanding. Adams had to decide about his

faith, and what he decided set him apart from most men, for despite the secularization of religion in New England, the God of John Calvin yet contended for the souls of men, and He won many of them. Most men, if they were not churchmembers, were at least firm believers.[4] At first, John Adams did not escape the force of the faith. Like probably most young men raised in the Calvinist tradition, Adams thought at one time that he would become a minister.[5] Later, a zeal for learning and examples set by Harvard lights changed that, and he became a mild heretic. He rejected the doctrine of original sin and doubted trinitarianism, but he never turned scoffer.[6] When he was almost forty, he would still prefer a church with Calvinist creeds, and one reason that he gave for the preference was typical -- he liked the Congregational way best next to that of the Independent, he said, and found both Episcopalians and Presbyterians equal as slaves to priesthood.[7] Adams preferred that church power rest in the congregation.

Although some Congregational doctrines fell easily from Adam's mind, its codes remained a way of life. At twenty-one his vision of "Eutopia" was that of a Biblical commonwealth.[8] At twenty-seven, his Calvinist

conviction sounded clear: "This world," he wrote, "was not designed for

a lasting and happy state, but rather for a state of moral discipline,

that we might have a fair opportunity and continual excitements to labour,

after a cheerful resignation to all events of providence, after habits of

virtue, self-government and piety."[9] Adams' sense of the world remained

the Puritans' sense of the world, where rules of conduct were found in

prescriptive and proscriptive codes outside the man. Having those codes

as a standard, Adams could quickly decide what he thought was right in

almost any given situation, and he was as quick to judge himself as

others.[10]

In one important particular, however, the Calvinist system of social

values that prevailed in Massachusetts made decision difficult. Calvinists

before, in the time of, and after John Adams had the same experience:

men were told that material success was meaningless, then told that if

they did not succeed that something was drastically wrong with them in

the eyes of God. When Adams moved from the farm to the city these

incongruities increasingly disturbed him. At first he compromised

and became a teacher. Finally he entered law. The faithful's proper

concern had always been laws governing men, and John Adams studied with

a passion. His reading confirmed his belief in and attachment to

prescriptive and proscriptive codes, whether they were to be found in

providential decrees, minute legalities, or the laws of nature and

nations which he read about in Grotius, Pufendorf, Locke and Montesquieu.

Adams put his faith and his trust there, in laws and not men.[11]

Whenever Adams looked for causes and solutions, he looked to government

and law. His profession became not only a means of success but also a

study of truth.

Adams' studies broadened his outlook. He learned more of the history

of his own province than he had known as a teacher. Tales he had

learned as a boy about the early Puritan removal from England became

detailed, substantive fact. Images of French "Popish" devils and

devilish Indians shed their scales, but the image of struggle to hold

the land remained. Adams himself remembered the battle of Louisburg,

and battles stretched back from Louisburg in endless number. The

English were still fighting the French during the months that he

pursued his studies.[12] For nearly a hundred and thirty years, war

and bloodshed had been part of Massachusetts. Battle was as nearly a

part of tradition as was his faith, and few in Massachsuetts thought of

the duties of the soldier as dishonorable, or wrong, if performed for

the right reasons. History told Adams that the French would not win,

that victory would go to the English, and it told him that the struggle

to hold the land would probably go on unabated.

The inhabitants of Massachusetts Bay, Adams learned, had not always

struggled with foes from without. Conflict among the early Puritans about

theology he wrote off as superstitions of a less knowledgeable age. But

the removal of people from England in search of a land apart from Europe

was real enough, and so too were the habits and practices of self-

government which they had sought and found. Students of Massachusetts

history knew that back in 1686, Massachsusetts Bay found itself in

turmoil over reorganization of its original charter.[13] Before that time,

they have been virtually independent of England. The first inhabitants

had settled the land at their own expense and had chosen their own

government -- governor, magistrates, and deputies. When Parliament passed

the first of the Acts of Trade and Navigation, the Acts produced a stir in

the General Court. The Massachusetts legislature remonstrated against

the Acts because, they said, the "representatives or deputies have full

power and authority, both legislative and executive, for the government

of all the people here."[14] Not until 1677 did the inhabitants conclude

that the Acts bound them; even then their understanding was that the

Acts of Navigation were not laws "without invading the liberties and

properties of the subject, until the General Court made provision therein

by law."[15] Then, in 1686, Edmund Andros, acting under commission of

the Stuart King, Charles II, had tried to reorganize Massachusetts Bay,

Plymouth, Rhode Island, and Connecticut under one central administration.

The Glorious Revolution knocked the Stuarts off the throne and took Andros

with them, but in 1692, Massachusetts men learned that henceforth the

crown would appoint their governor; they might elect their Representatives

and the Representatives, in turn, elected members of the Council.

To outsiders, these episodes were undramatic and pedestrian -- dry,

musty facts from times past -- but to those weaned in Massachusetts, they

meant much more. As an adolescent, Adams put his views in an unsophisticated

manner by noting simply that God had the whole plan of the universe in view

from all eternity.[16] Massachusetts was part of that plan. When he was

a mature individual of thirty-one, the study of history, natural law,

and the notion of providential purpose locked together. "I always

considered the settlement of America," Adams once wrote, "with reverence

and wonder -- as opening a grand scheme and design in Providence, for the

illumination of the ignorant and the emancipation of the slavish part of

mankind all over the earth."[17]

The turbulence and conflict of the years from the Stamp Act crisis

until the Battle of Lexington and Concord strengthened Adams' convictions

in the sanctity of America, and during those years, he emerged as one

of the principle spokesmen for opposition to Parliament in Massachusetts.

Like Dickinson and other theorists of the opposition, Adams maintained

that he sought to defend the rights of colonials within the Empire, and

he too forswore aspirations for independence. But unlike Dickinson, Adams

found that his attitudes and the political circumstances in Massachusetts

brought him to the brink of rebellion far in advance of most Americans.

During the years of conflict, he argued for the rights of colonials in

three ways: on the basis of the right of consent to all laws, on the

basis of historical events, and on the basis of his conception of

English government.

On at least two occasions, Adams argued that laws of Parliament did

not bind colonials because they had not consented to them. In December,

1765, Adams and two other lawyers appeared before the governor to present

a memorial from the town of Boston, and Adams found himself obliged to argue

a question for which he was not fully prepared: whether the courts

of law should be closed under the terms of the Stamp Act since the

people refused to comply with the law.[18] Being unprepared and not

having "one momen's opportunity to consult any authorities," Adams

instinctively grounded his argument "on the invalidity of the Stamp

Act, it not being in any sense our Act, having never consented to it."[19]

And later he argued against the Sugar Act in the same way, and more

forcefully. He made the broad assertion that a British subject could

"be subjected to no laws which he does not make, or constitute others

to make for him."[20]

His historical argument was more involved and less popular. In

an essay called "On the Canon and the Feudal Law," Adams postulated

that tyranny had existed from the earliest times, and that only

gradually had people come to know that they had God-given rights to

life, property, and freedom. Inspired by that knowledge, men began

to battle for their rights, and an incessant struggle between rulers and

the ruled ensued. In the Middle Ages priests and feudal princes

devised a scheme for establishing themselves as joint tyrants, and

through their cunning and force -- and the ignorance and timidity of

the people -- they were able to establish a despotism that lasted for

centuries. In the Reformation men rediscovered their rights, and the

struggle was born anew. Out of that struggle came the Puritan fathers,

who established the British colonies in America in a way that would

prevent the re-establishment of the power of priests and princes, and

they diligently established educational institutions for the purpose of

educating all men in the knowledge of their rights, and of the need for

vigilance in defending them. In recent times, however, the fiber of

Americans had loosened somewhat, and Americans had become increasingly

timid about standing up for their rights. In the immediate context that

timidity was extremely dangerous, for "somebody or other in Great Britain,"

actuated by the love of power that characterized all men, had "meditated

for us . . . a direct and formal design . . . to enslave all America." [21]

Adams' theoretical argument, the early version of what ultimately

became his celebrated doctrine of government by balance, was one which

he found useful on several occasions, until it led him into difficulties

that he was slow to understand and slower to resolve. In the eassay "On

Canon and Feudal Law," in an article signed "The Earl of Clarendon" and

published in the Boston Gazette in January, 1766, and in several

subsequent pieces Adams analyzed the British constitution. He believed

that the British were a free people because they had a mixed system of

government in which there were two (not three, as in later versions of

the theory) "grand divisions" of power: the legislative, in which king,

lords, commons, and people all had equal voices, and the executive

and judicial (considered as one), conducted by the king through the

people in grand juries. The two sets of powers and the king and the

people were in a continuous state of tension, each trying to

aggrandize itself at the expense of the other; the preservation of

balance between them was the safeguard of liberty. This theory
served Adams well until 1770, when the Boston Massacre made him suddenly
and painfully aware that in America the people's fierce opposition to
the encroachments from England could lead to violence, a dangerous
threat to the balance between the powers. [22]

These various ideas, unresolved as they were, were adequate for
Adams as a theorist of resistance; but from 1773 onward, as he moved
from advocating resistance toward advocating independence, they became
steadily less adequate. Either they must be resolved in a way that
justified independence, or a new theory, perhaps incorporating some
parts of the old theories, had to be devised.

Adams took his first step toward a public commitment to independence
in January, 1773, when, before news of the Tea Act reached Boston and
long before the Coercive Acts were passed, he locked in debate with
Thomas Hutchinson on the question of Parliament's power in America. Tory
and Patriot theoreticians demonstrated how far they differed on
historical interpretation, in their views of the colonies in the Empire,
and on where power lay. When Hutchinson said that, by their removal

from England, colonials had lost their right of representation in
Parliament, Adams rejoined that the charters provided colonials with
representation in America.[23]   When Hutchinson said that the Glorious
Revolution had made allegiance to the Crown synonymous with allegiance
to the Crown in Parliament, Adams rejoined that colonial legislatures
had given their consent to the ascension of the House of Orange and that
colonial laws were confirmed by the Crown alone, before and after the
Glorious Revolution.[24]   When Hutchinson said that colonials had
previously admitted that they were bound by laws made by Parliament,
Adams pointed out that this applied only to those laws to which colonials
had given their "cheerful consent."[25]   When Hutchinson attempted
to frighten the Representatives into retreat and said that he knew
"of no line that can be drawn between the supreme authority of Parliament
and the total independence of the colonies,"[26] Adams adroitly countered
that "If there be no such line, the consequence is either that the
colonies are vassals of Parliament, or that they are totally independent."[27]
Representatives allowed Adams' arguments to stand as their official
remonstrances against Hutchinson.

178

Thomas Hutchinson had hardly "forced" Adams to a new position. Adams could easily deny the legislative power of Parliament because he had never affirmed it. But neither can Hutchinson's role and responsibilities be minimized. Hutchinson had prepared the way for widespread popular hostility to royal power in Massachusetts, and he kept at it. The Massachusetts Representatives accepted the forward position of John Adams precisely because Hutchinson made such a forceful play for power and disruption of the Charter. The royal faction had frightened the popular leaders so badly that they called a constitutional radical to their defense. John Adams never relinquished his place in the Patriot movement, and his views were never up for compromise.

Soon after Adams' dispute with Hutchinson, news of the Tea Act arrived. Adams did not advance in his constitutional views, but the Tea Act pushed him into a political militancy commensurate with his ideas. Hutchinson said that he would land the tea consignments. Massachusetts men said that they would never buy the tea, for to do so would be to pay a tax. The Liberty Boys made certain, and destroyed the tea when it arrived. John Adams moved with them by calling their action

"absolutely necessary" and the tea party the most magnificent movement
of all in defence of liberty.[28]   In short, Adams, on word of the tea
party, resolved part of the problem that had bothered him in 1770: he made
a distinction between kinds of popular violence. He did not approve
of the irrational, petty violence of the mob, he said, but did approve
of violence and destruction of property when there was a purpose behind
it.

Retaliation by Parliament in the form of the Boston Port Bill only
increased Adams' antagonisms and militancy. He readily joined in the
movement for a general congress, and formed a plan of his own. Adams,
after a decade of conflict, put no faith in petitions or even economic
coercion. In June, 1774, he wrote that he thought that a congress was
a good idea, and that he was sure that the body would be composed of
prudent men. "But what avails prudence, wisdom, policy, fortitude,
integrity, without power, without legions," he said. "When Demosthenes
went as amabssador from Athens to the other states of Greece, to
excite a confederacy against Phillip, he did not go to propose a non-
importation and non-exportation agreement!!!"[29]

180

John Adams did not go from Boston to Philadelphia with only well-written petitions in his hand and optimism about reconciliation in his heart. Massachusetts had felt the brunt of Parliament's retaliation. Boston harbor was closed and that portended economic stagnation. John Adams thought that he personally verged on bankruptcy. Massachusetts' Charter was suspended, and a military officer appointed to the office of Governor. Royal troops descended on Massachusetts. Then, New Englanders learned that the Catholics in Quebec had been given leave to renew the power of their church. The situation, together with Adams' pessimism about his personal affairs, bred a decision for harsh action, not an inclination to strike a negotiable compromise with Parliament -- or with anyone else. Over the summer of 1774, he thought through what he ought to do as a delegate to Congress. He decided on four definite things. First, he wanted the Congress to be made a permanent, annual convocation of all the colonies.[30] Second, he wanted this Congress to resolve for some kind of general militia establishment.[31] Third, he wanted a formal resolution on exactly what America would consider an act of war.[32] And fourth, Adams hoped that he could induce Congress to

accept his views on colonial consent and the power of Parliament.[33]

Three of Adams' aims for Congress met with little success. In September and October of 1774, Adams found that Richard Henry Lee agreed to the idea of a militia establishment, but the two failed to get their resolution through Congress.[34] Adams sent a letter off to his wife and stated his hopes that at least Massachusetts ought to be prepared. Let men in Massachusetts follow the old axiom, he said, "In time of peace prepare for war."[35] And he pursued his object on a continental scale by meeting with Charles Lee and Thomas Mifflin and discussing America's manpower and revenue sources. Lee had either just completed or was completing a pamphlet on the topic of the power of American arms, and Adams either followed Lee or helped him with the pamphlet; Adams' notes and Lee's final publication contained similar figures.[36] On the matter of getting Congress to lay down a definite statement of what America would consider an act of war, Adams proposed that if any person were arrested under the statute of treason of Henry VIII, then the colonies should consider the arrest an act of war, "and reprisals ought to be made in all the colonies."[37] Congress refused that motion.[38] A few

days later, October 6, word arrived that such an arrest had been made.[39]

On the matter of an annual Congress, a compromise was reached. It was

agreed that if American rights were not redressed within a year, a second

Congress would meet.[40]

But the true test of Adams' skill came with his activity on the

committee of colonial rights and grievances. Adams found that he could

not be open about his views in Congress or on the committee, and he

resorted to political wire-pulling. The Massachusetts delegates, Adams

wrote, "have been obliged to keep ourselves out of sight, and feel the

pulse and sound the depths; to insinuate our sentiments, designs, and

desires, by means of other persons; sometimes of one province, and

sometimes of another."[41] Adams did not like to finagle but he proved,

with the help of others, successful at getting what he wanted.

As it turned out, the question of the power of Parliament was the

most controversial issue debated in the committee on rights, and everyone

seemed to have his own views.[42] Early in the sessions, Adams borrowed

notes on the power of Parliament from John Dickinson, a Patriot whom

Adams held in high esteem at the time.[43] With Dickinson's statements

before him and his ideas in mind, Adams threw himself into the committee

work. Christopher Gadsden of South Carolina asserted that if Congress

admitted the power of Parliament to regulate trade, then it admitted

Parliament's power in all cases. Adams denied that.[44] He knew a way to

admit the legality of the old Acts of Trade and Navigation which said

nothing about the sovereignty or legislative power of Parliament in

America. On the other hand, James Duane of New York wanted a phrase

descriptive of the actual charters and history of all the colonies. Some

colonies, Duane pointed out, had been founded after the Acts of Trade

and Navigation became law; Parliament's laws were part of the

governmental foundations of those colonies, and, therefore, fundamental

law in those colonies. For that reason, Duane wanted an admission that

the right to regulate trade was rooted in the British Constitution and

involved legal right. Duane asked that the right of Parliament be based

upon the British Constitution, charters, and, in order to accommodate

other colonies, necessity and compact.[45] Adams rejected three of Duane's

suggestions. He agreed on the use of "necessity," for that was in

accord with his own views, but he did not want the argument based upon

an admission of autonomous Parliamentary right, charters, or compact.

He favored consent alone.[46] And he held firm.

After nearly a month of tedious debate, Adams won. The fourth resolve

of the committee report first expressed the statement of John Dickinson

(and others) that colonials enjoyed free and exclusive power of internal

legislation through their assemblies; next came Adams' idea of citing

practical considerations as the reason for consenting to trade regulation

("from the necessity of the case, and with a regard to the mutual interest

of both countries, we cheerfully consent to the operation of such acts

of the British Parliament, as are . . . restrained to the regulation

of our external commerce . . .") and following that, an extraneous

denial of Parliament's right to tax, which was in accord with the

traditional colonial distinction between the right to legislate and the

right to tax.[47] Implicit in the resolution was the proposition that

Parliament had no legislative power over America, only a utilitarian

function that rested not on any autonomous right but on the fact that

colonials "cheerfully" consented to trade regulation. The document,.

styled a "Declaration of Rights and Grievances," was published and sent

throughout America and to Canada and England.

185

Upon returning to Massachusetts Adams once again took up his pen.

In the Novanglus Letters, published months before Lexington and Concord,

Adams made two significant modifications in his earlier positions. First,

he extended the conspiracy--the design of "somebody or other" to enslave

America--back twenty years, and way beyond the years of the first signs

of Imperial reorganization or attempts of Parliament to tax.[48] That

left a vacuum in Massachusetts government. If, indeed, the royal

executives were dedicated to tyranny, then government in the colony was

destined to remain a source of perpetual clash. Adams recommended that the

extra-legal organizations -- the Provincial Convention and the Congress --

stand as the guides to action until Massachusetts inhabitants could be

assured that good men would govern them.[49] And, secondly, as Adams

reached for a reasonable defense of the extra-legal bodies as de facto

powers, he broke through years of training and, for once, forgot the

scholastic political definitions. Though he did not specifically repudiate

his earlier theorizing about government by balance between its parts, he

did deny the charge that popular resistance had degenerated into the

tyranny of the mob, and declared that "a democratical despotism is a

contradiction in terms." For the ordinary polemicist, a turn of phrase might mean little during the heat of debate. For John Adams, this turn of phrase had awesome connotations, and he could not have used it had he not thought the issues through. That he did use it meant that he had concluded that the theory of balanced government , however applicable. in England, did not necessarily apply to the people of America, and they could cut themselves free of king and aristocracy, leaving the people alone to rule, and still preserve their liberty.

Although these minor themes in the Novanglus Letters and Adams' militant stance over the last six months were indicative of how dangerously near he stood to rebellion, his major theme in the Letters urged Parliament to retreat from its insistence on the right to legislate for the colonies in all cases and to confine itself to regulation of imperial trade and commerce. He openly avowed that the central aim of colonial resistance was to uphold colonial rights and liberties within the Empire. Thus, Adams' stated motives were those of a Patriot who had managed to retain a posture of loyal opposition to the mother country, but who had pieced together a loose framework of justifications for

extreme political action. He was trapped in a web of conflicting loyalties and aspirations.

The Battle of Lexington and Concord pushed Adams over the brink and ended his allegiance to the Empire. Adams felt the gravity of the situation, but the event lifted a burden from his shoulders. For the first time in months, his letters breathed a sense of elation and expectation. He set out for the Second Continental Congress convinced that America would act decisively. On one occasion, he wrote enthusiastically that "everyone must be a soldier," and as enthusiastically reiterated his own determination to pursue military studies.[50] He intended that America should be a separate power, and was sure that no alternative remained but to slice away the institutions of English authority. His despair for America in the Empire had been replaced with enthusiasm for America outside the Empire, and he was optimistic about Congress and its new task.[51]

But in May, June, and July, 1775, the clash in Congress shocked Adams awake to the harsh realities of politics. Few members of Congress agreed

with him--so few in fact, that he retreated into momentary silence.

Majority sentiment favored redress and reconciliation. Adams favored

a strong army, a navy, trade agreements with foreign powers, and a permanent

confederation.[52] In May and early June Congress moved slowly and took a

month to create an army and longer to get it into the field. The full

general staff did not leave for the scene of conflict at Boston until

after the battle of Breed's Hill.[53] Adams described the situation in a

letter to James Warren. "You will see," he said, "a strange escillation

between love and hatred, between war and peace -- preparations for war

and negotiations for peace."[54] Adams was not pleased, he dreaded

negotiation with England like death itself, but he saw ruinous division

if he pressed too strenuously for what he wanted. Adams wrote that all

the colonies ought to assume a government like that of Connecticut,

dissolve all "Ministerial tyrannies and customs," and confederate.[55] But

if he pressed the scheme, he said, "Discord and total disunion would be

the certain effect. . . ."[56]

Nevertheless, Adams grew irascible and flustered. When John

Dickinson introduced his second petition to the king, Adams attacked

the proposal in such a way that Dickinson apparently thought the attack

was personal. To Adams' surprise, Dickinson caught him in the foyer of Congress and dressed him down. Adams' fears of division were confirmed. Dickinson told Adams in no uncertain terms that if he persisted in his attacks upon redress and reconciliation, then Dickinson would withdraw from Congress and take the other delegates from the Middle Colonies.[57] Adams was not at all certain that John Dickinson would not do exactly what he threatened. He retreated for a few weeks. He also signed the "Olive Branch Petition."[58]

When measures that Adams supported came up for debate at the end of July, he was confident that some of them would pass. On July 21 and 22, Benjamin Franklin of Pennsylvania and Richard Henry Lee each submitted a report recommending trade with foreign nations. An intercolonial navy was implicit in their recommendations. Franklin also introduced a proposal for and a plan of confederation. Congress deadlocked and referred the matters to Monday, July 24, when another deadlock ensued.[59] Dickinson led the opposition, and all these proposals were blocked.

Adams had got nothing that he wanted, and he vented his feelings about Dickinson in a letter to his friend, James Warren. "In confidence,"

190

Adams said, "I am determined to write freely to you this time. A

certain great fortune and piddling genius, whose fame has been trumpeted

so loudly, has given a silly cast to our whole doings."[60] Dickinson's

insistence on another petition for redress of grievances without

corresponding measures in time of war, Adams thought, placed the colonies

"between hawk and buzzard." The members of Congress, Adams said, "ought

to have had in our hands a month ago the whole legislative, executive

and judicial of the whole continent, and have completely modeled a

constitution; to have raised a naval power, and opened our ports wide;

to have arrested every friend of [royal] government on the continent."[61]

Adams wanted America on an equal footing with England. With a general

government, Congress might then safely negotiate for peace. With definite

plans of organization, restoration of commerce, and a navy, America

would be prepared for a long war.

Adams and Dickinson parted ways. Adams never forgave the other

Patriot for his part in blocking measures Adams thought were necessary

for the defense of liberty and the war effort. Thirty years later the

very thought of Dickinson still rankled Adams. And Dickinson had his

own pride. The British intercepted and published Adams' letter.[62]

Dickinson became suspicious of Adams for he distrusted the New Englander's

aggressiveness and play for leadership; he stopped speaking to Adams and

treated him as if he did not exist.[63] Had that been all between the two men,

the situation might have been different. But they did more than cease

to speak and indulge in childish pretenses. They ceased to understand

or communicate with one another -- even on the floor of Congress. During

the critical months that lay ahead, neither Dickinson nor Adams fully

understood what the other was talking about. Dickinson aimed at a

flexible policy that he thought was crucial for the preservation of

colonial and Pennsylvania unity. John Adams thought that separation was

the inevitable path to unity and that the life of Massachusetts was

dependent upon strong, formal actions of Congress. Adams viewed his

own measures as forged in the fire of absolute necessity and absolutely

correct in the light of events. Dickinson looked upon his own policies

as good strategy and necessary for the war effort. The Patriots remained

in the same Congress only because the British lion was at the door and

threatened them all.

192

Adams' inquisitive mind led him to look into the causes of
disagreement among the Patriots. In June, 1771, he was considering
not only Dickinson but all the members of Congress when he wrote that
"those ideas of equality, which are so agreeable to us natives of
New England, are very disagreeable to many gentlemen in the other colonies."[64]
By November, he had concluded that men south of New England "are accustomed,
habituated to higher notions of themselves, and the distinction between
them and the common people, than we are . . . . I dread the consequences
of this dissimilitude of character."[65] The delegates from other colonies,
he wrote, had "Aristocratical impulses and monarchial attachments."[66]
Following his ideas out, Adams wrote a full description of his beliefs
on the spirit of liberty in New England. He said:

> New England has, in many respects, the advantage of every other
> colony in America, and, indeed, of every other part of the world
> that I know anything of.
>
> 1. The people are purer English blood; less mixed . . . than
>   any other; and descended from Englishmen, too, who left
>   Europe in purer times than at present, and less tainted with
>   corruption than those they left behind.
>
> 2. The institutions of New England for the support of religion,
>   morals, and decency exceed any other; obliging every parish
>   to have a minister, and every person to go to meeting, etc.
>
> 3. The public institutions in New England for education of
>   youth, supporting colleges at the public expense are not
>   equaled, and never were, in any part of the world.

193

4. The division of our territory . . . into townships;
empowering towns to assemble, choose officers, make laws,
mend roads, and twenty other things, gives every man an
opportunity of showing and improving that education which
he received at college or at school, and makes knowledge
and dexterity at public business common.

5.. Our law for the distribution of intestate estates occasions
a frequent division of landed property, and prevents
monopolies of land.[67]

Adams had at last found a means of defending aspirations for independence

by precise distinctions: on beliefs in human equality, on laws which

brought property holding to equal proportions, on general eduction of

the people at large, and on the people's public practices in "morality"

and government. He believed that he sought to protect the republican

nature of New England, and for him, separation would bring a renewal,

a restoration of liberty to his homeland and America at large.

Adams tried persuasion on his fellow delegates. He was convinced

that a transition from charter governments under the Crown to popular

republics would not necessarily involve disaster for the colonies. .

He argued the point verbally from the summer of 1775 into the winter,

and pointed to the government of Connecticut as a practical example

of what a good form of government was. But many individuals with whom

he spoke did not know exactly what he was talking about, and so he wrote

out several manuscript copies of his views, and these were circulating

in Virginia, New Jersey, and Pennsylvania in early 1776.[68] In fact, in

January, 1776, the North Carolina Provincial Convention applied to

John Adams for his thinking on new government.[69] He wrote these out

for John Penn of North Carolina. Adams pointed out that there were as

many varieties of republics as arrangements in the forms of society.

His own opinion, he said, was that the representative assemblies would

be an exact portrait of the "people at large, or in other words, equal

interests among the people should have equal interests in the representative

body."[70] He recommended a two-house assembly, and, for the time being,

during war, a governor elected by the assembly. He was emphatic that

the executor of the laws should have a negative but no other legislative

power, and he recommended that a "third branch" of government whose

function would be to interpret laws, be set up independent of assembly

and governor. After the war, he said, changes might be made so that

the governor would be elected by the people at large. Adams showed no

concern over property holding and the right to vote, and was not unduly

concerned with how the upper house of assembly was elected. He did

reiterate over and over again that men in power were not to be given
free rein. "Where annual elections end,"he said, "there slavery begins."[71]
Any government, he warned, could become corrupt; the virtue of any
society depended, in large measure, on the good character of its laws.[72]
Adams' rather calm and judicious approach eased the minds of those men
who had no inclination to advocate widespread reform in the midst of
a grave civil war.

In Congress, Adams pressed every resolution to its furthest
extremity in an attempt formally to commit the Congress to separation.
In late January or early February, 1776, he wrote a systematic program
for the delegates who favored independence. The program was no more than
he had advocated for six months past: new governments, a confederation,
trade with foreign nations, alliances with France, and independence.[73]
Dickinson was against all these, but was willing to investigate the
possibility of a French alliance. And, Adams himself despaired of a
systematic approach to independence before the attempts had quite gotten
underway. In March and early April, he and Richard Henry Lee decided
that they could force independence through recommendations from the
colonies alone, and both agreed that if Virginia could be induced to

lead the way, others would follow. [74]

Several events worked directly against Adams and Lee. First,

Thomas Paine's Common Sense, admirably written and full for independence,

had produced a grand stir among the people of all the colonies, but it had

also stirred men in Congress -- the wrong way. Paine frightened some. [75]

Adams thought Paine naïve in his views on government in the new states;

Paine's idea of a unicameral legislature did not, Adams said, insure

good laws or provide checks on the excesses of men in power. [76] Secondly,

the royal troops evacuated Boston, and third, rumors spread that the

British were going to sue for peace and that commissioners were on

their way from England. [77] Adams did not trust the situation, he

did not trust Paine, and he did not trust the British. In late April,

he tried to counter all three trends against independence by publishing

his own views on government. One part of the pamphlet, Thoughts on

Government, was a diatribe against Paine's recommendation of unicameral

legislature. Such a system, Adams said, was cumbersome, slow and subject

to the vices, avarice, and folly of a single person. More than that,

Adams said, it tended to be self-perpetuating; the members of a

single legislature would, he said, "make arbitary laws for their own

interest, and adjudge all controversies in their own favor." [78] He

hardened his position on indirect election of the upper house and

governor. [79] Then, Adams announced that local government was necessary,

since the king had discharged Americans from their allegiance by the

Proclamation of Rebellion. Without government, he implied, anarchy

reigned. [80] Thoughts on Government was another political maneuver. The

ideas in it expressed Adams' convictions about checks and limits on

power, but it also sought to ease fears about change, prevent decline

in the independence movement among more powerful men, and, then adroitly

played on the hostility of those same men toward disintegration of

authority, laws, and government.

In early May, Congressional affairs momentarily fell into the

hands of the independence-minded Whigs. Word arrived that North and

South Carolina had established temporary governments. [81] Adams, taking

the lead, argued that all the colonies must be given leave to do the

same, lest they fall into a state of anarchy. On May 10th, their

resolution passed, and Adams, R. H. Lee and Edward Rutledge were made

a committee to prepare the preamble. By chance, the delegates from

198

Maryland happened to leave Congress on the 14th, and that colony

was unrepresented on the 15th.[82] The traditional Whig bloc stood

depleted before the force of all New England and Virginia, and Adams

did not hesitate. He presented a preamble which advocated supression

of all authority under the Crown of Great Britain.[83] A long debate

ensued and New England, Virginia, and one other colony carried the preamble.

The maneuver worked beyond Adams' hopes; the resolution had an

immediate impact upon the standing assemblies of Pennsylvania, New Jersey,

and Delaware. The power structure in those colonies crumbled under the

stress, and Adams stated openly that if he had anything to do with it,

as he was accused, then he gladly accepted responsibility.[84]

The complexion of Congress altered twice in May and June. At

first, the advocates of independence sensed victory.[85] On June 7, Richard

Henry Lee announced that Virginia had declared independence, and moved

for a Congressional declaration of separation. The motion was postponed.[86]

Many of the delegates from the Middle Colonies and particularly John

Dickinson, began to insist that nothing should be done in regard to

independence until all the colonies had formed governments, Congress

had agreed on the form of confederation, and alliances had been concluded with France.[87]

The arguing and maneuvering continued for a month, until, on July 1, the resolution came up for debate. As Adams expected, Dickinson rose to speak against it. Adams did not listen carefully to Dickinson's speech; he had listened to the ideas in it for the last six weeks.[88] He knew that Virginia, Georgia, and the four New England delegations favored the resolution, but he could not be certain what the other colonies would do. He wanted only one more vote, and it would have to come, he thought, from among the Southern colonies.

200

VI

THE SOUTHERN COLONIES: AMERICAN ARISTOCRATS AND THE CRISIS IN EMPIRE

From the vantage point of the Southern colonies, whether Americans would seek to defend their status within the Empire or seek the status of an independent republic hinged on a tenuous balance of power. On the advent of crisis and war, Virginians were as forward as New Englanders. They hesitated only briefly, then united and drove the royal governor from the colony, and in May, 1776, inhabitants of the Old Dominion declared their colony an independent state.[1] But just to the north in Maryland, although westerners in Frederick County tried to follow Virginians, a strong traditional Whig and neutralist group held the movement back. Patriots in eastern Maryland controlled resistance to England, and they blatantly remonstrated against directives from the Continental Congress, refused to help Virginia, and expressed confidence that an early solution to the conflict could be found. By July, Maryland tottered between the two camps.[2] And in the lower South, division was sharper and more serious. Backcountry farmers in the Carolinas refused to follow Patriots of any

description, and thousands of them armed and threatened to fight for Great Britain.[3]   In North Carolina, Patriots divided nearly equally on the question of independence.[4]   In South Carolina a small group of more zealous Whigs, whose following came mainly from the city of Charleston, gathered a militia force and marched west to put down backcountry Loyalists, then found that most easterners abhorred the action and were against further aggression or separation from Great Britain. Loyalists, traditional Whigs, and proponents of independence spun a web of tensions that caught and held South Carolina.[5]   Further south, Georgians cast a gloomy eye on English power on the frontier and on the sea, and did nothing. Georgia went unrepresented in the First Continental Congress, and her inhabitants were slow to act.[6]   The first years of crisis found Southern farmers on opposite sides, Southern aristocrats at cross purposes, and urban dwellers in arms against yeoman farmers.

Nor were Southern leaders unified; Southern delegates in the Continental Congress were far more divided among themselves than were men who represented the other two regions in America. Even Samuel Adams was not as openly hostile toward England as Patrick Henry of Virginia. In the

initial debates of the First Congress, Henry asserted that all government

in the colonies was at an end and proposed that Congress formulate an

American constitution. By early 1775, Henry advocated alliances with

France and independence and led in organization of the Virginia militia.[7]

Richard Henry Lee of Virginia was indefatigable in support of separation,

though he decided for it later than Henry.[8] Christopher Gasden of

South Carolina, Button Gwinnett of Georgia, and William Hooper of North

Carolina also joined the independence-minded Whigs,[9] as did nearly half

of the Southerners who were elected as delegates to Congress.[10] Arrayed

against them were those Patriots who continued to espouse a policy of

redress and reconciliation and who hoped to remain in the Empire. Edward

Rutledge of South Carolina never equivocated on the question of inde-

pendence. He debated against it, tried to organize delegates to oppose

the measure, and voted against the Declaration on July 1. Later, rather

than abandon America, Rutledge signed the Declaration.[11] Robert Alexander

of Maryland, however, chose a different course. Alexander toyed with the

idea of independence, and at one time asserted that it could be justified

by necessity, but when the time came, he fled Congress and ended up as a

203

Loyalist.[12] Thomas Johnson of Maryland helped formulate traditional Whig policies in the Congress, and opposed independence. Maryland voters refused to elect him to the constitutional convention of 1776, and Johnson had to use devious means to gain a seat.[13] Other Southerners supported redress and reconciliation. Carter Braxton of Virginia was a notorious opponent of independence.[14] Joseph Hewes of North Carolina resisted independence to the last debates.[15] These five Patriots represented just over half of the delegates from the Southern colonies who opposed independence down to July, 1776.[16]

On the surface, little save the issue of independence seemed to divide Southern Patriots. Men in both camps belonged to the slaveholding aristocracy. Lee, Braxton, and Rutledge considered themselves among the first families of their colonies, all had held political power for some time, and all were Anglicans.[17] According to Southerners' standards, Thomas Johnson, Robert Alexander, Patrick Henry, and William Hooper belonged to a secondary but nonetheless powerful class of lawyers and landowners. Henry and Johnson had long held political office in their respective colonies, and both Hooper and Alexander were on the verge of

becoming politically prominent. All were Anglicans.[18] Joseph Hewes

was an eastern North Carolina merchant, Christopher Gadsden was an

eastern South Carolina merchant; Hewes was a Quaker, Gadsden an

Anglican.[19] Gwinnett, an immigrant to Georgia, was a sea-island farmer

and cattle raiser.[20]

But beneath the surface there were significant differences,

arising from the fact that the delegates came from different areas in the

South and conditions in those areas were not all the same. Each group

of Southern patriots sought and found its natural allies in the Congress --

most Marylanders and South Carolinians consistently sided with New

Yorkers and Pennsylvanians, and most Virginians and Georgians with New

England -- and these alliances were more than coincidence, for the

sentiments of the Southern delegates were rooted in conditions similar

to those of New England and the Middle Colonies. In the upper South,

colonials in Virginia, and to a lesser extent Maryland, found themselves

caught in a constricting economic situation after the French and Indian

War. At the same time, population expansion soared, agricultural

production for export did not keep pace with rising numbers of people. In

both Virginia and Maryland, land was apparently abundant at the end of

the war, but by the 1770's, land was growing more scarce and the slave

system in both colonies demanded extensive amounts of new land, if not

for expansion of the institution of slavery, then to bolster and

supplement income from the older plantations. Marylanders were able to

solve their problems in part; most Virginians were not. A decade of

Imperial crisis drove the eastern leaders in the two colonies to take

different stances, and the political structure in Maryland provided for

leaders that did not express Maryland sentiments directly, or only

expressed sentiments in part. In the lower South, in South Carolina and

eastern Georgia, the economic patterns were the reverse. South Carolina

contained an extremely strong group of merchants, and planters grew

crops that gave the colony, after the war, the most favorable balance of

trade of all the colonies. Eastern Georgians participated in a similar

rise. The means of growing plantation crops in both areas did not demand

extensive land, and population growth in both colonies relative to land

was moderate. Crisis drove tidewater Georgians to stand still, and the

colony ended by sending individuals to Congress who only partially

expressed local sentiment. North Carolina bridged the other two geographical areas in almost every respect: in economic conditions, population growth, and concern about England, and in the attitudes of its leaders. These colonial conditions laid the basis for American response to crisis as Parliament's attempts to tax and war sliced into and joined with political circumstances in each of the colonies.

Although Maryland and Virginia were among the oldest of the American settlements, time had not brought unified institutions to those colonies. Maryland, contiguous to the Middle Colonies, had a history of religious wars and bloodshed. Men had finally learned to live together, but religious diversity was a characteristic of the colony: it contained large numbers of Quakers who lived along the eastern shore, Germans and Scotch-Irish who lived in the backcountry, a large and powerful group of Anglicans who lived everywhere, and a number of Catholics.[21] Virginia was less diverse, but dissenter groups of all descriptions, mainly Baptists and Presbyterian Scotch-Irish, had settled the southwest and west.[22] In Maryland the Chesapeake Bay region was the seat of plantation slavery. Along the tidewater, aristocrats who worked their plantations

with slaves dominated life and culture. Virginia had an extremely

large and powerful group of slave owners, and in that colony the

plantation system extended into the interior along numerous rivers and

streams, and provided a bridge between sea coast and deep interior. But

in Maryland, the plantation system stopped slightly west of the Bay,

and the colony was more emphatically divided between slave-holding east

and yeoman-farmer west. In both colonies, large concentrations of

Negro slave-owners coincided with large numbers of Anglicans. For the

most part, eastern aristocrats controlled government, and, to a degree,

the established church.[23] They owned over two hundred thousand men

outright, without qualification and without intervention. They dominated

thinking, arts, letters, and education, and only their own consciences

and a few Imperial laws acted as restraints upon their power.

Three things prevented the rather sharp division between east and

west from erupting into ruinous strife. First, regardless of how

much dissenters detested Anglicans or yeomen farmers feared the

power of the eastern aristocracy, all men feared the possibility

of slave rebellion more. Over a century of fears of slave insurrection

had conditioned whites to habitual compromise. The

gentry was more flexible toward lower social groups, and lower social

groups were more timid about untoward political action.[24]   Consciously

or unconsciously, racial and class division in the south forced compromise

among the whites, and a hundred years of compromise had left its mark.

Second, the values of most men in Virginia and Maryland reflected respect

for the aristocracy: men admired the gentry, aspired to that class, and

usually voted for the planter aristocrat.[25]   And third, until the middle

of the eighteenth century abundant land and economic prosperity kept men

apart and engaged. The upper South was a mélange of unity and diversity

that rested precariously upon the most clear-cut class distinctions known

to man.

Then, events during and just after the French and Indian War

jeopardized the balance. In Virginia, and next in Maryland, the land

filled up. Virginians pressed outward into the Ohio, and met the French

and Indians and fought them, and at the end of the war, encountered

Pennsylvanians, Marylanders, and royal administrators. Maryland filled

more slowly, but eventually reached the point of explosion as Frederick

became the most populous county in the colony.[26]   Westerners turned back

toward the east. At the same time, prosperity vanished, and the Virginia

aristocracy fell into a downward spiral that led it to the very brink of

financial disaster. Marylanders followed Virginians briefly, then

recovered, and fended off ruinous debt. The aristocracy in the upper

South derived divergent benefits from the Empire, and a decade of

Imperial conflict underlined that divergence. The Virginia gentry,

trapped in a closing vise partially of their own making, launched out in

a series of attacks against royal authority, joined with popular dis-

content, and tumbled royal power in the colony. Maryland was caught by

the tensions of its greater diversity and the fact that its eastern

leaders had recovered from serious economic decline. Marylanders

accordingly struck a middle ground: they resisted the attempts of

Parliament to tax and movements for separation. Their leaders joined

those of the Middle Colonies. Virginians led in the movement for

independence.

Virginia's problem of land relative to the increase in the white

population was not as critical as New England's. Virginia contained a

greater amount of unsettled land, and when her inhabitants expanded, they

met Indians for the most part and not other Americans. Nonetheless, the colony reached the point of needing new and better land even before the French and Indian War, and, indeed, the expansion of Virginians into the Ohio was partly responsible for beginning the war in North America. The whole colony was in favor of expansion westward, easterners because it meant an opportunity to engage in extensive speculations in land, and perhaps provide a market for their own surplus of slaves, and the yeomanry because of the natural increase in population. Virginians, like New Englanders, fought long,often, and hard in an effort to win the land, but after the war the Proclamation Line and Pontiac's conspiracy threw the frontier into confusion. Although migrations continued for the next decade, they were halting and slow, and the western counties filled.[27] During these same years, Virginia's political leadership was typified by such men as George Washington, Patrick Henry, and Edmund Pendleton -- each in his own fashion expressing hopes for the expansion of Virginia.[28]

In the 1750's, an equally important development took place in the eastern counties: tobacco cultivation ceased to support the gentry in the usual manner. For half a decade, many eastern planters were forced

deeper into debt as nature laid a heavy hand on their crops. Since

tobacco was on the enumerated articles lists under the Acts of Trade and

Navigation, tobacco producers had to send their crop to the British Isles

exclusively; they had to pay the shipping costs and the customs at entry,

and they had to take the prices offered them by English and Scottish

merchants.[29]   Until the time of the crop failures in the 1750's and early

1760's, the system worked well enough, and the Virginia gentry matured

into one of the most wealthy and powerful groups in America.[30]   But after

the war, failures in tobacco crops coincided with recession, and the

system turned against the planter.

Virginians moved to meet the problem. Some converted to wheat and

flax, and some put their slaves to work in the manufacture of cloth.

Speculation in soldiers' patents to western lands also provided a means of

easing some of the burden on easterners. None of these measures proved

adequate since conversion to wheat was not always feasible or profitable and

men who purchased land paid the proprietors only meager fees, or did not

pay them at all; cloth manufacturing was open to only a few.[31]   Not to be

restrained by the laws of nature, Virginians turned to government in an

effort to extricate themselves. The House of Burgesses passed a law

prohibiting the slave trade. The reason was obvious: to block the

importation of slaves meant an immediate increase in the value of slaves

in the colony; easterners could themselves become the source of traffic

in human beings. England disallowed the law.[32] While paper currency

was abundant, Virginians were able partly to rectify the financial

imbalance by clearing their debts to English merchants in depreciating

paper currency, and when English administration rebuked them, they ran to

the protection of their own courts, passed a law allowing their judges

to set exchange rates, and found some relief.[33] The Currency Act

undermined the system slowly but surely, for as paper currency was retired,

the mechanism of clearing debts in paper disappeared. Some Virginians

found a way around that too. John Robinson, Treasurer of the colony,

had charge of disposing of all retired war currency. Robinson received

the currency, but instead of burning it, he used it as a means of building

a political faction second to none and of temporarily easing financial

strain. In a five-year period just after the war, Robinson reissued the

currency to his political allies and friends as personal "loans." His

account books revealed that over £100,000 had been put back into

circulation in this manner, but how much was actually loaned was a mystery,

and so was the amount that was returned through the treasury of the

colony as original currency, and thereby retired twice by taxation of

the inhabitants at large.[34] Financial manipulation on the part of the

House of Burgesses provided only a slight means of relief, and this

mode of retaliation against nature and English merchants was transient

and superficial.

The other means which Virginians chose to redress economic decline

was disastrous. They borrowed heavily from English creditors in the hope

of a renewal in tobacco crops. When tobacco began to renew the economy,

and for a brief time it appeared that Virginians would be able to

extricate themselves, credit crisis caught the tobacco planters in a

ruinous debt imbalance as credit sources tightened: total American

indebtedness to English creditors stood at around £3,500,000 and Virginia

owed over £1,500,000 of this, and the largest part of the debt fell on the

planter gentry. The rolls of debtors included the names of some of

the most prominent men in the colony. Thomas Robinson's loan lists had

included some of the same names.[35] The aristocracy of Virginia entered

a crisis period not unlike that of the nobility of southern France

in the eighteenth century, and it reacted in much the same manner: it

resisted Parliamentary taxation and fought Imperial centralization tooth

and nail.

Planter indebtedness and increasing population in the west set

the stage for Virginia politics in the early 1760's. Most members of

the House of Burgesses fought for local government control of the clergy.

They did not attack the Church, but contended for the right of the

Burgesses to dominate it. When tobacco failures induced a concurrent

rise in tobacco prices, the Burgesses passed a law allowing clergy fees

to be paid in either tobacco or paper currency (another financial

maneuver to relieve their own strains), but England disallowed the law.

Patrick Henry made the cause his own in a different way from most

Virginians. Dissenters disliked the clergy fees more than Anglicans

did because it hurt their consciences as well as their pocketbooks,

and when Henry agreed to defend citizens against the claims of a

clergyman for his fees in Hanover County, Henry struck out against

both local and Imperial laws. He denied the right of the Crown to disallow good laws passed by the House of Burgesses, he denounced the rapacity of the Anglican clergy, and he advocated exempting from the payment of clergy fees all dissenters in the colony.[36] Thereafter, Henry was the dissenters' undisputed leader and defender. While this was happening many of the eastern planters expressed discontent with executive interference in their attempts at financial relief. Aristocrat and yeoman were equally dissatisfied; each had his leader: Robinson went quietly about relieving the upper classes from strain, Henry loudly about his defense of popular rights.

When the Stamp Act crisis flared across the colony, Henry was immediately in opposition, and as a member of the House of Burgesses, submitted the most radical resolutions against the tax. Robinson called some of his remarks treason. Henry apologized, but retorted that his attachment to liberty in America had led him to his remarks.[37] At repeal of the Stamp Act, Patrick Henry was unassailable behind a wall of popularity that was not equalled by any other local figure in America, and he set himself outside the inner clique in the Burgesses. Most political figures

in the Old Dominion were content to move within the practical system

provided by Robinson's control and power.

Robinson's death and the Townshend Acts further disrupted the

political system in Virginia. Robinson died in 1766, and whether his

mismanagement of Virginia currency would be exposed hinged upon who

fell heir to the dual office of Speaker and Treasurer. Patrick Henry

refused to allow the change of power to take place with any measure of

regularity by advocating that the two offices be separated, and he was

supported by Richard Henry Lee. [38] Men loyal to Robinson scurried to

cover up the fraud, but they were unsuccessful. Henry's and Lee's

attack upon Robinson was in fact an attack upon the standing powers in

the Burgesses, and, just as important, upon the kind of political power

which proceeded from an official who controlled the currency, the tax

rolls, and extension of tax debts as well as the office of the Speaker.

Henry and Lee severed an arm of power from the old guard; the next

Speaker, Peyton Randolph, would never be as powerful a man as Robinson.

And as the Townshend Acts disrupted politics in Virginia, Henry and Lee

(though Lee had to be instructed on the exact constitutional violations

of American rights), were among the leaders of opposition.[39] Once again,

the Burgesses shared leadership of the American colonies with Massachusetts.

By the 1770's Virginia politics was typified by three groups of men

who expressed varying attitudes about Virginia and England. Peyton

Randolph led a large group that controlled the House of Burgesses with

little effort. Men like Richard Bland, Benjamin Harrison, Edmund Pendleton,

and the elder Thomas Nelson defended the power of the Burgesses against

Parliament, but were satisfied with their own local power and with

institutions in Virginia. Virginians could cooperate with royal officials,

but they were known to do so on their own terms. Most of the gentry

supported the Anglican establishment and never questioned slavery, and

they looked on the dissenter population with a critical and suspicious

eye. Most also resisted Parliament and did so vociferously because

Parliament threatened to undermine their rights and power. They were

convinced that they could not withstand any further financial strain.

England had its share of their property through trade.[40]

Richard Henry Lee typified another attitude of the gentry and

member of the Burgesses. A descendent of the House of Stratford, Lee

was not particularly disturbed by the aristocracy, but as early as

1766, he said that government in Virginia had lost its original form

and expression. Lee wrote that in England the aristocratic power of

government was actually protected and independent of the Crown, but

in Virginia, he said, the aristocracy was dependent on the Crown.

"With us, " he said, "the legislative power is lodged in Governor,

Council and the House of Burgesses. The first two appointed by the

Crown, and their places held by precarious tenure of pleasure only." This

system Lee wrote, offended English government, and destroyed the "just

equilibrium" among the powers of the king, aristocracy, and people.

That was only the beginning of his criticism: the Crown's appointees

to the Council also sat as judges in the courts, he said, and

tried all cases civil, ecclesiastical, and criminal. And, Lee, said,

"even the third or democratic part of our legislature is totally

in the power of the Crown!" [41] Lee meant that the power of gubernatorial

veto, the suspending clause, and right of disallowance blocked the

Burgesses' will. Yet there was something more to Lee's disgruntlement:

the system of privilege in Virginia was large enough for just as many men,

and though Lee sought the office of stamp collector in 1765, he was forced

quickly to disavow his intentions. He made several applications for an

appointive office after 1765, but did not get one. Lee supplemented his

income by management of his brother's estate, and in 1769 he complained

that his titles to land were exhausted and that he was without a means of

ready cash. Tobacco failures hit him as hard as they hit any man in

Virginia. By the early 1770's he was living on a precarious line between

solvency and insolvency. He had a difficult time collecting his own fees

and paying his debts.[42] Local conditions and Parliament's attempts to

tax alienated monarchy's best ally in Virginia: the slaveholding

aristocrat who preferred special privilege to reform, but would settle

for the latter if the former was not forthcoming.

Patrick Henry was a man of a different stamp, and he drew the

younger, disenchanted gentry to his side. Henry's career was born in the

atmosphere of attacks upon the men who ruled Virginia: first he attacked

the Anglicans, then the Burgesses themselves, and always Crown and

Parliament. By the 1770's younger men like Thomas Jefferson and James

Madison expressed attitudes similar to those of Henry. They questioned

the felicity of slavery, and they scoffed at the benefits of an

established church. Young Madison asserted that if the Anglican

establishment had been part of the New England system of government, then

tyranny would have long before swallowed up all of the colonies.[43]

Whatever the sources of Virginians' dissatisfaction, the attitudes

of their political leaders reflected ddeply rooted desires for change.

The gentry remembered a golden era of economic production, or so it seemed.

The past looked much brighter than the present. Like all aristocrats, the

Virginia gentry received the threats from Parliament with utter disdain, and

quite naturally, Virginians of this stratum of society would call for a

return to the past in an effort to recapture the time when their culture

was at its peak. But just as important -- and as indicative of the

desire for change -- was the way in which men born to the gentry tradition

defected from it and questioned the rightness of the tradition. Neither

attitude was expressed in a vacuum: Parliament's attempts to tax were an

integral part of Virginians' discontent, and so were local conditions.

The Intolerable Acts sent the varied groups of Virginia leaders into

rebellion, and war brought Virginia into the camp of the champions of

independence. Henry called for immediate severance of allegiance to the

Empire, went to the First Congress and asked for an American constitution,

and failing there, returned to Virginia and worked for independence among

the popular groups.[44]   Henry's feats in 1774 and early 1775 were little

short of astounding. For the fourth time in as many clashes with England,

Henry assumed the lead in the House of Burgesses. Outside the Burgesses,

he spoke and thousands rallied to his standard. He settled with actions

what he could not accomplish with oratory, and he forced the gentry at

large to take a stand. Henry's first feint at the royal government with

his yeomanry militia was turned aside, but when Governor Dunmore acted

hastily and threatened to use force, Virginians did not hesitate. Henry

led the militia to victory against royal forces.[45]   And the gentry

quickly followed: first men like Richard Henry Lee and the younger gentry

decided for independence, than came individuals like Edmund Pendleton, and,

finally, the gentry at large supported separation from the Empire.[46]

Accordingly, between 1774 and 1776, Virginia's delegates to the

Continental Congress were among the most aroused, the most belligerent,

and the most zealous. They numbered among them the first President of the

222

Congress, the first man to call for separation and a republic, a pillar
of the inner group of independence-minded Whigs in Congress, the
commander of military forces of the colonies, and the author of the
Declaration of Independence. On only one occasion, when Carter Braxton
and Benjamin Harrison were elected to Congress, did the Virginia
delegation include men whose loyalties were open to doubt, and the
Provincial Convention quickly recalled both from Congress, though they
did not receive word of it until after July 2.[47] Men from Virginia
favored independence for different reasons, but they presented a united
front on the question.

In the 1750's and 1760's, although easterners in Maryland
experienced an economic setback similar to that in Virginia, their
efforts at recovery were successful. Many found wheat a profitable
staple, and Baltimore slowly matured as a flour manufacturing center.
When tobacco crops renewed in late sixties and early seventies, the
eastern part of the colony moved out of its decline, and Maryland moved
virtually free of debt. At the same time, when currency retirements
after the war constricted, Marylanders met the problem in the same way as

223

Pennsylvania and New York did by issuing loan certificates to an amount

equal to Ł 219,000. By 1774, the colony, though one of the smaller in

America, had a larger currency supply than that in the whole of New

England, and while the colony was not in the midst of boom, most men

were doing moderately well and some were thriving.⁴⁸

Maryland politics was punctuated by a series of successful efforts

of the eastern leaders to pare the power of the executive authority.

Also, after 1765, Marylanders were always less concerned with Parliament

than Virginians were. By the 1770's, men like Matthew Tilghman, Robert

Goldsborough, John Hall, Thomas Johnson, William Paca, and Samuel Chase --

all later delegates to Congress -- had established the power of the lower

house over legislation , taxation, and clergy fees. Most people voted

for them and against the political factions that supported the governors.

Maryland Whigs were distinguished by their insistence upon subordinating

the power of the executive branch to that of the legislative, and in

Maryland that meant lodging power in the eastern gentry.⁴⁹

Between 1774 and 1776, Maryland's delegates to the Continental

Congress were controlled by the Provincial Convention and committees in

eastern Maryland. Westerners had little voice in the delegations, and
only one Marylander, Samuel Chase, worked for independence. Two of the
Maryland delegates fled Congress in late 1775; the remainder contended
against independence up until the last debates.[50] Maryland, less unified
internally, was less inclined to independence and less forward in the
defense of America.

In the lower South, the colonies of Georgia and South Carolina
showed signs of youth and immaturity in their political institutions, and,
compared to the upper South, these colonies were still rich in natural
resources. The planter aristocracy was small but powerful, and conflict
with England unfolded in the context of an extension of their power and
expansion of their wealth. South Carolinians, like eastern Marylanders
and men in the Middle Colonies refused to admit Parliament's right to tax,
and fought to stave off movements for separation. Georgia planters
refused to take part in the movement at all, and leadership fell to a
group of middling and professional men from St. John's Parish. In the
instance of Georgia, popular leaders in the most immature of the colonies

led the Patriots without interference from the planters.

Both Carolinas were apparently distinguished by rapid economic

expansion. The per capita accumulation of capital in the Carolinas was,

in the decade after the French and Indian War, greater than that in

the Middle Colonies and far greater than that in New England.[51] But the

lion's share of this expansion fell to South Carolina alone, and to

Charleston merchants and planters primarily.[52] Both rice and indigo

exports increased in volume and value, and Charleston merchants

serviced much of North Carolina and Georgia as well as their own colony.

In only one year during the decade did the value of Charleston's imports

exceed the value of its exports, and what might have seemed a backward

colonial settlement was an extremely successful commercial and

agricultural region.[53] South Carolinans reckoned wealth in terms of

slaves, and by that index they were wealthy indeed. In 1774, South

Carolina contained one hundred and five thousand slaves and only

seventy thousand whites.[54]

Economic affairs in Charleston were strikingly different from those

in other Southern colonies. Charleston lawyers collected fees in hard

specie and refused paper currency during the same years that Virginians were fortunate to collect fees at all. The combined annual incomes of three or four families in Charleston were on a scale with the profits that the whole colony of Connecticut made in its trade with the West Indies. South Carolinians invested in plantations in Barbados, and while Boston, for example, never recovered from the credit crisis, Charleston was hurt only momentarily, and the next year its trade balances were back to a high level. The colony was diversified, its merchants resilient, and its planters grew one of the most profitable staples in America.[55] A counter-trend marred the economic life of the city in the seventies: its artisans were struck by a decline in the prices of manufactured wood products, their most important single article.[56] But be that as it may, South Carolina inhabitants at large were not badly harmed by currency restriction. The small white population had more currency outstanding than did the whole of New England, and strain on the less wealthy classes came primarily from refusals to accept the currency and not by the absence of it.[57]

Except for participating in the outcry against the Stamp Act,

227

South Carolinians paid scant attention to what was happening in the

arena of conflict with Parliament, and their failure to do so lay

partly in their local circumstances. Easterners in the late 1760's

possessed a disproportionate amount of governmental representation,

they disregarded the problems of the frontier, and they intended to

prevent any threat to their power. The backcountry, seized by fears

of Indian raids and disgruntled by the fact that they had no courts

of law and had to travel east to obtain legal redress, set the frontier

aflame and fought a brief civil war against established authority.[58]

At the same time, the artisans and mechanics of Charleston supported

non-importation agreements and more direct actions against Parliament.

Charleston leaders suppressed the westerners and supported non-importation

half-heartedly. Between 1766 and 1774, South Carolinians were more

concerned about keeping order than opposing Parliament.

In 1774 Christopher Gadsden led the artisans and mechanics in the

movement for economic retaliation and a congress, and the backcountry

farmers, still nursing wounds inflicted earlier, rumbled out against

the east.[59] Leadership during the crisis fell to those already in power:

the Rutledges, Henry Laurens, Rawlins Lowndes, the Lynches, and

Henry Middleton. These men never relinquished their power, and Gadsden

was, for a time, isolated in advocacy of harsh action and a militia.

And, these same men dominated the South Carolina delegation to Congress

right down to the July, 1776, debates. When Henry Middleton and Thomas

Lynch did not go to Congress, they sent their sons. South Carolinians

demanded caution and moderation from their delegates, and their delegates

obliged. [60]

The planters in Georgia took a different course when the crisis

struck. For the most part, they did nothing, and their inactivity

was a third kind of response by the southern gentry. By early 1776,

the Virginia aristocracy advocated separation, the South Carolinians

acted, but acted for redress and reconciliation, the Georgia gentry

pulled in its head. As a result, resistance in Georgia fell to a group

of leaders of middling rank -- men like George Walton, John Houston,

Lyman Hall, and Button Gwinett. [61] Only one individual who represented

the Georgia planters ever attended Congress, and he eventually became

a Loyalist. [62] By late 1775, Georgians in Congress had attached themselves

to independence and consistently voted with New England.

From 1765 onward, North Carolina was divided against itself.

Geographical conditions isolated the east from the west, and large

numbers of Scotch-Irish occupied the backcountry. Over the decade

their numbers grew, and the antagonisms of the backcountry farmer were

expressed in an uprising against the east that ended in bloodshed;

the westerners complained of unequal representation in the assembly,

unfair taxation, and the lack of protection from the Indians. The

eastern seaboard had its problems. Charleston dominated commerce,

and North Carolina merchants could not always compete. The same price

recession that hit wood products in South Carolina touched North Carolina.

The Intolerable Acts threw the colony into confusion, and the Provincial

Convention was reticent until the Loyalists were defeated . All its

delegates were cautious on the question of separation and the one delegate

from the west refused to serve after the First Congress. Of the other

three, two took an open part in seeking independence from Great Britain,

and both arrived at the position comparatively late in the contest.[63]

230

Southern Patriots reflected immediate events in their colonies,

and they acted according to those immediacies and their estimation

of the Empire. Most Marylanders were for allowing Parliament legal

authority in the Empire, and consistently against abandoning their

government; war and fighting did not alter their stance.[64] A few

South Carolinians were more advanced in their ideas on the power of

Parliament, but even Thomas Lynch (who thought that Parliament had no

right to make any laws for America) opposed independence, discussed

reconciliation with unofficial peacemakers from England, and maintained

that separation from the Empire would mean republican government in

America, a form of government, he said, that worked best in theory.[65]

Edward Rutlege suspected New Englanders' ideas and feared their politics.

"I dread their low cunning," he said, "and those . . . principles which

men without character, and without fortune in general possess, which

are so captivating to the lower classes of mankind, and will occasion

such fluctuation of property as to introduce the greatest disorder."[66]

Virginians, however, soon joined themselves to New Englanders, Patriots

who thought and acted similar to themselves on the issues of Empire.[67]

231

Georgians were inarticulate about the power of Parliament; they complained about the planter aristocracy in their colony, and the delegates moved from resistance to revolution in one quick step.[68] The one Georgia delegate who favored traditional Whig policies said that a republican government was little better than a government of devils; he eventually became a Loyalist.[69] As Southern society split asunder on the advent of war, so too did Southern leadership, and what two of those leaders, Thomas Jefferson and John Rutlege, thought and did, provided the South with leadership that would have had colonials pursue entirely different courses.

232

VII

THOMAS JEFFERSON AND JOHN RUTLEDGE

Thomas Jefferson and John Rutledge were as different in their

views and their actions as any two Patriots could be. From 1774

onward, Jefferson dared what only the revolutionary dared, and though

he was often soft-spoken, men knew where Jefferson stood on the issues.

Rutledge was always reticent and he wore an inscrutable mask of pragmatism.

Often, Rutledge appeared to have no opinion on political issues. Jefferson

advocated rebellion and republicanism for Virginia, Rutledge hoped to

avoid armed conflict, much less outright rebellion in South Carolina,

and he detested full-fledged popular republicanism of any variety.

Jefferson was an intellectual, and his thinking was oriented to political

solutions of men's problems; he sought change in Virginia and hoped that

most men would benefit from it. Rutledge did not like men of ideas, he

looked on politics as a means to power, and he placed his concern for

economic affairs before utilitarian reform. Jefferson was first and

foremost an advocate of independence. He did not like the Imperial

yoke, and the crisis in Empire fulfilled his hopes for change.

Rutledge was and remained a man who found the Empire beneficent; the

first years of conflict changed none of his ideas and none of his habits.

A curious but revealing fact about the advent of revolution in America

was that both Jefferson and Rutledge met with considerable success in

their aims and hopes.

At the end of the summer of 1774, John Rutledge rode through

Philadelphia surrounded by servants, slaves, and all the bustle of

traveling retinue. "St. John" had come to Philadelphia, and he brought

as much of Charleston with him as he could. Rutledge's reason for

bringing his own household to the second largest city in the Empire

went deeper than whim or a love of comfort and outward display. Rutledge

relished inscrutability. His own retinue acted as a buffer against

exasperating intrusions and kept him aloof behind a troop of middlemen.

Rutledge found it advantageous to cultivate the image of political

and personal enigma, and of all the colonials who came to the First

Continental Congress, Rutledge was the most convinced believer in the

unstated and unrevealed as a means to political power. A personal

retinue was a finishing touch to Rutledge's deeper motivations. [1]

By 1774, Rutledge's career was replete with illustrations of the

fact that he was a man who made the practical his guide. At twelve years

of age, he thought that "literature and the arts were debilitating"

and that "batchelors of the library were idlers." [2] He shunned abstractions,

poetry, and fiction, and he had no interest in history. Rutledge was

a deist, but he was a member of St. Philips Church in Charleston, and

he used ecclesiastical power to his own advantage. [3] He was a confirmed

aristocrat who disliked democracy, and called backcountry farmers a

"pack of beggars," but he was a politician who wooed and won the

backcountry to his side in elections and who received votes from the

Charleston artisans. [4] Rutledge was often arrayed against the royal governors

in South Carolina, but he gladly accepted political preferment from

them. He asked for and got a place on South Carolina's delegation to

the Stamp Act Congress in order to protest Parliament's right to tax,

then wrote a petition to the House of Lords that said nothing about

the power of Parliament to tax America. Rutledge cultivated his mind

by the practice of law and study of the ledger-book, and the main

reason that he had come to Philadelphia was because the stir over the

Intolerable Acts had given him pause, and he wanted to know exactly

what it all meant for his position in South Carolina.

For Rutledge had learned to turn institutions and conditions

in South Carolina in his favor. In 1761, he returned from study in

England to find the family estates dilapidated and on the verge of

bankruptcy. By 1774, he had converted his legacy into a thriving family

enterprise that planted, reaped, and shipped rice and indigo crops.

Rutledge himself owned sixty slaves that worked five small plantations.

His total estate was valued at $70,000, and one of his residences was

popularly known as "St. John's Palace." His family owned thrice his

own holdings. Rutledge and a handful of other men dominated the courts

in South Carolina. On one occasion, he held three assembly seats. He

was Attorney General of South Carolina at the end of the 1760's -- an

office held by appointment. Rutledge's influence was everywhere: in

the legislative process, in the arm of the royal administration, and

in prosecution and defense before courts of law. In 1774, at the age of

thirty-four, he was one of the most wealthy and powerful men in

America, and he undoubtedly thought that his position rested on his

own ability and attention to hard work.[5]

If Rutledge had had his way, there would have been no South Carolina

delegation to the First Congress, but as he had learned, the crisis

of 1774 afforded him no other alternative. Back at the time of the

Townshend crisis, he had done all that he could to keep non-importation

agreements from going into effect. He opposed any extra-legal meeting

of citizens. On learning of the Boston Port Bill, he thought that

South Carolina's best course was to wait, and when the pressure of

popular sentiment resulted in a decision to send a delegation to Congress,

Rutledge used his power in the legislature to write the instructions of

the delegates. His instructions were a model of Rutledgian thinking.

South Carolina had to do nothing, agree to nothing, and the instructions

said little.[6] As Rutledge's activities would soon show, South Carolina

would join itself to the American cause on only those terms which

Rutledge found acceptable, and no one would know just what his terms

were until it was too late to prevent him from getting them.

237

As Congress got down to business, Rutledge hinted at the stand

he would take. During one of the first sessions, he told the delegates

that they should not let their imaginations run too far afield. "We have

no legal authority," he said, "and obedience to our determinations will

follow the reasonableness, the apparent utility and necessity of measures

we adopt. We have no legislative or coercive authority." [7] Those few

sentences were full of meaning, for in the light of what Rutledge did in

Congress and afterward in South Carolina, Rutledge meant that Congress

should be a petitioning body and nothing more. Before the month of

September was out, he had aligned himself with men who thought the same.

Joseph Galloway of Pennsylvania engineered the leadership of those

who thought that any action beyond petitioning was beyond the duty

of the Congress. The "Plan of Union" which Galloway had drawn up in

preparation for the Congress was his solution to the disagreements

between England and its colonies, and he sensed that South Carolinians

would support him. When Galloway tested South Carolina's sentiments,

he learned that the delegates were already familiar with a plan which

resembled his own. William Henry Drayton, a member of the South Carolina

238

Council and Supreme Court turned pamphleteer, had written and published

a proposal for Anglo-American union. Though Drayton was overtly

hostile to England and recommended a "temporary suspension of the rules

of constitutionality" in dealing with the Intolerable Acts, he also

advocated a general government for America to decide on tax payments

to England. "Without a system of a general nature," Drayton wrote, "the

colonies . . . will scarce agree upon proportional quotas of a general

aid to the crown."[8] Drayton recommended that the Congress propose that

the two houses of assembly in each colony appoint deputies to a high

court of the colonies, and that the court set Imperial tax quotas for

each of the colonies. Galloway's plan went further by providing for

a President-General appointed by the Crown and a balanced representation

from the colonies. South Carolina delegates liked Galloway's Anglo-

American union.[9]

Galloway waited for a propitious moment to present his plan. At

the end of September, Congress joined in debate on whether the delegates

should propose a non-importation agreement, and whether a non-exportation

agreement should be appended to non-importation. The delegates met an

impasse. John Rutledge chose that moment to interject a single phrase: all ways and means ought to be proposed, he said.[10] If the men in Congress thought that he favored non-exportation, then they were dead wrong. When the debates resumed, Galloway, hoping to take advantage of the deadlock over non-exportation, threw his "Plan of Union" into the debates, and Rutledge immediately supported him. The strategy was good. If Congress could be persuaded to support the plan, then Congress might be induced to do little more than that. Debates proceeded quickly, Rutledge spoke full in favor of the plan. A vote was called on postponement of consideration of Galloway's motion; non-exportation was at stake in the voting, if not the entire Association. Galloway and Rutledge suffered a bare defeat: six colonies voted for postponement, five against postponement, and one colony divided.[11] Advocates of non-exportation would, it appeared, probably succeed.

But John Rutledge had no intention of allowing Congress to cut off South Carolina's exports. When disagreements on the utility and the time for non-exportation were settled, Rutledge let Congress know that South Carolina would not be bound by it unless her crops of

rice and indigo were excepted from the Association. Other Patriots

rejoined that such obvious favoritism would destroy colonial unity,

and with that Rutledge stood and walked out of Congress. In haste to

rectify the damage that lack of unity meant for economic coercion,

Congress offered South Carolina a compromise: She might have one of

the crops excepted, but not both.[12] South Carolina chose rice. The

Continental Association was published in America with the phrase"excepting

rice to Europe" affixed to the non-exportation clause. John Rutledge

had what he wanted all along: protection of South Carolina commerce.

On other issues in Congress, Rutledge appeared to be anything but

an obstructionist. As a member of the committee on rights and grievances,

he listened carefully to the various arguments, and particularly those

of Duane and John Adams. Finally, he threw his support in favor of

basing Parliament's power on John Adams' distinction of Parliament's

right to regulate trade by necessity and colonial consent.[13] Members of

the committee did not know that a major issue of the June Provincial

Convention in South Carolina had been that some South Carolinians feared

participating in a Congress with New England precisely because, as Rawlins

241

Lowndes had said, New Englanders "deny the super-intending power of Parliament."[14] John Rutledge, trained at the Inns of Court, could not have overlooked the full meaning of John Adams' phrasing. Adams' position afforded him a rationalization for obstructing if it suited his interests to do so: he could press the statement on rights to any conclusion that he wished in order to prevent South Carolina from a general, inordinate allegiance to Congress' resolves.

When the First Congress adjourned, Rutledge did not have all that he wanted, but he did not come away from Philadelphia empty-handed. South Carolinan rice growers were excepted from the Association by the clause relating to non-exportation, and he and others could deal with non-importation locally. If need be, timid men could be intimidated by the statement relating to the power of Parliament. Moreover, the remainder of the delegates had kept Christopher Gadsden from any mischief.[15] John Rutledge did not expound on his successes. To have done so would have been self-defeating. He simply collected his retinue and went home.

Back in South Carolina, Rutledge's obstructionist inclinations and actions bore fruit. At the first Charleston committee meetings,

he said nothing in support of Congress or any of its resolves. For

nearly three months, Gadsden advocated full enforcement of the non-

importation agreement, [16] but Charlestonians in general were half-hearted

about it, and the issue was still in doubt when the Provincial Convention

convened in January of 1775. Men who grew crops other than rice descended

on the Convention with a vengeance, and men who supported Congress found

themselves in a dilemma. They were against the favoritism shown rice

growers, but unless they approved the Association, then the resolves of

Congress would go unapproved. The atmosphere of the Convention was

electric, and men were loud, noisy, and grumbling. Christopher Gadsden

stood, proclaimed that he had fought the favoritism and denied any

part in the affair.[17] The burden of explanation fell on John Rutledge.

He made no plea for colonial unity or South Carolina sacrifices, and

he made no mention of Parliament's threat to liberty. Rather, he introduced

a theme of economic conflict among the colonies. Non-exportation was, he

said, "upon the whole . . . rather like a commercial scheme, among

the flour colonies, to find a better vent for their flour through the

British Channel; by preventing, if possible, any rice being sent to those

markets . . . ."[18] As debated continued, the Convention hall grew

more unsettled. Delegates made several motions, one of which called

for approval of the Association on condition that the exception of rice

be expunged at the next Congress. Nonetheless, the solidarity of the

rice growers and some confusion on the part of others were sufficient

to gain approval of the Association as it stood by a vote of eighty-seven

to seventy-five.[19] Rutledge's leadership gave a little and got much.

The issue of whether to allow the exception of rice to stand

in the non-exportation section of the Association kept the planters

united, but between early January and mid-March, several important

individuals joined Gadsden. The first significant dispute came over

formal announcement of the necessity of militia training. William

Henry Drayton, a planter himself, had become increasingly angered by

royal administration in South Carolina. At the time of the Regulator

uprising in 1769, he had supported suppression of the backcountry

because he said, it represented an unconstitutional demoracy. In 1774,

he supported resistance to Parliament, he said, because the Coercive

Acts represented unconstitutional threats to charters.[20] By early 1775,

244

Drayton was in open opposition to standing legislative powers in

South Carolina, favored the Congress, and proved slightly more forward

than most traditional Whigs. Drayton insisted that South Carolina ought

to initiate formal militia training, and the Convention formed a secret

committee for military preparations. Drayton accepted the chairmanship;

neither Edward nor John Rutledge, Henry Laurens, nor any of the old

guard cared to serve, but Arthur Middleton, son of Henry Middleton,

took a place on the committee.[21] In March, the Rutledges reached a point

of decision in regard to the Association. John Rutledge had assumed

all along that the planters and merchants in Charleston would only be

lukewarm about non-importation. The committee which enforced the

agreement contained a large number of men of this disposition. When

goods arrived from England, the committee decided on each case, and

it tendened to make loose judgements on what could come in and what

could not. The mechanics and artisans, on the other hand, were for

enforcement without distinction and without qualification. In March of

1775 the two groups clashed over admission of an order from England that

had been placed prior to the date of the agreement not to import.

245

The committee ruled in favor of admission, and the Rutledges sided
with it, but that proved insufficient, and Gadsden demanded a
full meeting of citizens to settle the issue. At the meeting, Edward
Rutledge demanded that the citizens allow the committee to decide on
all cases, for otherwise, he said, chaos would rein in South Carolina.
Drayton picked that moment to sever ties with the planters and merchants.
He leaped to his feet, shouted "No! No!" and told the meeting that
the committee should be responsive to the will of the people as the
Senate of Rome had been responsive to the desires of the Roman people.
In the voting that followed, the committee retracted its ruling by
one vote. Drayton led part of the planters away from John Rutledge
and into an alliance with Gadsden and the artisans. And a little
later, Drayton forced Rutledge to come out into the open by setting
the militia in motion in a move to take gunpowder magazines at Hobcaw
and Cochran. Rutledge found that he could do nothing, thereby risking
Drayton's moving in full power, or act on the seizure of military
stores. He took a stance that was ambiguous. He favored having men
of repute go in broad daylight and request gunpowder stores. South

246

Carolina's planters and merchants, formerly fairly united, split into two groups: by far the larger stood with redress and reconciliation and for the least possible amount of friction. Drayton and Arthur Middleton joined with Gadsden and the small group that, at this time, advocated complete autonomy in the Empire. News of Lexington and Concord would send these groups scattering in diverse directions.[22]

In April, John Rutledge himself was superficially an exponent of the traditional Whig policies, but in fact his sources of power and popularity were not directly based upon any particular position he had taken. His support of rice growers stood him in good stead with one of the more powerful groups in South Carolina. His view of a loose enforcement of the Association had won the confidence of the merchants in Charleston, and in the backcountry where men were antagonistic to the Patriots, people thought that Rutledge and his brother Edward were inclined to Loyalism. Moreover, Rutledge's insistence that Patriots request military stores, rather than take them, won the confidences of supporters of royal authority and those men who were absolutely against any show of force. Gadsden and Drayton

were Rutledge's only real antagonists. The turmoil and crisis

did not hurt him personally. During the first months of resistance,

Rutledge's income was larger than at any time in the previous decade.[23]

Men looked on Rutledge in various ways: the planter and merchant saw

him as a sensible protagonist of Charleston commerce; others saw him

as a moderate defender of American rights; others thought him secretly

a Tory, and still others looked on Rutledge as a defender of law and

order. As Rutledge prepared to leave for the Second Continental Congress,

his power was certainly threatened but unbroken. That April when he

left Charleston, he did not know that news was on its way that would

shake the colony to its foundations and produce civil war in South

Carolina.

That same month in the colony of Virginia, another man born to the

southern planter aristocracy prepared to leave for the Second Congress.

Thomas Jefferson was younger than Rutledge, but both were lawyers, both

plantation and slave owners, both were deists, and both opposed Parliament's

assertion of the right to legislate for the colonies in all cases.

248

The similarities ended there. Though by heritage Jefferson was a member of the oligarchy that ruled Virginia, professionally and economically he was a member of an upper middling class of planters.[24] In 1770, his family home at Shadwell had burned, and Jefferson had moved to Monticello, where he lived for a time in one room. He also had rights to land grants left him by George Jefferson, and he practiced law to supplement his income. In 1771, Jefferson had aided a friend with a small investment in a mercantile venture and wrote that he was concerned over the prospects of the scheme. "Should my friend prove unsuccessful (and ill fortune may render any person unsuccessful), " he said, "it might sweep away the whole of my little fortune."[25] In 1773, Jefferson and five other lawyers had had such difficulty in collecting their fees that they had announced that they would no longer take any cases without advances.[26]

In April, 1775, Jefferson differed from Rutledge in another respect: Jefferson was an intellectual, a "batchelor of the library," a man with deep concerns about things of the mind, for Jefferson took the patrimony of the gentry with a severe seriousness, and he excelled

at the studies which traditions of gentry education imparted. Planter

aristocrats thought that the study of languages, history, science, and

law made a well-rounded man. Jefferson mastered the tradition.

Study of the law and legal theory, history and government absorbed him.

He viewed science as a means of human improvement, and put some of

his ideas into practice on his own plantation. In fine, Jefferson was

the kind of individual that Rutledge thought ineffectual and useless,

and Rutledge the kind of man Jefferson respected little or not at all.

    Whereas Rutledge had accepted the culture of South Carolina and

made himself an important participant in trade and commerce, Jefferson

had become a critic. Jefferson's culture, indeed, Virginia society

rested on slavery, but Jefferson himself was not convinced that slavery

was either beneficial or right. He thought the institution inhuman

and its influences debilitating, and with that, cut himself off from

elementary adjustment to the society around him. That was not all.

Jefferson considered it an honor to be out of sorts with Anglican

authorities. He thought that an established church was archaic; he

was against laws that forced dissenters to pay clergy fees, and against

prosecution of non-Anglicans in the courts.[27] Jefferson placed his

faith in education and enlightenment, thought the best of men, and

looked to government to protect and insure liberty. Between 1774 and

1776, Jefferson would make concrete contributions to reform of institutions

and government in Virginia while Rutledge made none for South Carolina.

And Jefferson and Rutledge responded differently to an American

congress. While Rutledge had been obstructionist regarding the First

Congress, against non-exportation, and disgruntled with non-importation,

Jefferson had advocated a close union of the colonies, and had led

the inhabitants of the county of Albemarle to request Virginians

to accept both measures of economic coercion.[28] The Virginia Provincial

Convention's instructions to its delegates to the First Congress had

not suited Jefferson. By the instructions Virginians, he had said,

"are to conform to such resolutions only of the Congress as our deputies

assent to: which totally destroys that union of conduct in the

several colonies which was the very purpose of calling Congress."[29]

But it was Jefferson's responses to the news of the Coercive Acts

that truly set him apart from men of Rutledge's stamp: he dared what

only a few dared and called for extensive reform of the Empire. In

a pamphlet which he had written for his personal acquaintances and

which had appeared in mid-1774 as A Summary View of the Rights of British

America.[30] Jefferson had begun with the rights of men and the nature of

government in "original societies, " and he had finished by up-ending

the whole Imperial structure. He not only attacked the errors of

Parliaments, but also levelled a series of accusations against George III

and the Crown, and before Jefferson was done, he had made evident his

belief that the last one hundred years of colonial history had been

one hundred years of tyranny, for which the kings of England shared

equal responsibility with Parliament. Accordingly, Jefferson's con-

ception of reconciliation with Great Britain entailed sweeping away

that hundred years of abuse of executive authority. Only such reform,

Jefferson said, would prevent recurrence of English usurpation of

American liberty.

In his Summary View, Jefferson asserted that the first settlers

of America had come as free and independent men who established governments

in America by agreement. They owed no loyalty to any ruler, and they

admitted no power of any governing body except their own. The first

colonial communities, by circumstances and natural law, contained all

aspects of sovereignty, Jefferson thought, and whatever was law in those

societies was law by agreement among the first settlers. Colonials,

Jefferson said, agreed to be bound by the common laws of England, they

agreed that the kings of England would be their rulers, and they saw

fit to grant England a share of their trade. Jefferson insisted that

the conflicts between Virginia and England proceeded from tyrannical

usurpation of the original rights and powers of colonials by both

Crown and Parliament: kings had abused their prerogative powers in

America and Parliament had assumed the right to legislate in all cases.

Jefferson speedily dispatched the question of the power of Parliament.

Virginians, he said, might send to England what products of their labors

they thought proper or convenient to send. The first colonials granted

England a share of their trade, and Parliament has erroneously assumed

that this gave it legislative authority in America. Parliament might

make no laws to bind Americans. As for the power to regulate trade and

the Acts of Trade and Navigation, Jefferson was blunt: "The true ground

on which we declare these acts void, "he said, "is that the British parliament has no right to exercise authority over us."[31]

But Jefferson labored over the question of the power of the Crown in Virginia. As he turned to consideration of the kings, he soon made it clear that responsibility for tyranny lay with the Crown as much as with Parliament. First, Jefferson said, the Stuarts had assumed the right to reorganize governments in America, and thereby they had laid the basis for usurpation of colonial liberty. Next, he said, they had approved of the right of Parliament to regulate colonial trade. Neither action of the Crown had any basis in law. Then, Jefferson noted, the Crown had proceeded to build an edifice of tyranny on the basis of illegal assumptions of power. Also, Jefferson maintained that the threat to Virginia came primarily through extension of prerogative power over legislation enacted by the House of Burgesses. He listed some of these: the Crown had disallowed prohibition of the slave trade and scoffed at "the rights of human nature deeply wounded by this infamous practice;" the Crown had extended the right of disallowance to the power to force Virginians to include a suspending

clause in their laws and left the colony helpless before contingency

and emergency; the Crown had extended its power to include jurisdiction

over the organization of new counties and the extent of representation

in the Burgesses; the Crown had abused the power of dissolution of

colonial assemblies and used that prerogative beyond the limits provided

for by the laws of England. Should such abuse continue, Jefferson said,

the full power of legislation would revert back to the people "who may

use it to an unlimited extent." And, finally, Jefferson's last important

criticism of the extension of the prerogatives of the Crown in America

struck at the basis of the power of monarchy in America. The Crown,

he said, had assumed that all ungranted land in North America belongs

to it. In short, the Crown had robbed colonials for a century and a

half: "From the nature and purpose of civil institutions," Jefferson

said, "all the lands within the limits which any particular society

has circumscribed around itself, are assumed by that society, and subject

to their allotment only." Jefferson said that Parliament might not

legislate for America, and he said that the Crown could not tax by

way of fees on land since the land did not belong to it in the first

place. He reduced the colonial connections to England to the Crown's limited use of the right of disallowance and dissolution.[32]

Jefferson did not stop here, but went on to propose concrete measures of reform that would end the Imperial conflict: George III must have the Coercive Acts repealed, he must dispense with unlimited use of the prerogative, and he must give up claims to ungranted land. George III held the power of peace in his hands, Jefferson said, and he should first insure that a century of the usurpation of colonial liberty be swept away.[33] Then, the Crown ought to re-establish its prerogative power over the affairs of the Empire by reviving the power to veto Parliament's laws relating to Imperial affairs. George III should become the mediator between the different parts of the Empire and check any effort of Parliament to usurp rights and powers of government in America. In 1774, Jefferson was not content to protect what colonials had in the way of self-government, he called for restoration of full self-government of men in original societies, requested that the Crown retract a hundred years of rule, and advocated that the Crown renew its power over laws enacted by the English Parliament.

256

Jefferson called for reconciliation _via_ a proclamation of reform.[34]

Had those reforms come to America, the colonies would have become

self-governing republics checked only by occasional disallowance and

appointment of governors.

As Jefferson set out for the Second Continental Congress in 1775,

he was disgruntled with the state of affairs in America and with

what Virginians had actually done to preserve liberty. From the beginning,

he had been of the opinion that the resolutions of Congress should take

priority over resolutions of individual colonies. He had sided with

Washington, Henry, and Richard Henry Lee in their effort to erect formal

control of the Convention over militia groups in Virginia. And,

Jefferson had thought to have the Virginia Convention use unusual

wording in making an inquiry about New York's separate plea for recon-

ciliation. The language Jefferson used when he first composed the

inquiry revealed his feelings. Had New York, he wrote, "altered from

the confederacy with other American states"? The meaning and intent

of such wording proved overly strong, and he later replaced "confederacy"

and "states" with "union" and "colonies" respectively.[35] But his

attitude toward the power of Congress was openly unionist. By

April of 1775, Thomas Jefferson hovered at the door of rebellion, and

news of the Battle of Lexington and Concord sent him across the

threshold. Like John Adams, Jefferson quickly abandoned the positions

held during a decade of colonial resistance and rejected the grounds

of reconciliation stated in the resolves of the First Congress. The

First Congress, he said, had stated a minimum of what colonials would

accept; now blood had been shed, and America would probably not settle

on those terms. Jefferson himself had not liked the terms of

reconciliation to begin with. The reformer had become the rebel.

When Jefferson and Rutledge came together in the same general

conference, they immediately picked different allies and supported

different proposals. Jefferson joined with the Adamses, Franklin, and

Richard Henry Lee. Rutledge continued his support of New Yorkers and

most Pennsylvanians, but if he had had his way, he would have

left Congress and returned home for good. Jefferson took Franklin's

proposal of a confederation seriously, made a copy of it, and was

well on his way to a solution of the problem of forming a general

government in America. Rutledge, as chairman of a committee on government

in the colonies, tried to thwart the effort of Massachusetts delegates

to get Congress to recommend a popular form of government for their

colony and thereby move the people nearer separation. His maneuver

was clever, and his use of his power typically obstructionist. In

June, when the matter was referred to Rutledge's committe, he reported

with a counter-proposal. "Send letters to prominent men in each section,"

Rutledge said, "who shall choose, after conference with fellows,

representatives . . . who will elect councillors . . . and these acting

as a Council shall take over affairs of government until such time

as the government of His Majesties appointment shall consent to govern

the colony according to its charter."[36] The reconciliatory nature of this

proposal defeated the whole intent of the proposition for change in

Massachusetts, for it would restrain rather than encourage sentiment for

independence. During the remainder of 1775, Jefferson sent barb after

barb at George III; he said that the king was motivated by an "incendiary

purpose," that "ignorance and wickedness somewhere controls him," and

that he was running the Empire to ruin,[37] and by so doing, struck at

the only symbol that he felt bound the colonies to Great Britain;

Rutledge sought to block colonial action that tended to upheaval and

change.

Rutledge quickly perceived the threat that war posed to his

power in South Carolina, and from the fall of 1775 onward, he was more

concerned with protection of that power than with anything else. In

late July, 1775, Congress adjourned briefly, and Rutledge made a hasty trip

back to South Carolina. As the conflict deepened, he was forced further

into the open. He found that there were whispered rumors about the

honesty of his commitment to opposition to England, and worse, he

found that William Henry Drayton had nearly managed to send a militia

force to attack the backcountry farmers. Traditional Whigs regrouped on

Rutledge's return, prevented the march, and affairs settled somewhat.

Then the Convention instructed Rutledge to return to Philadelphia in

September. He had no more than arrived when he learned that Drayton had

been elected President of the Convention, and that the tidewater and

upcountry were in open war. He asked to be recalled, but the Convention

refused to honor his request.

In the meantime, Rutledge acted on his own. Congress had received and confirmed the South Carolina Convention's request regarding establishment of a temporary government. Rutledge stopped the recommendation of Congress from going to South Carolina; he took Congress' official communication to the Convention, and kept it with him. The recommendation did not reach the colony for four months, and when it did, John Rutledge presented it in person. [38] Once again Rutledge blocked, obstructed, and delayed Patriot action on his own authority and initiative, and by so doing, molded resistance to Parliament and Patriot action in a perceptible manner.

On the other hand, Jefferson fostered rapid governmental establishment in Virginia. In the late winter of 1775, he joined with Henry, R. H. Lee, and George Wythe in support of concrete proposals for a new, popular government in the colony. Virginia Patriots, sensitive to the clash between their militia and Governor Dunmore, moved rapidly in debate about the form of government for the colony. By early 1776, Lee, Henry, and Wythe were in full support of Adams' Thoughts on Government. [39] Another

group of Patriots disagreed, and Carter Braxton suggested a form of
government for Virginia that would have given the planter class power
in perpetuity.[40] Lee and Henry were violently antipathetic to Braxton's
ideas, and feared that their adoption might destroy the movement for
independence. Thomas Jefferson struck out on his own, and by the spring
of 1776, he had conceived a set of governmental changes in Virginia
that extended beyond those contained in Adams' Thoughts on Government.

No more striking contrast between Jefferson and Rutledge existed than
in the way the two men faced new government in their colonies. Rutledge
abandoned Congress in 1776, and never returned. When he got to South
Carolina, he found that Drayton had markedly advanced in his power,
but that most Charlestonians were against independence and inclined
toward allowing the standing committees to direct resistance. Henry
Laurens, for one of the old guard, thought that some kind of temporary
government was necessary. Another divisive opinion came from
Christopher Gadsden. On February 8, Gadsden put in an appearance in
the Convention, and when Rutledge submitted Congress' resolves for
government in South Carolina, Gadsden was immediately on his feet.

262

He waved a copy of Paine's Common Sense at the delegates and declared

that he was for Paine's form of government and for complete independence.[41]

Rutledge protested, and stood full against independence. He said that

he "abhorred the idea; and that he was willing to ride post day and

night, to Philadelphia, in order to assist in re-uniting Great Britain

and America."[42] The Drayton faction drew to Rutledge because they

thought that Gadsden was impudent in openly declaring for independence

at that time.[43] And, John Rutledge became chairman of a committee

to consider the Congress' recommendation. For the first time Rutledge

seemed to turn on his own class, but the first draft of a temporary

government which he submitted to Convention was coldly calculated,

first, to delay South Carolina from taking on the matter of establishing

a government, and, second, to inform men like Laurens on what the

provisions of a new, temporary government could do to the power of the

tidewater aristocracy. Rutledge accomplished both his aims, and got

the kind of temporary constitution that he wanted. When the committee

reported a series of recommendations that allowed for more extensive

participation of the west and the popular eastern elements in the

revolutionary tribunals, Laurens said that he would never assent to it. [44] The report was recommitted. Not until April did South Carolina have a government, and John Rutledge had a large hand in shaping it and running it. The preamble openly stated that the government was temporary, and that when reconciliation between the colonies and mother country took place, South Carolina would revert to its charter government. Under the temporary government the people at large who could vote by law were to elect an assembly, and the assembly would elect councillors, a president, a vice-president, and chief justice of the supreme court. The president would have veto power over all money bills. [45] Tensions within South Carolina did the remainder: in the balloting for the office of president Rutledge received thirty-eight votes, Laurens thirty-two, and Drayton thirty-one. [46] What South Carolina would do in regard to separation from the Empire rested in large measure on what its new president-elect would do.

John Rutledge did nothing to upset his precarious balance of forces. On April 11, 1776, he issued a new statement of the purposes of American resistance that hewed to the path marked out by traditional

opposition to England. He asked that Parliament restore trial by jury, and that the colonies be taxed only by their consent. He did not hesitate to say that the colonies were not in rebellion and that he was disheartened by accusations of treason levelled against the colonies. Americans, Rutledge said, desired peace, and with peace they would return to their former status under the charters.[47] Gadsden and Drayton opposed Rutledge's position, as usual, and South Carolina Patriots splintered into three competing groups, but John Rutledge still dominated the political arena. Crisis and war had forced Rutledge to side with the advocates of resistance. Only English invasion of South Carolina and the Congress' Declaration of Independence could force him to side with separation from England. Nothing could make him side with the advocates of unmitigated popular republicanism.

Thomas Jefferson's attitudes and actions about government were precisely opposite. In early 1776, he thought that a new constitution for Virginia was the whole object of the controversy with England, and he wrote a constitution for Virginia that rested partly upon his hostility toward English authority and partly upon his dissatisfaction with

265

Virginia government as it stood under the charter.[48] In his preamble

he proclaimed that English authority in America was dissolved . Then

with a few bold strokes of the pen and in a few scattered sentences

Jefferson sought to lay the basis for popular power and universal

manhood suffrage. He paid homage to the tradition of having property

qualifications for the right to vote, providing that voters must have

a quarter of an acre of town property or twenty-five acres of country

property. Then he made every adult male in Virginia a property-holder:

with the influence of the Crown gone, he said, all land reverted to the

state, and accordingly, the government of Virginia, under Jefferson's

constitution, would allot each adult male enough land to bring his

property holding to fifty acres, if he did not already have that amount.

Jefferson proposed thereby to insure, first, that every adult male in

the revolutionary generation might vote, and, second, that minimal

property holders might divide their estates with the next generation

and thus enfranchise their sons. Jefferson's views on new government

rested on a principle that departed from colonial traditions: that the

legislature should act positively in economic affairs (by the distribution

of land to the landless and minimal property holders) in order to

insure liberty (the right to vote).[49] Under Jefferson's constitution

Virginia would place no other qualifications on the right to hold

office save the right to vote and an oath of allegiance, and the

legislature would consist in two branches with effective control of

all power in the republic.

Jefferson next turned to standing institutions in Virginia which

he thought threatened a popular republic. He proposed to eradicate the

church establishment and to institute full liberty of "religious opinion."

Thus far, Jefferson's constitution did not touch on the power of the

gentry or on slavery. Jefferson hoped for laws to restrain both,

and it was here that he revealed his feelings about society, property,

and caste in his native colony. He proposed that henceforth all landed

estates be handed down to the whole blood in equal proportion with the

heir at law,[50] and to insure the demise of slavery, he advocated prohibition

of the introduction of any new slaves into the state of Virginia.[51]

Jefferson offered a constitution for his colony that involved far-reaching

change in basic institutions and advocated rule of the people. No colonial

rebel was more radical than Jefferson on the point of reformation

of America on the advent of war with Great Britain. For Jefferson,

the promise of revolution was the promise of equality in the state,

not merely the hope of protecting what colonials had, and his subsequent

career rested on the conscious conviction that the future could bring

a better world than had existed in the past.

By the spring of 1776, Jefferson and Rutledge presented contrary

images of colonial leadership in the face of crisis and upheaval.

Jefferson had made up his mind, worked for institutional change in

Virginia, then returned to Congress and worked for independence. John

Rutledge evaded and avoided the question of revolution and continued to

invoke the dictums of traditional opposition to Great Britain. Jefferson

encouraged zealous Whigs and fought against Patriots who thought the

Empire to the best advantage of the colonies. Rutledge sought to hold

zealous Whigs at bay and prayed for news of reconciliation, peace, and

an end to upheaval. And, Rutledge remained in South Carolina; protection

of his power and property depended on his presence. Jefferson went

back to Philadelphia: the course that America would take would be

decided in the arena of national debate.

268

VIII

THE CONGRESS AND AMERICAN INDEPENDENCE

Throughout the twenty-two months of the last Imperial crisis,

events had unfolded in three theaters: the British government,

the several colonies, and the Continental Congress. Now, as the crisis

neared culmination in June of 1776, actors in the first two theaters

had committed themselves to postures of mutual hostility, and had done

so in a way that prevented either from easily turning back. But the

meaning of what they had done depended upon what Congress would do.

Since the passage of the Intolerable Acts in the spring of

1774, England had followed a policy of war and suppression. Crown

and Parliament had brushed aside Congress' petitions, proclaimed that

the colonies were in rebellion, and prohibited colonial trade. The

royal army had descended upon Boston and Quebec, made a feint at North

Carolina, and, by late June of 1776, was laying seige to Charleston.

The colonials, for their part, had thrown up a wall of resistance

against British demands as well as against British arms. By late June,

that resistance had achieved widespread , though not uniform, success.

The continental forces had freed Boston after a year of sporadic

fighting, and Americans had defeated the English in Quebec, only to

suffer defeat in their turn, and then to be routed by disease and forced

to retreat to their own soil. North Carolina Patriots suppressed an

internal Loyalist uprising, and South Carolinians held the English

at bay in Charleston. Meanwhile, the Congress had retaliated against

Parliament and Crown by issuing letters of marque for seizure of English

vessels and by recommending that all the colonies suppress the authority

of the Crown. Congress had created an army and a navy, and had begun

diplomatic negotiations with France. Moreover, colonists had forged

temporary governments and forced royal officials to flee the provinces.

Thus as the situation stood in late June of 1776, England could

do little other than increase its war effort; the colonies, severally,

could do little other than continue to resist. Only the men in Congress,

representing the colonies collectively, still had a choice. And even

they had only an either-or choice: to continue the official policy of

reconciliation or to sever the bonds of Empire.

270

As late as the fourth week of June, what the members of Congress would do about the resolution for independence was not irrevocably established, either in fact or in the minds of the Patriots. Advocates of independence had made gains, but they had not broken the power of their opponents. In fact, they had managed only one unmistakable victory: their preamble to the recommendation for new government. That victory had not materialized until May 15th, 1776, but it had helped independence-minded Whigs in Congress and their supporters throughout the colonies. The preamble gave proponents of separation a specific issue around which they could rally, and they gained force in late May and early June. Benjamin Franklin of Pennsylvania, Caesar Rodney of Delaware, Samuel Chase of Maryland, Jefferson and Lee of Virginia, and William Hooper of North Carolina, all used the recommendation to move the people a step nearer independence. However, the colonies did not tumble like dominoes into the independence camp, and when R.H. Lee introduced the resolution for independence in Congress, traditional Whigs quickly postponed the motion. Later in June, most of the colonies had issued instructions to their delegates expressly permitting them

to vote for independence if they so chose. As July approached, some

men were confident that the resolution would pass.[1]

But the exponents of redress and reconciliation had not capitulated,

and they had no intention of giving up the principle of liberty within

the Empire without a fight. They still received the impact of English

action from without and independence action from within with marked

resilience. In June, traditional whigs made a concession: they finally

agreed on a committee to consider a formal American confederation. They

did so only after they had thrice defeated confederation movements

within the Congress.

The worst thing that had happened to the men who continued to call

for colonial rights within the Empire had taken place within their own

ranks. Pinioned by the English and Americans alike, some traditional

whigs had been seized by apprehensions about the war and their local

power and abandoned Congress for their provinces. Some gave over their

responsibilities and withdrew from the conflict; others moved to insure

their power in local government. By late June, their numbers in Congress

had dwindled, and though they attempted to rectify the balance, July

came upon the traditional Whigs before they were fully prepared

to meet the question before the Congress.[2]

Nonetheless, the balloting power of the men who favored liberty

within the Empire was strong. In late June they still controlled the

votes of five states: New York, Pennsylvania, New Jersey, Maryland,

and South Carolina; and the delegations from Delaware and North Carolina

were divided. On the other side, advocates of independence controlled

the same six states they had controlled when Lee first introduced the

resolution, the four New England colonies, Virginia, and Georgia.[3]

There was another potential barrier to independence, and a vital

one: the question whether the traditional Whigs (and the colonies

they represented) would have to accept the decision if a bare majority

of the delegates in Congress did vote for independence. Until just now,

the traditional Whigs had themselves had a bare majority, and again and

again they had used external threat -- and the need for a united front

that it imposed -- as a means of persuading the independence faction to

go along with them. Thus advocates of independence had not only to win

control of another delegation; they had also to force the traditional

273

Whigs to become victims of their own logic.

These political circumstances in Congress made Thomas Jefferson's task as author of the Declaration of Independence more difficult than it appeared on the surface to be. Jefferson favored the creation of an American republic, and had radical and well defined ideas about the governments and reforms that should follow the destruction of English authority in America. But in the present context he had to keep such ideas to himself; he had to talk preservation, not innovation; he had, in short, to accept ten years of Dickinson-like argument, but turn it upside down so that it justified a course which colonials had previously denounced. During the month of June he labored over a statement of the case for independence that would do just that.

On Friday, June 28, Jefferson delivered a draft of a declaration of independence which anticipated his opponents' arguments by using them, and which relegated his own views on the principles of government to a subsidiary role. He made no new departure from the previous framework of argumentation: Americans did what they did only because they were driven to it and not because they desired or aspired to sedition, war ,

or revolution. Now, Jefferson said, Americans were forced to declare

independence in order to preserve their rights and liberties, and

they did so because England left them no alternative. "Prudence, indeed,"

Jefferson said, "will dictate that governments long established should

not be changed for light and transient causes." And, when Jefferson

turned to the causes which impelled America to sever the governmental

bonds of Empire, he did not attack the form of Imperial governmental,

but the corruption of government in the hands of George III and,

secondarily, of Parliament. In twenty-nine separate clauses, Jefferson

drove home the assertion that the reign of George III had been a

history of tyranny that had at last reached the point where it was the

right and duty of Americans to declare their independence. By adroitly

shifting the major focus of previous antagonisms from Parliament to

Crown, Jefferson shifted responsibility for conflict to the only link

that bound the colonies to the Empire. What colonial Whigs had

heretofore used to justify resistance, Jefferson used to justify

independence. Jefferson placed the full weight of the Declaration here.

He argued forcefully, he argued directly, and he marshalled an array

of facts to prove what he said.

But that was not all the Declaration of Independence was, nor was it all that Jefferson intended that it be. He lifted the conflict from the level of a civil war to the level of the defense of the rights of mankind. He did so in an astute fashion. Attuned to the realities of the situation in Congress, Jefferson used a simple formula for avoiding antagonizing Americans: he avoided areas of controversy between the Patriots. Jefferson laid down no directives for the individual colonies, he did not elaborate on the consequences of independence, and while he was detailed and factual about the tyranny of England, he was general and vague about the nature of American government. What Jefferson delivered to Congress consisted largely in those maxims of government which Americans, monarchists and republicans alike, could accept. He said that all men were created equal, that government derived its just powers from the consent of the governed, and that men were obliged to suffer a considerable amount of oppression for a considerable period before they had the right and duty to revolt -- all innocent enough proposals. Only hints of Jefferson's complete views

were **visible** in the Declaration of Independence. He put these into the

preamble and allowed the indictment against England to carry the

justification for independence. Jefferson wanted the Declaration

accepted, not caught up in endless and, perhaps, ruinous debate.[4]

When Congress convened on Monday, July 1, independence-minded
Whigs learned that the traditional Whigs intended to hold firm, and

during the course of the debates, John Dickinson rose in an attempt to

postpone the resolution. He made only a passing remark about Jefferson's

Declaration: its language was too vehement. Then Dickinson joined

the issue directly and told the men in Congress that independence was

nonsensical: it was reckless, it served no purpose in foreign or

domestic relations, it did not take into account the nature of the

colonies or the aims of France, it undermined former arguments and

aims of resistance, it defied the practical necessities of a people

engaged in war, and it was a measure that was more in the interests of

New England than in those of all the colonies. He asked Congress to wait.

John Adams rebutted. He argued that Americans had waited long

enough for word of reconciliation and had done all that reasonable men

could be expected to do. Independence, he said was necessary for

the protection of liberty, for the colonial war effort, and for the

prevention of anarchy in the colonies. American independence was

already a fact, Adams said, for the Crown had already declared the

colonies outside its protection; it only remained for Congress to

affirm this reality. Furthermore, until the colonies did affirm that

they were irrevocably committed to the dissolution of the British

Empire, they could expect no aid from France.[5]

For hours the delegates hassled, and then the issue was decided

by something that had to do with neither logic nor argument: a new

delegation from New Jersey entered the hall. The delegation was headed

by John Witherspoon, Presbyterian minister and proponent of independence,

a man who had been in several local disputes about independence and

had on one occasion been roundly defeated on the measure. Two other

New Jersey delegates arrived with him: Richard Stockton, a former

member of the New Jersey Council, and known to favor independence, and

Abraham Clark, called the "Poor Man's Advocate." A fourth member

had already taken his seat and probably heard the debates: Francis

278

Hopkinson, deist, impecunious poet and literato, had bolted Governor

William Franklin's faction in 1775. These men had been elected to

Congress only nine days earlier, and they represented the impact of

May 15th preamble on politics in New Jersey. Governor William Franklin

had continued to exert influence and power in the colony until the

Provincial Convention acted on the recommendation of Congress. John

Adams summarized the debates for the New Jersey men, and New Jersey

registered its approval of independence. The traditional Whig block

was severely shaken.[6]

Independence Whigs pressed their new advantage and demanded an

unofficial ballot in the committe of the whole . The roll call began

with the northernmost colony of New Hampshire and proceeded to the

southernmost of Georgia. New England voted four colonies for independence.

New Yorkers, sensing the result of the balloting and divided among

themselves, abstained. With that, the Middle Colonial block fell

apart as New Jersey voted yes, Pennsylvania no, and Delaware divided.

Traditional Whigs were beaten. Marylanders reconsidered; William Paca

told Congress that his colony would be bound by a majority. Virginia

voted yes. Rather than divide North Carolina's vote to no purpose,

Joseph Hewes capitulated and voted yes with John Penn. South Carolina

remained adamant and voted no. Georgia's vote gave independence

nine colonies--a clear majority.[7] Congress then assembled in its

official capacity, but before the question could be put, South Carolina

requested that the vote be postponed until the next day.[8]

That evening and night, men who espoused redress and reconciliation,

knowing what the next day would bring, decided how they would meet the

fact of independence. Some decided to change their vote, others decided

to abstain, others decided to absent themselves, and still others

decided to make one final gesture to the past and vote no.

When Congress opened on July 2, it was clear that the traditional

Whigs were badly beaten. John Dickinson and Robert Morris were

conspicuously absent. That left Pennsylvania favoring independence

by a scant majority of three to two. During the night two other colonies

had gone over to independence: South Carolina agreed to be bound by the

majority, and Caesar Rodney had ridden all night and now made the

Delaware vote two to one in favor. When the question was put for the

final time, only New York refused to concur; instead, it abstained
from voting. Twelve colonies voted in favor of the resolution and
Jefferson's Declaration of Independence. Independence had been declared
at last, and the American rebellion entered a second and more radical phase.

That was the end. It was also the beginning. The time to rend had
found its season and expired. The time to build had come to be. Men
perceived the change each in his own fashion, and what they did refracted
the change and recast that change in their several images and kinds.
Men could do no other.

In the short run, meeting the change suddenly became more important
than what had produced the change. John Adams, Puritan rebel, welcomed
the rebirth of liberty and looked to laws to protect a cleansed people.
"Power follows property,"Adams said, and suggested laws that would
lodge the greater mass of property in the hands of the great mass of
people. The many, he had decided, were the true defenders of good
government when they had an interest in government. John Rutledge,
aristocrat and opportunist, received the change with comparative

equanimity, then threw himself into an effort to build so that ordinary

men would have no power at all. John Dickinson retired into seclusion

and waited. He would think over what was to come, and the Quaker idea of

community would renew itself. Dickinson was most interested in the

general good of the whole community and said so. Finally, Jefferson

viewed the change as merely the first of a series of reformist acts that

would be necessary before man could be truly free. Change brought conflict

about how to build.

In the long run, that was what made men forget. Though the Patriots

may have had serious limitations, most ceased to dispute the obvious.

Invariably, they even ceased to dispute what had brought the change to

be, and in their turn, placed a new face on the years before the time

to build, and, in turn, altered the past, present and future. There was

less malevolence in their forgetfulness than good sense in a time of war

and revolution. Yet, even a generation after the decision for independence,

men would seek to recapture their old selves in a fleeting moment before

they died, and the question would return, and return in a guise molded

in a different time, when men had different hopes and aspirations.

282

That was why Adams and Dickinson argued as they did in the early

nineteenth century. Not all that either they or others said was exactly

right. So would it be with men who came after them. And the men who

came after would have less excuse for error, for they were not caught

in the throes of war, rebellion, and bloodshed that brought independence

to be.

Notes

and

Bibliographical Essay

NOTES

Chapter 1: Introduction

1

Writings on John Adams are extensive. For the most thorough study see Page Smith, John Adams (2 vols., Garden City, N.Y., 1962). The discussion on Adams' recollections is taken from his autobiography in Lyman H. Butterfield and others, ed., The Adams Papers, Diaries and Autobiography of John Adams (4 vols., Cambridge, Mass., 1961), 3: 309-398. Since the Butterfield edition of John Adams' works is not yet completed, it is necessary to supplement it by using Charles F. Adams, ed., The Life and Works of John Adams (10 vols., Boston, 1850-1856).

2

Butterfield, ed., Adams Papers, 3: 317.

3

Butterfield, ed., Adams Papers, 3: 316.

4

Butterfield, ed., Adams Papers, 3: 383.

5

By way of Mrs. Mercy Warren's History of the Rise, Progress, and Termination of the American Revolution (3 vols., Boston, 1805), 1:307-314. Mrs. Warren requested Dickinson's opinion of the work: Charles J. Stillé, Life and Times of John Dickinson, (Phil., 1891), 194-195.

6

Letters from a Farmer in Pennsylvania (Phil., 1768); for Lee's response to the Townshend Acts: R.H. Lee to _____, March 27, 1768 in J.C. Ballagh, ed., The Letters of Richard Henry Lee (2 vols., New York., 1911-1914), 1: 27, and Lee to Dickinson, July 25, 1768, Ballagh, ed., Lee Letters, 1: 29; Samuel Adams use of Dickinson: H.A. Cushing, ed., The Writings of Samuel Adams (4 vols.,

285

New York, 1904-1907), 1: 136, 165, 201, and 2: 221.

7
   Dickinson's recollection is taken from a letter to Mercy Warren,
September 9, 1807, quoted in Stillé, Dickinson, 195-196.

8
   Two brief essays contain general accounts of historiographical
disagreement on Patriot conflict at the outset of the Revolution: Edmund S.
Morgan, The American Revolution, A Review of Changing Interpretations
(Washington, 1958), and Jack P. Greene, "The Flight from Determinism: A Review
of Recent Literature on the Coming of the American Revolution," South
Atlantic Quarterly, 61 (Spring, 1962), 235-259.

9
   This was still true some fifteen years later: Forrest McDonald, We The
People (Chicago, 1958), passim.

10
   Richard Upton, Revolutionary New Hampshire (Hanover, N.H., 1936);
Robert E. Brown, Middle-Class Democracy and the American Revolution 1691-1780
(Ithaca, 1955); David S. Lovejoy, Rhode Island Politics and the American
Revolution (Providence, 1958); Oscar Zeichner, Connecticut's Years of Controversy,
1750-1776 (Williamsburg, 1949); Carl L. Becker, The History of Political Parties
in the Province of New York, 1760-1776 (Madison, 1909); Leonard Lundin on New
Jersey: Cockpit of the Revolution (Princeton, 1940); on Pennsylvania: David
Hawke, In the Midst of a Revolution (Phil., 1961), and Theodore Thayer,
Pennsylvania Politics and the Growth of Democracy, 1740-1776 (Harrisburg, 1953);
John A. Munroe, Federalist Deleware, 1775-1815 (Wilmington, Del., 1954); Charles
A. Barker, The Background of the Revolution in Maryland (New Haven, 1940);
Robert E. and B. Katherine Brown, Virginia, 1705-1786: Democracy or Aristocracy?

286

(East Lansing, Mich., 1964) : E. W. Sikes, The Transition of North Carolina from Colony to Commonwealth (Baltimore, 1898) ; Edward M. McCrady, The History of South Carolina under the Royal Government, 1719-1776 (New York, 1899); and a general survey: Allan Nevins, The American States during and after the Revolution, 1775-1789 (New York, 1924) are indicative of the intensive research on the local level. On colonial society and government, Alice M. Baldwin, The New England Clergy and the American Revolution (Durham, N.C., 1928); Carl Bridenbaugh, Cities in Revolt: Urban Life in America, 1743-1776 (New York, 1955), and Mitre and Sceptre: Transatlantic Faiths, Ideas, Personalities and Politics, 1689-1775 (New York, 1962) ; Elisha P. Douglass, Rebels and Democrats (Chapel Hill, 1955); Jack P. Greene, The Quest for Power: The Lower Houses of Assembly in the Southern Royal Colonies, 1689-1776 (Chapel Hill, 1963); and A. M. Schlesinger, The Colonial Merchant and the American Revolution (New York, 1917), comprise a partial listing of studies of this nature. Biographies are too numerous to list here, see the Bibliographical Essay, Secondary Sources, Biographies, below. General surveys: George Bancroft's volumes on the Revolution in History of the United States (10 vols., Boston, 1834-1875); John C. Miller's The Origins of the American Revolution (2nd ed., Stanford, 1959), and Triumph of Freedom, 1775-1783 (Boston, 1948) are two of numerous milti-volume treatments; E.C. Burnett, The Continental Congress (New York, 1941), Burnett, editor, Letters of Members of The Continental Congress (8 vols., Washington, 1921) -- cited hereafter as Burnett, ed., Letters-- and W. C. Ford, editor, The Journals of the Continental Congress, 1774-1789 (34 vols., Washington, 1904-1937), cited hereafter as, Ford, ed., Journals.

11
On the level of Imperial government, George L. Beer's British Colonial

287

Policy 1754-1765 (New York, 1907) broke new ground in interpretation, and Lawrence H. Gipson's monumental The British Empire before the American Revolution (9 vols., to date, New York, 1936---) discusses the full scope of the Empire. Several studies have been done on special aspects of the Imperial administration: Oliver M. Dickerson, The Navigation Acts and the American Revolution (Phil., 1951), Carl Ubbelohde, The Vice-Admiralty Courts and the American Revolution (Chapel Hill, 1960), and Dora Mae Clark, The Rise of the British Treasury: Colonial Administration in the Eighteenth Century (New Haven, 1960).

12
    Randolph G. Adams, The Political Ideas of the American Revolution (3rd. ed., New York, 1958), first published in 1922; Charles H. McIlwain, The American Revolution: A Constitutional Interpretation (New York, 1923); Robert L. Schuyler, Parliament and the British Empire; Some Constitutional Controversies Concerning Imperial Legislative Jurisdiction (New York, 1929); Edmund S. and Helen M. Morgan, The Stamp Act Crisis: Prologue to Revolution (Chapel Hill, 1953); Carl L. Becker, The Declaration of Independence (2nd. ed., New York, 1942); David Hawke, A Transaction of Free Men (New York, 1965); Merrill Jensen, The Articles of Confederation (Madison, 1948).

13
    Lawrence H. Gipson, The Coming of the American Revolution 1763-1775 (New York, 1954) contains a general survey of Parliament's legislative enactments and colonial responses thereto.

14
    See Morgan and Morgan, Stamp Act Crisis, passim.

15
    Morgan and Morgan, Stamp Act Crisis, 276.

288

16
Peter Force, ed., American Archives: Consisting of a Collection of AuthentickRecords, State Papers, Debates and Letters. . . (9 vols., 1837-1853), 4th Series, 1 : 5-66, 111-129, 165-170. A convenient reference to important parts of the texts of the acts is Henry S. Commager, ed., Documents of American History (7th ed., New York, 1963), 71-76.

17
For various responses to Adams' call for economic coercion see Force, ed., American Archives, 4th Series, 1: 297, 304, 333, 341, 347, 350. Adams' responses to these, Cushing, ed., Adams Writings, 3: 125-126.

18
Force, ed., American Archives, 4th Series, 1: 746, 787, 1022, 1041, 1042-1043, 1081. Connecticut's General Assembly had gotten war preparations well underway by October, 1774, The Public Records of the Colony of Connecticut (15 vols., Hartford, 1850-1890), 14: 343-346.

19
Force, ed., American Archives, 4th Series, 1 : 297, 304, 333, 341, 347, 350.

20
Force, ed., American Archives, 4th Series, 1 : 793.

21
Burnett, The Continental Congress, 23-32.

22
The approval of the Suffolk Resolves (Force, ed., American Archives, 4th Series, 1 : 777-778) was twice debated in Congress: Ford, ed., Journals 1 : 39 and 58. Later, Philip Livingston of New York, elected to Congress but not in attendance denied Congressional approval in The Other Side of the Question . . . (New York, 1774), 26.

23
Gage had instructions to prevent colonials from arming, Force, ed., American Archives, 1 : 245.

289

Chapter II. The Middle Colonies: Liberty and Empire

1

William H. Nelson, The American Tory (Oxford, 1961), 87.

2

Quakers remonstrated against the Association in November, 1774, Force, ed., American Archives, 4th Series, 1: 963, and against Congress in January, 1775, Force, ed., American Archives, 4th Series, 1: 1093-1094, 1176-1177.

3

Force, ed., American Archives, 4th Series, 1: 1164, 1191, 1203; 2: 304, 314. Alexander Flick, Loyalism in New York during the American Revolution (New York, 1901), 14-20, 36-40. George Dangerfield, Chancellor Robert R. Livingston of New York, 1746-1813 (New York, 1960), 57.

4

Force, ed., American Archives, 4th Series, 6: 808, 833; John Haslet to Caesar Rodney, May, 1776, George H. Ryden, ed., Letters to and from Caesar Rodney...(Phil., 1933), 87; Harold Hancock, The Delaware Loyalists (Wilmington, Del., 1940).

5

Dangerfield, Livingston, 60; debates on Congress in the Assembly: Journal of the Votes and Proceedings of the General Assembly of the Colony of New York from 1766 to 1776...(Albany, 1820), Jan. 20-March 24, 1775; Flick, Loyalism in New York, 30-31, 46-47, 49; Pennsylvania:Archives of the State of New Jersey, 1st Series, 10 (Newark, 1886), 580-584; Thayer, Pennsylvania Politics, 164-165; New Jersey: Archives of New Jersey, 1st Series, 10: 575-578.

6

One group of delegates from the Middle Colonies was prepared to agree that England had acted tyrannically in 1774, but refused to support Congress

by mid-1775: Joseph Galloway and Samuel Rhoads of Pennsylvania; Isaac Low and
Simon Boerum of New York; and John DeHart and James Kinsey of New Jersey.
Another and by far larger group was willing to fight, but not to declare
independence: John Dickinson, Robert Morris, Edward Biddle, Thomas Willing,
Charles Humphreys, James Wilson, John Morton, and Andrew Allen of Pennsylvania;
John Jay, R.R. Livingston, Jr., Philip Livingston, John Haring, John Alsop,
Philip Schuyler, Lewis Morris, James Duane, Francis Lewis, and Henry Wisner of
New York; William Livingston, Stephen Crane, and Richard Smith of New Jersey,
and George Read of Delaware. Though these men were not present in Congress at
the same time, they made their views known. Galloway: his own A Candid
Examination of the Mutual Claims of Great Britain, and the Colonies...
(New York, 1775); Rhoads, though a Philadelphian, refused to attend Congress
regularly and dissented on enforcement of the Association: Force, ed.,
American Archives, 4th Series, 1: 486, and Butterfield, ed., Adams Papers,
2: 177, n.3; Low was very timid after the first Congress, and, at first,
refused to serve in the April, 1775, Provincial Convention, Force, ed.,
American Archives, 4th Series, 1: 294-295; see W.H.W. Sabine, ed., Historical
Memoirs of William Smith (2 vols., New York, 1956-1958), 1:220 for Smith's
evaluation of Low's hesitancy; Boerum of King's Co. represented an extremely
lethargic populous: E.B. O'Callaghan, ed., Calendar of Historical Manuscripts
Relating to the War of the Revolution in New York (2 vols., New York, 1866-
1868), 1: 41-42, and he retired from Congress in June of 1775: Burnett, ed.,
Letters, 1: lii. John De Hart and James Kinsey resigned from Congress in
late 1775: Archives of New Jersey, 1st Series, 10: 680-683; For Dickinson's
views see Ch. III; Morris to _____, Dec. 9, 1775, Burnett, ed., Letters, 1: 271,

and Morris' and Willing's statements in Thomas W. Balch, ed., Willing,
Letters and Papers (Phil., 1922), xxxvii-xxxviii. Biddle was undoubtedly
prepared to fight, but suffered a stroke in May, 1775: Pennsylvania
Magazine of History and Biography, 1 (Phil., 1877), 102. Humphreys supported
the war effort, but voted against independence: Penna. Mag. of Hist. and Bio.,
1:85; Wilson: Richard Smith, Diary, in The American Historical Review, 1
(Jan. and April, 1896; 288-310, 493-516), 307; John Morton opposed independence
until the last debates, then voted in favor on July 2: Penna. Mag. of Hist.
and Bio., 1: 1-2; Andrew Allen and Thomas Willing were on the same "anti-
independence" election ticket: George Read to his wife, May 1, 1776,
William T. Read, Life and Correspondence of George Read (Phil., 1870), 157--
Allen eventually became a Loyalist, Penna. Mag. of Hist. and Bio., 1:207-208;
9(July, 1885), 177, and see his antagonism to independence in Burnett, ed.,
Letters, 1: 398. Emphatic evidence for Jay, Duane, and R.R. Livingston's
opposition to independence still exists: Jay to Edward Rutledge, July 6, 1776,
Henry P. Johnston, ed., The Correspondence...of John Jay (4 vols., New York,
1890-1893), 1: 70, and Frank Monaghan, John Jay (New York, 1935), 80-81;
Livingston: Burnett, ed., Letters, 1: 477, Dangerfield, R.R. Livingston, 73;
See Duane's letters to Livingston and Jay in Burnett, ed., Letters, 1: 464, and
to R.R. Livingston, March 20, 1776, Robert R. Livingston Papers, 1775-1777,
New York Public Library, wherein Duane states he is against any "irrevocable
measure." John Alsop: Burnett, ed., Letters, 2: 12-13. Philip Schuyler:
John R. Alden, The American Revolution, 1775-1783 (New York, 1954), 84, n.22.
Evidence concerning other New Yorkers is less emphatic; Lewis Morris was
more militant than some New Yorkers (Force, ed., American Archives, 4th Series,

292

2: 323-324), but no evidence remains that either he or Henry Wisner proposed that the colonies declare independence, and John Haring, President of the New York Provincial Convention, must have concurred in John Jay's successful efforts to keep secret Congress' request for a census of New Yorker's sentiments on the question in June of 1776. Francis Lewis and Philip Livingston were opponents of independence and refused to exert themselves in any way to aid the measure, Johnston, ed., Jay Correspondence, 1: 67, Burnett, ed., Letters, 1: 524-525. For William Livingston's outspoken animosities to independence, see Theodore Sedgwick, A Memoir of the Life of William Livingston (New York, 1833), 173-174; Crane and Smith had to be replaced by the New Jersey Convention, and Smith never mentions any intention of supporting independence in his Diary, he finally resigned in mid-June: Force , ed., American Archives, 4th Series, 6: 1618. The single Delaware delegate who opposed independence was clearly against separation in the last months of debate, George Read to his wife, May 1, 1776, Read, Read, 161.

Those Middle Colonials who served as delegates and favored independence by late 1775 or early 1776 included George Clinton and William Floyd of New York, Benjamin Franklin, Thomas Mifflin, and George Ross of Pennsylvania, John D. Sergeant of New Jersey, and Thomas McKean and Caesar Rodney of Delaware. Clinton had given up hope of reconciliation: Hugh Hastings, ed., The Public Papers of George Clinton (10 vols., 1899-1914), 1: 216-217, but nevertheless remained relatively quiet on the topic of independence so that as late as June 1776, Edward Rutledge of South Carolina thought Clinton against the measure, Johnston, ed., Jay Correspondence, 1: 67; William Floyd to William McKesson, May 9, 1776, O'Callaghan, ed., Calendar of Historical

293

Manuscripts, 1: 304; Franklin's initial confederation proposal entailed a formal break with England, John Bigelow, ed., The Works of Franklin, 7 (Federal ed., New York, 1904), 80, 94-100, 123. Mifflin, Ross and McKean were all actively engaged in moving Pennsylvania to independence: Force, ed., American Archives, 4th Series, 6: 962, Thayer, Pennsylvania Politics, 178-180. Ryden, ed., Rodney Letters, 79, 85; Sergeant to John Adams, June 15, 1776, Adams, ed., Adams Works, 9: 425, n. 1-4, and Butterfield, ed., Adams Papers, 2: 177.

7
Burnett, ed., Letters, 2: 12-13.

8
Alden, American Revolution, 84, n. 22.

9
Livingston to Henry Laurens, Feb. 5, 1778, Sedgwick, Wm. Livingston, 173-174.

10
De Hart to the General Assembly of New Jersey, Nov. 13, 1775, Archives of New Jersey, 1st Series, 10: 682-683; Sedgwick, Wm. Livingston, 169.

11
Considerations on the Nature and Extent of the Legislative Authority of the British Parliament (Phil., 1774); Richard Smith, Diary, 307; Charles Page Smith, James Wilson: Founding Father (Chapel Hill, 1956), 74-75, 89.

12
Robert Morris to Horatio Gates, April 6, 1776, Burnett, ed., Letters, 1: 416; See also 2: 19; Balch ed., Willing Letters, xxxvii-xxxviii; Clarence VerSteeg, Robert Morris Revolutionary Financier (Phil., 1954), 6.

294

[13] George Read to his wife, May, 1776, Read, Read, 161, and Ford ed., Journals, 5: 515.

[14] Alsop: Virginia Harrington, The New York Merchant on the Eve of the Revolution (New York, 1935), 220; Morris and Willing: VerSteeg, Robert Morris, 5; Smith, James Wilson, 23 and 49. De Hart and Livingston: Sedgwick, William Livingston, 158, 160; Benson J. Lossing, The Life and Times of Philip Schuyler (2 vols., New York, 1860), 1: 46, 202-204; Read, Read, 22-23.

[15] Louis B. Wright, The Atlantic Frontier (New York, 1947), Ch. IV.

[16] For a discussion of Anglicans in New York on the advent of rebellion, see Flick, Loyalism in New York, 10.

[17] Ruth M. Keesey, "Loyalism in Bergen County, New Jersey," William and Mary Quarterly, 3rd Series, 18 (Jan., 1961), 558-562. Lundin, Cockpit of the Revolution, 13.

[18] Lundin, Cockpit of the Revolution, 36.

[19] Hancock, Delaware Loyalists, 44-50.

[20] Thayer, Pennsylvania Politics, 1 ff., discusses cultural population ratios in that colony, and for population growth, see Bureau of the Census, Historical Statistics of the United States (Washington, 1957) 756; this work is the best available source on colonial trade and commerce, population estimates, wholesale commodity prices, paper money emissions, and colonial taxation. Though historians should use any statistical compilation with

caution, this particular publication has a great deal to recommend it.
First, many of the figures on colonial trade and commerce have been checked
against the original sources in the Public Records Office in London; second,
Section Z contains statistical studies previously unpublished; third, of
the twenty-seven tables given, twenty-two are based on recent studies by
some of the most reputable economic and statistical historians in the U.S. All
things considered, Historical Statistics is the most sound, up-to-date
reference for colonial economic data. See 743-755 for a full explanation
of each table, the reliability of the data, and the extent of research on
colonial statistics.

21
    Force, ed., American Archives, 4th Series, 1: 963, 1093-1094, 1176-1177.

22
    Sabine, ed., Wm. Smith Memoirs, 1: 169

23
    E. P. Alexander, A Revolutionary Conservative, James Duane of New York
(New York, 1938), 45; Sabine, ed., Wm. Smith Memoirs, 1:34; Lundin,
Cockpit of the Revolution, 61-68.

24
    New York alone contained well over two million acres of unsettled,
available land: U.P. Hedrick, History of Agriculture in the State of New York
(Albany, 1933), 45-48, contains a listing of major land patents for the
years 1763-1770; Harrington, New York Merchants, 141-142. The New Jersey
proprietors controlled over a million acres, and the Penns perhaps twice
that amount.

25
    Butterfield, ed., Adams Papers, 2: 107. The inhabitants of the Middle
Colonies felt the full impact of these events in this sequence, though Pontiac

had begun his raids before the news of the Proclamation Line reached America.
In 1774 John Morin Scott told Adams that some people in New York were
"intimidated by the levelling spirit of the New England Colonies . . . ."
Butterfield, ed., Adams Papers, 2: 106.

26
Lundin, Cockpit of the Revolution, 61-68.

27
See Chapter III.

28
Hedrick, Agriculture in New York, 45-48. Few Livingstonians got major
land grants of over 10,000 acres.

29
Joseph Galloway, A Speech of Joseph Galloway Esq. . . . (Phil., 1764);
John Dickinson, A Speech Delivered in the House of Assembly . . . (Phil.,1764);
Thayer, Pennsylvania Politics, 93-99.

30
Sabine, ed., Wm. Smith Memoirs, 1: 34.

31
Butterfield, ed., Adams Papers, 2: 107; Burnett, ed., Letters, 1:173;
for an example of Middle Colonial feelings in Congress, see: Andrew Allen
to Philip Schuyler, March 17, 1776, Burnett, ed., Letters, 1: 398, where
Allen writes of the "dark designs" of New Englanders.

32
Charles B. Kuhlman, The Development of the Flour Milling Industry in
the United States (New York, 1929), 14-22; Harrington, New York Merchants,
208-213, 215-216. Carl and Jessica Bridenbaugh, Rebels and Gentlemen:
Philadelphia in the Age of Franklin (New York, 1942), 3-13.

33
Gipson, American Revolution, 18.

297

34

Historical Statistics, 772.

35

Historical Statistics, 758.

36

Historical Statistics, 756, 757, 758-760, 772. These estimates are made to indicate the general situation in the Middle Colonies. Anyone familiar with the available data knows that present knowledge of commercial figures does not permit an exact, mathematical computation of economic growth in the colonies. Instead, Historical Statistics contains sufficient information for a studied judgment and nothing more (see n. 20 above).

37

Historical Statistics, 773.

38

Historical Statistics, 774.

39

Historical Statistics, 756.

40

Journal of the New York Assembly, April 4, 1769 ff.

41

Livingstonians were constantly in a minority: see votes in Journal of the New York Assembly from May 12, 1769, when Philip Livingston's seat was contested, through March, 1775.

42

Sabine, ed., Wm. Smith Memoirs, 1: 54, 55, 63-34, 67-68, 132-133. Journal of the New York Assembly, Nov. 17, 1768; May 12, 1769; May 17, 1769; Nov. 25, 1769; Dec. 7, 1769; Dec. 13, 1770.

43

Hedrick, Agriculture in New York, 45-48; Harrington, New York Merchants, 141-142.

298

44
Boreum maintained a fair degree of dependence on the DeLanceys, but had joined Livingstonians by late 1774; see his voting record in the *Journal of the New York Assembly*, Jan. - March, 1775.

45
Low, President of the New York Chamber of Commerce, had hopes of becoming mayor in 1775 and sought DeLancey support, Sabine, ed., *Wm. Smith Memoirs*, 1: 220.

46
Sabine, ed., *Wm. Smith Memoirs*, 1: 265.

47
Dangerfield, *R.R. Livingston*, 56

48
See note 6 above, and Burnett, ed., *Letters*, 1: 524-525.

49
Burnett, ed., *Letters*, 1: 524-525.

50
Archives of New Jersey, 1st Series, 10: 680-683; Burnett, ed., *Letters*, 1: 348, 412.

51
Archives of New Jersey, 1st Series, 10: 680-683; Sedgwick, *Wm. Livingston*, 173-174; Burnett, ed., *Letters*, 1: 340; Sergeant replaced Crane in Feb., 1776: Burnett, ed., *Letters*, 1: 347, and see Sergeant's statements in Adams, ed., *Adams Works*, 9: 425, n. 1-4.

52
Ryden, ed., *Rodney Letters*, 79, 85; Force, ed., *American Archives*, 4th Series, 6: 962; Burnett, ed., *Letters*, 1: 528.

53
Read, *Read*, 161. The "Court-Party" in Kent Co. was strong enough to prevent Rodney's election to the Delaware Constitutional Convention of 1776: Ryden, ed., *Rodney Letters*, 104. Hancock, *Delaware Loyalists*, 56-57.

299

Chapter III: John Dickinson

1

Dickinson wrote a revealing self-appraisal in the first of the Letters from a Farmer; by the 1770's his estate was taxed ₤711--an amount greater than that of the senior partner of the wealthiest merchant firm in Philadelphia, Thomas Willing--and was probably worth upwards of ₤50,000: Pennsylvania Archives, 3rd Series, 14: 385, and the article signed "Senex" in Force, ed., American Archives, 4th Series, 2: 212; Stillé, Dickinson, Chs. 1 and 2.

2

Frederick B. Tolles, Meeting House and Counting House: The Quaker Merchants of Colonial Philadelphia, 1682-1763 (New York, 1948), 234 ff.

3

Tolles, Meeting House and Counting House, Appendix B, 251-252.

4

P.L. Ford, ed., The Writings of John Dickinson, Memoirs of the Historical Society of Pennsylvania, 14 (Philadelphia, 1895), 21-49, 462.

5

In his pamphlet The Late Regulations Respecting the British Colonies (Phil., 1765), Dickinson cites, among other economic authors, Sir Josiah Child, A New Discourse on Trade (1668).

6

For changes that took place in Pennsylvania in these years see Bridenbaugh, Cities in Revolt, 332-333; Thayer, Pennsylvania Politics, 1-8; Tolles, Meeting House and Counting House, 234 ff.

7

Bigelow, ed., Franklin Works, 4: 65-66; "Introduction to A Speech by Joseph Galloway, Esq.," 4: 72-118. Compare this interpretation to that given by Thayer, Pennsylvania Politics, 93-94, 96.

300

8

John Dickinson, A Speech Delivered in the House of Assembly . . . (Phil., 1764), and also in Ford, ed., Dickinson Writings, 21-49.

9

Ford., ed., Dickinson Writings, 77-119.

10

Commager, ed., Documents, 40-41.

11

The change of government never took place, although only four assemblymen voted against it; Bigelow, ed., Franklin Works, 4: 134-137; Thayer, Pennsylvania Politics, 95.

12

(Phil., 1764), 8, 9 n., 10 n., 20-22, 25.

13

Morgan and Morgan, Stamp Act Crisis, 246-247; Gipson, American Revolution, 78 n. 22, 83; Julian P. Boyd, Anglo-American Union: Joseph Galloway's Plans to Preserve the British Empire, 1774-1778 (Phil., 1941), 22.

14

Dickinson's own progression is easily followed in The Late Regulations ... (1764), "Resolutions of the Stamp Act Congress," Ford, ed., Dickinson Writings, 183-187 (1965), An Address to the Committee of Correspondence in Barbados (Phil., 1766).

15

Compare Dickinson's draft with the final Resolutions, Ford, ed., Dickinson Writings, 183-187.

16

Ford, ed., Dickinson Writings, 183-187.

17

Address to Barbados, 4-5.

18

Address to Barbados, 5, 9-10.

301

19
  The Late Regulations, 33.

20
  In the elections of October, 1765, while he was attending the Stamp Act Congress.

21
  The first "Letter" was published in the Pennsylvania Chronicle and Universal Advertiser on December 2, 1767, and the last "Letter" appeared on February 15, 1768. Other colonial newspapers ran the series, and the first pamphlet edition of the Letters from a Farmer was published in Philadelphia in 1768. Subsequent editions were published in Boston, Williamsburg, New York, London, and in Amsterdam. The pamphlet was even translated into French and read in the salons.

22
  Letters from a Farmer, 5.

23
  Letters from a Farmer, 9, 12, 13.

24
  Letters from a Farmer, 14,16.

25
  Letters from a Farmer, 23 ff.

26
  Commager, ed., Documents, 66–67.

27
  Gipson, ed., American Revolution, 187.

28
  Stillé, Dickinson, 94.

29
  After the Earl of Hillsborough's own letter denouncing non-importation agreements in April, 1768. Galloway had already led the Assembly to reject Massachusetts' action: Thayer, Pennsylvania Politics, 142.

302

30
    Thayer, Pennsylvania Politics, 149-50.

31
    Thayer in Pennsylvania Politics, 8 and 150, describes the nature of factions in Pennsylvania after 1757; Smith, Wilson, 45.

32
    Thomas Wharton to Samuel Wharton, Nov. 30, 1773, Selections from the Letter-Books of Thomas Wharton . . . Penna. Mag. of Hist. and Bio., 33 and 34 (2 Parts, Phil. 1909 and 1910), Part 1: 319. Gipson, American Revolution, 221.

33
    Ford, ed., Dickinson Writings, 462. William Smith of New York had earlier ursurped the pseudonymn of "Pennsylvania Farmer," Sabine, ed., Wm. Smith Memoirs, 1: 76.

34
    Wharton Letter-Books, Part 1: 319, 323; Kenneth R. Rossman, Thomas Mifflin and the Politics of the American Revolution (Chapel Hill, 1952), 21; Ford, ed., Dickinson Writings, 497.

35
    Archives of New Jersey, 1st Series, 10: 389-391; Force, ed., American Archives, 4th Series, 1: 341, 485-486; Ford, ed., Dickinson Writings, 491-500; Rossman, Mifflin, 21.

36
    Archives of New Jersey, 1st Series, 10: 389-391. Boyd, Anglo-American Union, 48.

37
    Ford, ed., Dickinson Writings, 491, 497, 500; Jared Ingersoll to Jonathan Ingersoll, Feb. 11, 1775, F.B. Dexter, ed., Jared Ingersoll Papers, Papers of the New Haven Historical Society, 9 (New Haven, 1918), 450. Rossman, Mifflin, 25.

303

38
A New Essay on the Constitutional Power of Great-Britain Over the Colonies in America . . . (Phil., 1774).

39
Force, ed., American Archives, 4th Series, 1: 560; Boyd, Anglo-American Union, 27 ff.; Thayer, Pennsylvania Politics, 158-163; Pennsylvania Archives, 8th Series, 8: 7173-7174.

40
Butterfield, ed., Adams Papers, 2: 147.

41
For example of the feelings of one Tory see Wharton Letter-Books, Part 1: 329, 338, 433.

42
Thomson's statement: "What Congress adopted, I committed to writing; with what they rejected, I had nothing further to do . . . ." Cited in Lewis R. Harley, The Life of Charles Thomson (Phil., 1900), 95.

43
Ford, ed., Journals, 1: passim.

44
Ford, ed., Journals, 1: 102.

45
Ford, ed., Journals, 1: 58.

46
Archives of New Jersey, 1st Series, 10: 579-586.

47
Wharton Letter-Books, Part 2: 43; Force, ed., American Archives, 4th Series, 1: 1270, 1275-1280.

48
The Candid Examination ... which was under preparation since the Congress had convened: Boyd, Anglo-American Union, 48.

304

49
Force, ed., American Archives, 4th Series, 1: 963, 1093-1094, 1176-1177.

50
Thayer, Pennsylvania Politics, 163.

51
Dickinson to Arthur Lee, Oct. 27, 1774, Burnett, ed., Letters, 1: 83, and to Samuel Ward, Jan. 29, 1775, Bernard Knollenberg, ed., The Correspondence of Samuel Ward. . . (Providence, 1952), 32-33.

52
Jared Ingersoll to Jonathan Ingersoll, Feb. 11, 1775, Dexter, ed., Ingersoll Papers, 450.

53
Burnett, ed., Letters, 1: 83.

54
C. C. Vermeule, "Number of Soldiers in the Revolution," New Jersey Historical Society Proceedings, New Series, 7 (July, 1922), 224-226 (based upon the Henry Knox returns); Vermeule's estimates of the number of adult males is based upon less accurate figures than those given in Historical Statistics and the ratios of adult males to soldiers in service should be figured consonant with the more accurate population studies.

55
Rossman, Mifflin, 38.

56
Bigelow, ed., Franklin Works, 7: 80, 123.

57
Dickinson to Arthur Lee, July 7, 1775, Burnett, ed., Letters, 1: 157

58
This account of the dispute is taken from Adams' autobiography written some thirty years after the event (Butterfield, ed., Adams Papers, 3: 317-318); whether the two men encountered one another on this date and in this manner

is debatable. In view of the fact that Adams intended to sign the Olive
Branch Petition without much opposition: John Adams to James Warren,
July 6, 1776, Warren-Adams Letters, Collections of the Massachusetts Historical
Society (2 vols., Boston, 1917-1925), 1: 75, and that he did not attack
Dickinson personally until July 24: Warren-Adams Letters, 1: 88-89, it
seems possible that the confrontation may have taken place as a result of
Adams' attempt to press the proposal for a confederation on July 21-24,
Ford, ed., Journals, 2: 195 ff. Eliphalet Dyer indicates a heated dispute to
William Judd, July 23, 1776, Burnett, ed., Letters, 1: 173.

59
   Based on Dickinson's statements in a letter to Arthur Lee, July 7, 1775,
Burnett, ed., Letters, 1: 157.

60
   Butterfield, ed., Adams Papers, 2: 173

61
   Commager, ed., Documents, 96; The Proclamation had been issued in
August, 1775.

62
   Archives of New Jersey, 1st Series, 10: 389-391.

63
   Archives of New Jersey, 1st Series, 10: 389-391.

64
   A majority of delegates from the Middle Colonies, Maryland, South
Carolina, and perhaps North Carolina; see note 6, Ch. II and James Duane
to R. R. Livingston, March 20, 1776, R. R. Livingston Papers, Bancroft
Collection, New York Public Library: the intercourse between the five
Middle Colonies (the fifth being Maryland) and South Carolina has, Duane
wrote, "suffered no dimunition. "Joseph Hewes of North Carolina to Samuel
Johnson, July 28, 1776, Emmet Collection, New York Public Library.

306

65
    Note 6, Ch. II.

66
    Sam Adams to John Adams, Jan. 15, 1776, Cushing, ed., Adams Writings, 3: 258-260.

67
    Janet B. Johnson, Robert Alexander Maryland Loyalist (New York, 1942), 75, and Proceedings of the Conventions . . . of Maryland . . . (Baltimore, 1836), 83.

68
    Ford, ed., Journals, 3: 456; Burnett, ed., Letters, 1: 311.

69
    Butterfield, ed., Adams Papers, 2: 231

70
    Ford, ed., Journals, 4: 357-358. The preamble seems to have been purposely delayed until, or perhaps re-introduced on, the 15th of May when Marylanders were absent from the Congress. On the 14th, Marylanders withdrew and gave the Congress "to understand that they should not return nor deem further resolutions /of Congress_7 obligatory . . . . " The next day the resolution passed by a vote of six to four: Carter Braxton to Landon Carter, May 17, 1776, Burnett, ed., Letters, 1: 454. For the effects of the Resolution in Pennsylvania: Force, ed., American Archives, 4th Series, 6: 517-519, 560, 784-786, 1021.

71
    Ford, ed., Journals, 5: 425.

72
    Read, Read, 161.

73
    Robert Morris to Horatio Gates, April 6, 1776, Burnett, ed., Letters, 1: 416.

307

74
J. H. Powell, ed., "Speech of John Dickinson Opposing the Declaration of Independence , July 1, 1776," Penna. Mag. of Hist. and Bio., 65: 458-481. Parts of the sequence of Dickinson's speech have been transposed.

75
A majority of New Yorkers and Pennsylvanians in the Congress were opposed: n. 6, Ch. II, James Duane to R. R. Livingston, March 20, 1776, R. R. Livingston Papers, Bancroft Coll., New York Public Library. It was probably known that the Delaware delegation was divided, one in favor and one opposed (Read, Read, 161), and so too were the North Carolina delegates (Joseph Hewes to Samuel Johnston, 28 July, 1776, Emmet Collection, New York Public Library). At the time the debates began, New Jersey was unrepresented, and both Maryland and South Carolina had repeatedly opposed the measure: see Ch. VI. From the viewpoint of an opponent of independence like Dickinson, there was a good possibility that Congress might deadlock on the issue or, perhaps, that the vote would be considered inconclusive and postponed.

308

Chapter IV. The New England Colonies: Liberty and Independence

1

Joseph Hawley to Samuel Adams, April 1, 1776, relates that he had heard that a "great Mobb" will "drive down" on Congress. "The people are now ahead of you and the only way to prevent discord . . . is to strike while the iron is hot." Adams' response is in Cushing, ed., Adams Writings, 3: 277-281.

2

In May and June of 1774, New Hampshire, particularly Portsmouth, was somewhat lethargic in support of Boston, but that colony moved into step with the remainder of New England, and declared independence in June, 1776. For silencing of the Tories, see the names on the Portsmouth petition of Dec., 1775, in Force, ed., American Archives, 4th Series, 4: 459, and in the Provincial Papers . . . Documents and Records Relative to the Province of New Hampshire (31 vols., Concord, etc., N.H., 1867-1907), 8: 16, compared to those men who accepted new offices, Provincial Papers of New Hampshire, 8: 28, 29, 55, 95, 111, 121, and John Langdon's comments on this head to Josiah Bartlett, June, 1776, Historical Magazine, 6 (1862), 239.

3

Josiah Bartlett and John Langdon to the New Hampshire Provincial Convention, Oct. 2, 1775, and Nov. 3, 1775, in Burnett, ed., Letters, 1:213,246.

4

Provincial Papers of New Hampshire, 7: 204-296

5

Robert J. Taylor, Western Massachusetts in the Revolution (Providence, 1954), 64 ff.

309

6

John Hancock to Thomas Cushing, Feb. 13, 1776, "Letters of John Hancock, 1776, "Massachusetts Historical Society Proceedings, 60 (Boston, 1927), 102, discusses Cushing's removal as a delegate to Congress. John Adams was probably responsible: Adams, ed., Adams Works, 9: 367-368.

7

Records of the Colony of Rhode Island and Providence Plantations. . . (10 vols., Providence, 1856-1865), 7: 325, 522.

8

Zeichner, Connecticut, 203 ff.

9

Force, ed., American Archives, 4th Series, 2: 899.

10

While the Middle Cononies' inhabitants still debated the question whether merely to change instructions to their delegates in the Congress, New Englanders had settled the question of independence. Although Rhode Island had a strong Tory group in Newport (Livejoy, Rhode Island, 184-191), it declared independence in May, 1776, Force, ed., American Archives, 4th Series, 6: 1669, and the townships of Massachusetts acted as soon as feasible after Gage had evacuated Boston: American Archives, 4th Series, 6: 533, 552, 698-706. Connecticut: American Archives, 4th Series, 6: 902. New Hampshire: American Archives, 5th Series (3 vols., Washington, 1846-1848), 1: 49.

11

The fifteen men who represented New England at various times and who supported independence early were John Langdon, Josiah Bartlett, and William Whipple, Burnett, ed., Letters, 1: 213, 246, 456; John Sullivan, Provincial Papers of New Hampshire, 8: 686; Nathaniel Folsom, Proceedings of the New Hampshire Historical Society, 4 (1906), 253-267; John Adams, Adams, ed., Adams Works, 9: 356; Samuel Adams, Cushing, ed., Adams Writings, 3: 277-281.

310

Elbridge Gerry, James T. Austin, The Life and Times of Elbridge Gerry
(2 vols., Boston, 1828-1829), 1: 174; Samuel Ward: Knollenberg, ed.,
Ward Correspondence, 116; when Rhode Islanders declared independence,
William Ellery was elected to replace Ward who had died in March, 1776,
Force, ed., American Archives, 4th Series, 6: 1669, and see Ellery to
Benjamin Ellery, July 10, 1776, Penna. Mag. of Hist. and Bio., 10 (1886),
320-321, and Livejoy, Rhode Island, 192. Silas Deane eventually became a
loyalist, however, the circumstances surrounding his defection were unusual
and as early as February, 1775, Deane favored a formal confederation of
the colonies independent of England, The Deane Papers, Collections of the
New-York Historical Society for the Year 1886, 19 (New York, 1887), 38,
cited hereafter as Deane Papers (1887); Eliphalet Dyer, George C. Groce,
"Eliphalet Dyer: Connecticut Revolutionary," The Era of the American
Revolution, ed. by R. B. Morris (New York, 1939), 290-304; Sherman was reticent
at first, but joined the movement in 1776, Roger S. Broadman, Roger Sherman
(Phil., 1938), 132-134, 155 ff.; both Oliver Wolcott and Samuel Huntington
were elected by the Connecticut legislature because of their staunch support
of the Patriot movement; A. H. Clapp, "Samuel Huntington," The Congressional
Quarterly, 6 (Oct. 1864), 320 and see Burnett, ed., Letters, 1: 355-356.

Of the four recalcitrant members of Congress from New England--John
Hancock, Robert T. Paine, Thomas Cushing, and Stephen Hopkins--only Cushing
remained adamant in his opposition while the remainder favored independence
in the last month prior to the Declaration: Massachusetts Historical Society
Proceedings, 60: 98-116; "Letters of Thomas Cushing, from 1767 to 1775,"
Collections of the Massachusetts Historical Society, 4th Series, 4 (Boston,
1858), 347-372; Burnett, ed., Letters, 1: 447.

311

12
Burnett, ed., Letters, 246. Bartlett Manuscripts, New Hampshire Historical Society, 1: 26. George Sanderson, Biography of the Signers of the Declaration of Independence (2nd ed., Nashville, 1831, 1: 268-270; cited hereafter as Sanderson, Bio. of the Signers; Provincial Papers of New Hampshire, 7: 686.

13
Cushing, ed., Adams Writings, 3: 277-281.

14
Hancock to William Cooper, July 6, 1776, Massachusetts Historical Society Proceedings, 60: 113.

15
Burnett, ed., Letters, 1: 447.

16
Copy of a letter of William Ellery to Samuel Ward, Feb. 4, 1769, Ward Manuscripts, Rhode Island Historical Society, 1: 85; Ford, ed., Journals, 4: 353, and Force, ed., American Archives, 4th Series, 6: 1669; Ellery to Benjamin Ellery, July 10, 1776, Penna. Mag. of Hist. and Bio., 10: 32-321.

17
Burnett, ed., Letters, 1: 154, and Broadman, Sherman, 155 ff.

18
A. H. Clapp, "Samuel Huntington," The Congressional Quarterly, 6 (Oct., 1864), 320.

19
Durham, N.H., (Sullivan), Kingston, N.H. (Bartlett), Boston (Adams, Hancock), Providence (Hopkins), New Haven (Sherman), Newport-Bristol (Ellery), Norwich, Conn. (Huntington).

20
Only Ellery did not hold some office in 1774, and he became clerk of the Assembly that year: Col. Recs. of Rhode Island, 7: 5.

312

[21] On Sherman: Silas Deane to Mrs. Deane, Jan. 21, 1776; The Deane Papers (1887), 349.

[22] Hopkins was a late convert to Quakerism: William E. Foster, Stephen Hopkins (2 vols., Providence, 1884), 1: 34, but had been disowned in 1773.

[23] W. B. Baxter, The House of Hancock . . . (Cambridge, Mass., 1945), 236 ff., 279, 286-287.

[24] Broadman, Sherman, 71

[25] Lovejoy, Rhode Island Politics, 14.

[26] Channing-Ellery Papers, Rhode Island Historical Society, 1 (1765-1777), 55.

[27] John Adams to Abigail Adams, June 29, 1774; C.F. Adams, ed., Familiar Letters of John Adams to His Wife . . . (Boston, 1875), 2-3.

[28] Charles P. Whittemore, A General of the Revolution, John Sullivan of New Hampshire (New York, 1961), 5.

[29] Charles B. Kinney, Church and State: The Struggle for Separation in New Hampshire (New York, 1945), 54, 78, describes the situation in New Hampshire which was generally true for Massachusetts and Connecticut as well.

[30] Kinney, Church and State, 69.

313

31
For the ill will of Massachusetts Baptists in 1774, see J. Adams, Papers, 2: 153, n. 3.

32
In 1768, Samuel Adams thought the people inattentive to the threat of Anglicanism, Cushing, ed., Adams Writings, 1: 201-203, 203-207, 208-212.

33
See Zeichner, Connecticut, passim.

34
Benjamin Gale to Jared Ingersoll, Jan. 13, 1765, Dexter, ed., Ingersoll Papers, 373.

35
Lovejoy, Rhode Island Politics, passim.

36
Isabel S. Mitchell, Roads and Roadmaking in Colonial Connecticut (New Haven, 1933).

37
Charles S. Grant, Democracy in the Connecticut Frontier Town of Kent (New York, 1961) gives an account of this process in miniscule; see also: William D. Miller, The Narragansett Planters, Proceedings of the American Antiquarian Society, 43 (1933), 108.

38
Silas Deane to Josiah Trumbull, Aug. 10, 1774, Force, ed., American Archives, 4th Series, 1: 710.

39
The militias of New Hampshire, Massachusetts, and Connecticut continued training after the War, and in 1772, Connecticut passed new and more rigid training laws: Col. Recs. of Connecticut, 14: 3.

40
Schlesinger, The Colonial Merchant, 25. (New York, 1917), 25.

314

41
Schlesinger, The Colonial Merchant, 25-26.

42
For a detailed account of the endeavors of one New England mercantile family, see James B. Hedges, The Browns of Providence Plantations, Colonial Years (Cambridge, Mass., 1952).

43
Kuhlmann, Flour Milling Industry, 8.

44
The tightening of customs after the war revealed that New England was exporting to England between £125,000 to £140,000 during the latter part of the war. See the jump in values, Historical Statistics, 757.

45
Beverly McAnear, "Mr. Robert R. Livingston's Reasons Against a Land Tax, "Journal of Political Economy, 48 (Feb.-Dec., 1940), 63 ff., contains the text of Livingston's observations on the New England land system.

46
McAnear, "Robert R. Livingston," Jour. of Pol. Eco., 48: 87.

47
McAnear, "Robert R. Livingston," Jour. of Pol. Eco., 48: 89.

48
Historical Statistics, 756.

49
Miller, Narragansett Planters, 108.

50
Historical Statistics, 756.

51
Deane to Patrick Henry, Jan. 2, 1775, Deane Papers (1887), 36-38.

52
Precise figures for the amounts of land of various descriptions--first class, plow, brush, and meadow--are not available for the 1770's, but the

government of Connecticut did compile such figures in a survey completed
in 1785. It is extremely unlikely that a survey made in 1774 would
have been very different from that made a decade later; the total amount
of land was, of course, fixed, and given the technology and stage of
agricultural development at the time, it seems improbable that any appreciable
changes could have been wrought in the quality of the land in so short
a period. Also, population figures used here are, of course, for 1774.
In any event, the figures given here are cited as being symptomatic, and even
if they were in error by as much as twenty-five or thirty per cent, the
generalizations made here would not be greatly altered. The 1785 survey is
in Manuscript Volume 5, "Finance and Currency," page 229a, in the Connecticut
State Archives, Hartford. The colony population returns by county are
in Col. Recs. of Connecticut, 14: 485-491.

53
"Remarks on Dr. Gale's Letter to J. W. Esq." in Julian P. Boyd, ed.,
The Susquehannah Papers (4 vols., Wilkes-Barre, 1930-1933), 3: 261.

54
Historical Statistics, 772.

55
An estimate based on actual exports recorded for West Indies, Historical
Statistics, 758, 759-760.

56
Based on the ratio of values to tonnage for 1769 used as a constant
for the decade. If anything, New England export values relative to tonnage
probably declined more rapidly than the estimate given. Historical Statistics,
759-760.

57
Historical Statistics, 758.

316

58
  Richard Barry, Mr. Rutledge of South Carolina (New York, 1942), 149.

59
  Historical Statistics, 772.

60
  Historical Statistics, 768.

61
  Historical Statistics, 756.

62
  Provincial Papers of New Hampshire, 7: 274.

63
  Provincial Papers of New Hampshire, 7: 292-296.

64
  Bowdoin to Alexander McKay, Boston, Nov. 20, 1770; Bowdoin and Temple Papers, Collections of the Massachusetts Historical Society, 6th Series, 9 (Boston, 1897), 241.

65
  Bowdoin to Alexander McKay, Boston, Nov. 20, 1770; Bowdoin and Temple Papers, 241-242.

66
  Historical Statistics, 773; and see the analysis of Lawrence H. Gipson, "Connecticut Taxation, 1750-1775," in Essays in Colonial History (New Haven, 1931).

67
  Col. Recs. of Connecticut, 13: 300-301; 512-513; 14: 94.

68
  Col. Recs. of Rhode Island, 7: 24, 33, 54, 208.

69
  Henry M. Baker, "General Nathaniel Folsom," Proceedings of the New Hampshire Historical Society, 4 (1906), 254.

70
  Sanderson, Bio. of the Signers, 5: 289. Lawrence Shaw Mayo, John Langdon

of New Hampshire (Concord, N.H., 1937), 40 ff.

71

Hancock to Bernard and Harrison, July 29, 1867, A. B. Brown, ed., John Hancock, His Book (Boston, 1898), 139. And, Baxter, The House of Hancock, 286-287.

72

Cushing devoted most of his time to politics after 1765; Collections of the Massachusetts Historical Society, 4: 347-372.

73

Gerry expressed the decline for Massachusetts generally in a letter to Samuel Adams, Nov. 2, 1772, Elbridge Gerry, 1: 13-14.

74

Channing-Ellery Papers, 1: 55, 125.

75

Broadman, Sherman, 71.

76

Glenn Weaver, Jonathan Trumbull (Hartford, 1956), 134.

77

Broadman, Sherman, 103, notes the failures in these years, but fails to interpret Sherman's closing his business as due to decline in retail profits.

78

Adams, see Ch. V; Paine: Ralph Davol, Two Men of Taunton (Taunton, 1912), 24 ff., and 231.

79

Ward MSS, 1: 84; 2: 103, 110.

80

Dyer was president of the company; Huntington, a lawyer who represented his family's interests in the Company, Susquehannah Papers, 2: 53-54; 234, n. 3; 3: 9.

318

81
    Force, ed., American Archives, 4th Series, 2: 215, 430. Alexander, Duane, 44- 87-92.

82
    Lawrence S. Mayo, John Wentworth (Cambridge, Mass., 1921), passim.

83
    Mayo, Wentworth, passim.

84
    Col. Recs. of Connecticut, 14: 156-161.

85
    Susquehannah Papers, 3: 237, 289; Force, American Archives, 4th Series, 1: 161.

86
    Wittemore, Sullivan, 5.

87
    See Adams, ed., Familiar Letters, 121, for his description of New England and local government.

88
    Francis G. Walett, "The Massachusetts Council, 1766-1774," William and Mary Quarterly, 3rd Series, 6 (Oct. 1949), 605-627.

89
    The court faction in western Massachusetts was strong: Taylor, Western Massachusetts, 11.

90
    History of the Province of Massachusetts Bay, From the Year 1750 until June 1774 (3 vols., London, 1828), 3: 103-104.

91
    Brown, Middle-Class Democracy, 228-231; 259-263; 287.

92
    Morgan and Morgan, Stamp Act Crisis, 124-128.

93
    To Reverend G_____ W_____, Nov. 11, 1765, Cushing, ed., Adams Writings, 1: 27-28.

319

94
Brown, Middle-Class Democracy, 258-263.

95
For a good analysis of the British financial situation see Richard

B. Sheridan, "The British Credit Crisis of 1772 and the American Colonies,"

Journal of Economic History, 20 (June, 1960), 161-186.

96
Sheridan, "British Credit Crisis," Jour. of Eco. Hist., 20: 161 ff.

97
Historical Statistics, 757.

98
Historical Statistics, 758.

99
Brown, Middle-Class Democracy, 289 contains returns in general elections

for that year.

100
Brown, Middle-Class Democracy, 289-299.

101
Cushing, ed., Adams Writings, 2: 347 ff.

102
Historical Statistics, 756-759.

103
Sheridan, "British Credit Crisis, "Jour. of Eco. Hist., 20: 174.

104
The unabridged debates between the Representatives and Hutchinson

are published in the Appendix of James K. Hosmer's Life of Thomas Hutchinson

(Boston, 1896), 363-428.

105
Adams to Elbridge Gerry, March 25, 1774, in Austin, Gerry, 1: 37 ff.

106
Ford, ed., Journals, 1: 15-16

320

107
   Ford, ed., Journals, 1: 32-36.

108
   Mayo, Wentworth, passim.

109
   Provincial Papers of New Hampshire, 7; 292-293; Mayo, Langdon, 46-60.

110
   Provincial Papers of New Hampshire, 7: 369.

111
   Mayo, Langdon, 55 ff.

112
   Zeichner, Connecticut, 114-117.

113
   Cited in Lewis H. Boutell, The Life of Roger Sherman (Chicago,1896), 78.

114
   Boyd, ed., Susquehannah Papers, 2: 279, 290, 292, 304; 3: 237, 289;
Dexter, ed., Ingersoll Papers, 428-429.

115
   The Deane Papers (1930), Collections of the Connecticut Historical
Society, 23 (1930), 129, cited hereafter as Deane Papers (1930); Ford, ed.,
Journals, 1: 18-19. In 1774, Deane conceived of a semi-military republic
in the Mississippi region which would be completely free of England, Deane
(1930),
Papers,/131-132.

116
   Foster, Hopkins, 1: 104-117.

117
   Lovejoy, Rhode Island, 179-184.

118
   See Stille, Dickinson, 174.

119
   Deane Papers (1930), 151-155.

120
   Baldwin, New England Clergy, passim.

321

121
    Adams and Cushing to Rev. G_____ W_____, Nov. 11, 1765, Cushing ed., Adams Writings, 1: 27-28; John C. Miller, Sam Adams: Pioneer in Propoganda (Boston, 1936), 126. John Adams: Butterfield, ed., Adams Papers, 1: 266, and Adams, ed., Adams Works, 2: 310-311; Roger Sherman to Thomas Cushing, April 30, 1772, in Broadman, Sherman, 117; Ward MSS, 2: 142; Hopkins: see Lovejoy's full analysis in Rhode Island, 73-78.

122
    Deane Papers (1887), 38.

123
    Cushing, ed., Adams Writings, 3: 258-250; Warren-Adams Letters, 1: 88-89; Knollenberg, ed., Ward Correspondence, 32, 158; Deane Papers (1887), 38.

322

Chapter V. John Adams

1
John Adams to Moses Gill, June 10, 1775, Adams, ed., _Adams Works_, 9: 356.

2
This description of Adams is taken from his writings, and from illustration n. 14 in Gipson, _American Revolution_.

3
Catherine D. Bowen, _John Adams and the American Revolution_ (Boston, 1950) Chs. 1-13, _passim_.

4
Butterfield, ed., _Adams Papers_, 1: 14-15.

5
Butterfield, ed., _Adams Papers_, 1: 1-37

6
Butterfield, ed., _Adams Papers_, 1: 24-25.

7
To Abigail Adams, Oct. 9, 1774, Adams, ed., _Familiar Letters_, 46.

8
Butterfield, ed., _Adams Papers_, 1: 9.

9
Butterfield, ed., _Adams Papers_, 1: 41.

10
Butterfield, ed., _Adams Papers_, 1: 37, 2: 72-72, 76.

11
Smith, _John Adams_, 1-76, _passim_.

12
Butterfield, ed., _Adams Papers_, 1: 48-49.

13
See Adams on Massachusetts history, Adams, ed., _Adams Works_, 4: 313-314.

323

14
    Article VI. of a reply by a committee of the Massachusetts General Court respecting liberties, June 10, 1661, Commager, ed., Documents, 34.

15
    Massachusetts General Court to the Lords of Council, Oct. 2, 1678, Commager, ed., Documents, 31-32.

16
    Butterfield, ed., Adams Papers, 1: 30.

17
    Butterfield, ed., Adams Papers, 1: 257.

18
    Commanger, ed., Documents, 55.

19
    Butterfield, ed., Adams Papers, 1: 267.

20
    Adams, ed., Adams Works, 3: 482.

21
    Adams, ed., Adams Works, 3: 448-464.

22
    Adams, ed., Adams Works, 3: 477-483. For Adams' reaction to the Boston Massacre: Butterfield, ed., Adams Papers, 1: 260-261, and Smith, John Adams, 1: 124-125.

23
    Questions exist as to Adams' full authorship of the remonstrances, but parts are no doubt his own. See C.F. Adams' analysis in Adams Works, 3: 310-311. This and the following citations are from the unabridged debates between the Representatives and Hutchinson, republished in the Appendix of James K. Hosmer's Life of Thomas Hutchinson (Boston, 1896), 363-428.

24
    Hosmer, Hutchinson, 390.

324

25
Hosmer, Hutchinson, 427.

26
Hosmer, Hutchinson, 367.

27
Hosmer, Hutchinson, 394.

28
Dec. 17, 1773; Butterfield, ed., Adams Papers, 2: 85-86.

29
Warren-Adams Letters, 1: 29.

30
Adams to James Warren, June 25, 1774: "I am for making it annual, and for sending an entire new set every year. . . ." Adams, ed., Adams Works, 9: 339.

31
Warren-Adams Letters, 1: 29; and see n. 76, below. Butterfield, ed., Adams Papers, 2: 145, under "Preparations for War," no. 6 and no. 7.

32
Undoubtedly Adams wished a full commitment on the part of all the colonies respecting open war in Massachusetts, Ford, ed., Journals, 1: 52, n. 2.

33
Adams still thought Parliament had the right to regulate trade, but as he had said in 1773, that right was based upon "necessity" and colonials' consent: Adams, ed., Adams Works, 4: 99.

34
Lee, on Oct. 3, 1774, introduced a motion to put the colonies in a state of defense by recommending a militia establishment to the colonies; Ford, ed., Journals, 1: 54, n. 1.

35
Oct. 7, 1774, Adams, ed., Familiar Letters, 44.

325

36

Butterfield, ed., Adams Papers, 2: 145; Charles Lee, Strictures on a Pamphlet Entitled, "A Friendly Address to All Reasonable Americans" . . . (New London, 1775)--first published in Oct., 1774.

37

Sept. 30, 1774, Ford, ed., Journals, 1: 52, n. 2.

38

Ford, ed., Journals, 1: 52, n. 2.

39

Ford, ed., Journals, 1: 57.

40

Henry's speech in the early part of the 1774 session, Butterfield, ed., Adams Papers, 2: 125.

41

Ford, ed., Journals, 1: 40, n. 1.

42

A vote was taken on the issue; it ended in a tie, five colonies in favor, five opposed, and two divided; Butterfield, ed., Adams Papers, 2: 151.

43

Butterfield, ed., Adams Papers, 2: 137.

44

Butterfield, ed., Adams Papers, 2: 133-134.

45

Ford, ed., Journals, 1: 23-26, 38-44, 71-74.

46

Butterfield, ed., Adams Papers, 2: 151.

47

"Cheerfully consent" was the same phrasing used in Adams' dispute with Hutchinson in 1773, and this particular part of the Article is undoubtedly his, Adams, ed., Adams Works, 3: 310-311, 9: 350; Hosmer, Hutchinson, 427.

48

Adams, ed., Adams Works, 4: 19-28.

326

49
Adams, ed., Adams Works, 4: 19-28.

50
Adams, ed., Familiar Letters, 59.

51
Adams, ed., Familiar Letters, 59.

52
John Adams to James Warren, July 24, 1775; Warren-Adams Letters, 1:
88-89.

53
Washington left Congress on June 23.

54
July 6, 1775; Warren-Adams Letters, 1: 75.

55
Warren-Adams Letters, 1: 75.

56
Warren-Adams Letters, 1: 75.

57
Butterfield, ed., Adams Papers, 3: 317-318

58
July 8.

59
Ford, ed., Journals, 2: 177ff.

60
July 24, 1775; Warren-Adams Letters, 1: 88-89.

61
Warren-Adams Letters, 1: 88-89.

62
Adams, ed., Adams Works, 1: 174, n. 1.

63
Butterfield, ed., Adams Papers, 2: 177.

64
To Elbridge Gerry, June 18, 1775; Adams, ed., Adams Works, 9: 358.

327

65
To Joseph Hawley, Nov. 25, 1775; Adams, ed., Adams Works, 9: 367.

66
Adams, ed., Adams Works, 9: 368.

67
To Abigail Adams, Adams, ed., Familiar Letters, 120-121.

68
Adams' letter to R.H. Lee, Nov. 15, 1775, Adams, ed., Adams Works,
4: 186-187.is a brief version of Thoughts on Government, published in
April, 1776. He calls this assumption of government a "total" revolution.
John D. Sergeant had a manuscript version of Adams' views: Warren-Adams
Letters, 1: 230-231.

69
Adams, ed., Adams Works, 4: 203.

70
Adams, ed., Adams Works, 4: 205.

71
Adams, ed., Adams Works, 4: 205.

72
Adams, ed., Adams Works, 4: 203-209.

73
Butterfield, ed., Adams Papers, 2: 231-233.

74
See Lee to Henry, April 20, 1776, Ballagh, ed., Lee Letters, 1: 177-179.

75
John Adams to Abigail Adams, March 19, 1776, Adams, ed., Familiar
Letters, 146.

76
Thoughts on Government (Phil., 1776), 10-13.

77
Warren-Adams Letters, 1: 247-248.

328

78
Thoughts on Government, 10-13.

79
Thoughts on Government, 14-15.

80
16-17, 26. Adams was frank about the nature of Thoughts on Government:
"In New England . . . they will be disdained because they are not popular
enough; in the Southern Colonies, they will be despised and desulted because
too popular." Warren-Adams Letters, 1: 242.

81
The North Carolina delegates William Hooper and John Penn had asked
Adams for his views on new government; Hooper had taken a copy of these back
to North Carolina: Warren-Adams Letters, 1: 230-231.

82
Marylanders made their sentiments known on the 14th May, 1776, Burnett,
ed., Letters, 1: 454.

83
Ford, ed., Journals, 4: 357-358.

84
Warren-Adams Letters, 1: 250-251.

85
Warren-Adams Letters, 1: 245.

86
Ford, ed., Journals, 5: 425.

87
Adams, ed., Adams Works, 9: 399-400.

88
Adams, ed., Adams Works, 9: 415.

329

Chapter VI. The Southern Colonies: American Aristocrats and

The Crisis in Empire

1

Force, ed., American Archives, 4th Series, 2: 477 and 6: 461; for a good discussion of Virginia and her declaration of independence, see David J. Mays, Edmund Pendleton (2 vols., Cambridge, 1952), 2: 40 ff.

2

As late as May 21, 1776, Maryland instructed her delegates not to assent to independence without the Convention's knowledge, Proceedings of the Conventions . . . of Maryland . . . (Baltimore, 1836), 141-142, and its governor was still in the colony as late as June 8, 1776; Force, ed., American Archives, 4th Series, 6: 754.

3

John R. Alden, The South in the Revolution 1763-1789 (1957, Baton Rouge), 182-183, 197-202. Force, ed., American Archives, 4th Series, 2: 115-116; 116-117.

4

Nelson, American Tory, 111.

5

John Drayton, Memoirs of the American Revolution . . . (2 vols., Charleston, 1821), 2: 172-173, and see Ch. VII. The post-independence spelling for Charleston (prior to that, Charles-Town) is used throughout.

6

Force, ed., American Archives, 4th Series, 1: 773; Alden, South in the Revolution, 183-184.

7

Butterfield, ed., Adams Papers, 2: 125. In 1774, Adams found Henry's politics more agreeable than Dickinson's: Adams, ed., Familiar Letters, 133 ff. Robert D. Meade, Patrick Henry, Patriot in the Making (Phil. and N.Y., 1957),

330 ff.

8

Ballagh, ed., Lee Letters, 1: 129, 173, 177-179.

9

Drayton, Memoirs of the American Revolution; 2: 173; Richard Smith, Diary, 310; Burnett, ed., Letters, 1: 313; Charles F. Jenkins, Button Gwinnet (New York, 1936), 65 ff.; Adams, ed., Adams Works, 9: 415.

10

Maryland: Samuel Chase, Sanderson, Bio. of the Signers, 5: Appendix 4, 363-372, and Adams, ed., Adams Works, 9: 397. Virginia: only Carter Braxton and Benjamin Harrison were recalcitrant; Mays, Pendleton, 2: 40 ff; Henry, n. 7 above; Julian P. Boyd, ed., The Papers of Thomas Jefferson (Princeton, 1950 _____), 1: 159 ff., and Ch. VIII; Ballagh ed., Lee Letters, 1: 129, 173, 177-179; F.L. Lee, Burnett, ed., Letters, 1: 417; John C. Fitzpatrick, ed., The Writings of George Washington (39 vols., Bicentennial Edition, Washington, 1931-1944), 4: 321, 454. George Wythe: among other things, see Richard Smith, Diary, 511, 514. Thomas Nelson, Jr., was one of five the Burgesses allowed to represent Virginia after independence was favored by that colony's convention, while Harrison and Braxton were recalled, June 20, 1776, Boyd, ed., Jefferson Papers, 1: 407; Ballagh, ed., Lee Letters, 1: 190; See also, Nelson to Mann Page, Jan. 22, 1776 in Sanderson, Bio. of the Signers, 5: 51. Peyton Randolph died in 1775, and Richard Bland was old and infirm, though known as a "Tory," Wm. T. Hutchinson, ed., The Papers of James Madison (Chicago, 1962), 1: 157. North and South Carolina, n. 9 above, and John Penn: Adams, ed., Adams Works, 9: 230-231; Hooper and Gadsden, n. 9 above; Arthur Middleton: "Correspondence of Honorable Arthur Middleton, "South Carolina Historical and Genealogical Magazine, 27 (July, 1926), 118,123. Georgia: Archibald Bullock, Lyman Hall, Button Gwinnet, note 9 above, Adams, ed.,

331

Adams Works, 9: 415. Two men, George Walton and John Houston of Georgia, remain illusive, but probably favored independence: Adams, ed., Adams Papers, 2: 183.

11
    Rutledge to John Jay, June 29, 1776; Johnston, ed., Jay Correspondence, 1: 67.

12
    Alexander to the Maryland Council of Safety, Feb. 27, 1776, Archives of Maryland (Baltimore, 1892), 11: 189. Johnson, Alexander, 95 ff.

13
    Ballagh, ed., Lee Letters, 1: 214; Edward S. Delaplaine, The Life of Thomas Johnson (New York, 1927), 28 ff.

14
    Burnett, ed., Letters, 1: 420.

15
    Burnett, ed., Letters, 1: 267, 301, 401; and Hewes even retarded the news of new instructions from his colony which would have aided independence - minded Whigs: Herbert Friedenwald, The Declaration of Independence (New York, 1904), 97.

16
    Maryland: Wm. Paca did not join the independence Whigs until the last moment; Adams, ed., Adams Works, 9: 396, 416; Warren-Adams Letters, 1: 251; Matthew Tilghman mocked Robert Goldsborough and John Hall because they were frightened by war preparations; later the two men abandoned Congress; so did Tilghman: Oswald Tilghman, History of Talbot County Maryland (2 vols., Baltimore, 1915), 1: 432; Ballagh ed., Lee Letters, 1: 214, and Force, American Archives, 4th Series, 4: 712. Thomas Johnson and Robert Alexander, notes 12 and 13 above. Thomas Stone and John Rogers: Burnett, ed.,

332

Letters, 1: 431; Ballagh, ed., Lee Letters, 1: 214. Virginia: Braxton,
Harrison, Bland, notes 10 and 14 above; North Carolina: Richard Carswell,
from a hot-bed of Loyalism at Hillsborough, declined to serve in Congress
after 1774; Hewes: n. 15 above; South Carolina: the Rutledges, Drayton,
Memoirs, 2: 173 and Ch. VII; Thomas Lynch, Sr., Sabine, ed., Wm. Smith Memoirs,
1: 262-263. Thomas Lynch, Jr., probably agreed with his father, and Henry
Middleton held aloof from politics after reception of the Proclamation
of Rebellion, Barry, Rutledge, passim; J. J. Zubly of Georgia left Congress
and became a Loyalist. Butterfield, ed., Adams Papers, 2: 404. Thomas
Heyward, Jr., of South Carolina probably joined the traditional Whigs;
he was appointed when Gadsden left Congress, Ford, ed., Journals, 4: 305-306.

17
    Ballagh, ed., Lee Letters, 1: 71; Barry, Rutledge, passim. See
Braxton's An Address to the Convention of the . . . Colony of Virginia . . .
(Phil., 1776), 10-14; Hutchinson, ed., Madison Papers, 1: 170-179.

18
    Barker, Maryland, 45-46; Johnson, Alexander, passim; Meade, Henry,
215, 236, 259; Sanderson, Bio. of the Signers, 5:115 ff.

19
    Gadsden's property, however, was mainly in docks and wharves, Leila
Sellers, Charleston Business on the Eve of the Revolution (Chapel Hill, 1934),
186.

20
    Jenkins, Gwinnett, 23 ff. Gwinnett also practiced law and ran a
retail store.

21
    The Catholic population was considerably smaller than one might think.
For the actions of one leading Catholic who thought independence inevitable,

see Ellen H. Smith, Charles Carroll of Carrollton (Cambridge, Mass., 1942).

Barker, Maryland, 43-49.

22
Washington tried but could not get Germans to immigrate to Virginia;
Fitzpatrick, ed., Washington Writings, 3: 185-186.

23
The vestries were powerful, no doubt, but they could not control the
clergys' education, ordination or appointment; Boyd, ed., Jefferson Papers,
1: 49-51.

24
Southerners themselves admitted similar views: see Houston's comments
in Adams, ed., Adams Papers, 2: 183.

25
Charles Sydnor, Gentlemen Freeholders: Political Practices in Washington's Virginia (Chapel Hill, 1952), passim. Barker, Maryland, 183.

26
Virgina probably filled as rapidly, Historical Statistics, 756.

27
Population jumped in both colonies: Historical Statistics, 756.

28
All speculated in western land: Washington lived furtherest west.
See Mays, Pendleton, 1: 68-70. Fitzpatrick, ed., Washington Writings, 3: 1-4,
144-146. Meade, Henry, 233-234.

29
Curtis Nettels, George Washington and American Independence (Boston,
1951), 65-66.

30
Tobacco crops alone averaged an estimated ₤200,000 to ₤300,000 sterling
a year to the middle 1750's, Historical Statistics, 767.

31
Mays, Pendleton, 1: 117 ff.

334

32
   See Jefferson's comments, Ch. VII.

33
   Gipson, American Revolution, 43-46.

34
   A full transcription of the loan lists appear in Mays, Pendleton,
1: 181-183. Just before Robinson died, he sought to have the colony
borrow ₤240,000; where all would have gone in anyone's guess; ₤140,000
was to be loaned at 5% interest; presumably the other ₤100,000 would go
into the treasury to cover Robinson's fraud: Meade, Henry, 164-166.

35
   Sheridan, "British Credit Crisis," Jour. Eco. Hist., 20: 175-182,
shows that Virginia debtors numbered over 1, 100 with no prospects of
immediate ability to pay. The full meaning of the situation is best
demonstrated by the fact that a man like Edmund Pendleton was verging on
bankruptcy in the 1770's and this despite the fact that he had several means
of income from his profession, offices, and land investments, and had
converted his crops to wheat: Mays, Pendleton, 1: 117.

36
   Meade, Henry, 132.

37
   Meade, Henry, 172-174.

38
   Meade, Henry, 195-196.

39
   See Lee to ____, March, 1768, where he calls the Townshend duties
"not perhaps literally, a violation of our rights," and, later, to Dickinson,
July 25, 1768, where he acknowledged a debt to the Pennsylvanian; Ballagh, ed.,
Lee Letters, 1: 27 and 29.

335

40
Indebtedness among them to the Treasurer of Virginia ranged from £100 to £14,921, Virginia currency, and to English merchants from £100-£18,900, sterling.

41
Ballagh, ed., Lee Letters, 1: 19, 177-179.

42
Ballagh, ed., Lee Letters, 1: 40, 68, 72, 86, 93-94, 105.

43
Hutchinson, ed., Madison Papers, 1: 105.

44
Meade, Henry, 330 ff.

45
May, 1775, and the brief battles with Dunmore's troops thereafter, Force, ed., American Archives, 4th Series, 2: 477.

46
Follow May's analysis, Pendleton, 1: 276-2: 139.

47
Boyd, ed., Jefferson Papers, 1: 407. Benjamin Harrison was also suspected of being an anti-independence Whig. Both men were recalled, June 20, 1776; however, neither went home before July 2, 1776. Braxton had, without question joined the Dickinson forces: Burnett, ed., Letters, 1: 420 ff.

48
Historical Statistics, 767. Although the figures for Virginia and Maryland are given together, the tonnage values for each colony are given in 1769, and these can be assumed as a constant for the decade. Maryland expanded relative to Virginia and her own economy previous to the 1770's. Also, see Barker, Maryland, 341 ff.

49
Barker, Maryland, 350-365.

50
See notes 10 and 16 above. The popular support of Maryland

traditional Whigs was strong: in August, 1775, Tilghman, Johnson, Paca, Goldsborough, received 16 votes for positions of control within the Council of Safety; Thomas Stone, 15, and Alexander 12. Chase polled 13, and, as yet, he had not declared for independence. Cal. Md. State Papers, 8. In Nov., 1775, Alexander received more votes for the delegation of Cecil County to the Provincial Convention than any other candidate (131), Johnson, Alexander, 53.

51
Historical Statistics, 768, 772, compared to New England, 757; 758, 759-60.

52
The breakdown in Carolina exports and imports can be obtained by use of the statistics in Historical Statistics, 768, and those given in Charles C. Crittenden, The Commerce of North Carolina 1763-1789, passim., and Sellers, Charleston Business, passim.

53
The backcountry contained over one-half the white population. The large proportion of returns on rice and indigo crops, fell then, to an extremely small white population, 30,000-34,000, less the number of men in Charleston who were not planters, perhaps not more than 3,000 heads of families.

54
Historical Statistics, 756.

55
Rice prices remained above recession year prices, and in 1772 hit an all-time high; at the same time volumes increased far beyond proportional population growth: Historical Statistics, 756, 768, 772.

56
Richard Walsh, Charleston's Sons of Liberty (Columbia, S. C., 1959), 56-58.

337

57
New England had a population approaching 700,000 and around 175,000 outstanding; South Carolina with 70,000 whites and 106,000 in 1768, issued more in the 1770's, and had 298,000 outstanding in 1774, Historical Statistics, 773-774.

58
Alden, The South in the Revolution, 146-152.

59
"Middleton Correspondence," S. C. Hist. and Genea. Mag., 27: 123.

60
Drayton, Memoirs of the American Revolution, 2: 172-173.

61
Walton was an apprentice carpenter in the 1760's, and admitted to the bar in 1774; Hall was from Connecticut and main instigator of the Association; Houston was a critic of the planter class, and Gwinnett a newcomer to politics: Sanderson, Bio. of the Signers, 5: 263 ff.; Butterfield, ed., Adams Papers, 2: 183, Jenkins, Gwinnett, 63 ff.

62
J. J. Zubly, a Swiss immigrant; see Butterfield, ed., Adams Papers, 2: 204.

63
Hooper and Penn; in April, 1776, the Convention provided that the delegates might vote for independence, but it did not feel it necessary to remove Hewes. Force, ed., American Archives, 4th Series, 5: 859-860. Hewes held the news from Congress, Friedenwald, Independence, 97.

64
Burnett, ed., Letters, 1: 89; Proceedings of the Conventions of Maryland, 83-84, 141-142.

65
Butterfield, ed., Adams Papers, 2: 147 ff. Sabine, ed., Smith Memoirs, 1: 262-263.

338

66
  Johnston, ed., Jay Correspondence, 1: 67.

67
  See n. 10 above. Other than Henry, Virginians to the first Continental Congress took the position that Parliament had the right to regulate trade: see Butterfield, ed., Adams Papers, 2: 120.

68
  Butterfield, ed., Adams Papers, 2: 183.

69
  J. J. Zubly: see his own The Law of Liberty (Phil., 1775), and Butterfield, ed., Adams Papers, 2: 204.

Chapter VII. Thomas Jefferson and John Rutledge

1
I have relied heavily upon Richard Barry's biography of John Rutledge
for this and much of the material that follows. Rutledge, having been the
sort of man that he was, remains an illusive, vague individual, and Barry
has dealt admirably with the interpretive problems Rutledge left behind.
On one issue, however, Barry over-estimates Rutledge's actual influence,
namely, that Rutledge was responsible for the phrasing of the power of
Parliament in the First Congress' Declaration of Rights and Grievances:
Rutledge, 162-163. Compare his interpretation to that given here and in
Ch. V.

2
Barry, Rutledge, 12.

3
Barry, Rutledge, passim.

4
Alden, South in the Revolution, 150-151; Barry, Rutledge, 135-154.

5
Barry, Rutledge, 29-32, 149-150.

6
Ford, ed., Journals, 1: 24.

7
Butterfield, ed., Adams Papers, 2: 126.

8
A Letter From Freeman of South Carolina, to the Deputies of North-
America . . . (Charles-Town, 1774), 15.

9
Galloway had discussed his plan with John Rutledge even before Congress
began. He wrote William Franklin on Sept. 3, 1774, that he had talked with
Rutledge "whose sentiments and mine differ in no one particular . . . ."

340

Aspinwall Papers, Collections of the Massachusetts Historical Society, 4th Series, 10 (Boston, 1871), 706.

10
  Butterfield, ed., Adams Papers, 2: 137.

11
  Butterfield, ed., Adams Papers, 2: 143-144 n.; Burnett, ed., Letters, 1: 51-59.

12
  Barry, Rutledge, 165 ff.

13
  See n. 1 above, and Barry, Rutledge, 162-163.

14
  McCrady, South Carolina, 735 ff.

15
  Edward Rutledge to Thomas Bee, Oct., 1774, Burnett, ed., Letters, 1: 80.

16
  At Congress, Gadsden had become "more violent" about retaliation against England: Burnett, ed., Letters, 1: 80; Barry, Rutledge, 169-170.

17
  Drayton, Memoirs, 1: 169.

18
  Drayton, Memoirs, 1: 170.

19
  Drayton, Memoirs, 1: 172-173.

20
  Drayton's career and politics are interesting. As one of the wealthiest men in South Carolina and a member of the Council, he was against economic coercion in 1769, and in 1774, he supported Rutledge in the Convention. Then, he broke completely with his previous stance, and supported Gadsden and non-importation. See his own Letter From Freeman, 4; Drayton, Memoirs, 1: 171, 186; he was an exponent of independence by April, 1776, Drayton, Memoirs, 2: 254-255.

341

21
McCrady, South Carolina, 780 ff.

22
Drayton, Memoirs, 1: 183-186.

23
Barry, Rutledge, 149.

24
Jefferson's property holdings in 1774 included 42 slaves, though
he was forced, from time to time, to sell slaves in order to pay his debts,
and around 3,000 acres of land (which had grown to 10, 647 acres by 1794):
Jefferson's Farm Book, ed. by Edwin M. Betts(Princeton, 1953), 5, 15, 32.

25
Boyd, ed., Jefferson Papers, 1: 61.

26
Boyd, ed., Jefferson Papers, 1: 98-99.

27
Boyd, ed., Jefferson Papers, 1: 51.

28
July 26, 1774, Boyd, ed., Jefferson Papers, 1: 117-118

29
Boyd, ed., Jefferson Papers, 1: 143-144.

30
(Williamsburg, 1774). The following discussion is taken from the
manuscript copy of the Summary View in Boyd, ed., Jefferson Papers, 1: 121-135;
see 1: Appendix 1.

31
125.

32
133.

33
134.

34
134-135

Chapter VIII. The Congress and American Independence

1
Burnett, ed., Letters, 1: 514

2
Johnston, ed., Jay Corespondence, 1: 67.

3
Archives of Maryland, 11: 477-479.

4
The committee had made some revisions, but the only major one was that pertaining to the slave trade.

5
Adams' probable remarks, Adams, ed., Adams Works, 9: 409-410; Burnett, ed., Letters, 1: 416-417.

6
The New Jersey delegation had not been elected until June 22, 1776, and there is some question whether Richard Stockton was present on July 2. Francis Hopkinson, John Witherspoon and Abraham Clark were all expected to vote for independence: John D. Sergeant to John Adams, June 15, 1776, Adams, ed., Adams Works, 9: 425, n. 1-4.

7
Unfortunately, only Jefferson's account of the actual votes on July 1, remains: Boyd, ed., Jefferson Papers, 1: 306-315. Jefferson worked from notes, but his acccunt was written a month after the event. There is some reason to think that New York may have voted no on July 1st, and that Jefferson confused New York's action on that day with New York's refusal to vote on July 2. Paca's probable action is derived from John Adams' letter to Samuel Chase, July 1, 1776, Adams, ed., Adams Works, 9: 416; cf. Archives of Maryland, 11: 277-279.

35
Boyd, ed., Jefferson Papers, 1: n. 1, 159-160.

36
Ford, ed., Journals, 2: 79, 81, 84; Burnett, Letters, 1: 118-119;
Barry, Rutledge, 177.

37
Boyd, ed., Jefferson Papers, 1: 165, 269.

38
Barry, Rutledge, 188-190.

39
Ballagh, ed., Lee Letters, 1: 177-179, 184-185.

40
Braxton, Address to the Convention of Virginia, 10-14.

41
Drayton, Memoirs, 2: 172

42
Drayton, Memoirs, 2: 173.

43
Drayton, Memoirs, 2: 173. It is clear that Drayton and Arthur Middleton
were using Gadsden, and had little sympathy for him, "Middleton Correspondence,"
S.C. Hist. and Genea. Mag., 27: 124.

44
Barry, Rutledge, 191-192.

45
Barry, Rutledge, 192.

46
Barry, Rutledge, 192-193

47
Journal of the General Assembly of South Carolina, 1776 . . . (2 parts,
Columbia, S.C., 1906-1909), 1: 69-71.

48
The following discussion is from Jefferson's second and third drafts
of a constitution for Virginia in Boyd, ed., Jefferson Papers, 1: 34 ff.

49
and 358; 352 and 362.

50
353 and 363.

51
353 and 363.

345

8

Again, evidence is scant, but it is probable that some New Yorkers, Pennsylvanians, and South Carolinians hoped to obstruct the next day. Caucuses revealed that there was no hope for such an action. At any rate, John Adams remained restrained until July 2nd; Adams, ed., Familiar Letters, 193-194.

BIBLIOGRAPHICAL ESSAY

In the main, this dissertation is based upon the correspondence and writings of over eighty members of the First and Second Continental Congress. A search was made on each member of the Congress in an effort to find sufficient evidence for a fair judgment on the man's views of government and independence, and to place the individual in the proper social context. The papers of the more outstanding members of the Congress have received attention from archivists and editors, and their more pertinent works have been published. Materials on Patriots of secondary standing were more difficult to find, but a careful search of the numerous collections mentioned below revealed a fair number of letters by men long forgotten. Moreover, an attempt was made to accumulate evidence on the Patriots by researching the voting records of individuals in their local assemblies. All this information provided a substantial basis for a revaluation of political division in the Continental Congress and in the colonies. The holdings of the John Carter Brown Library, Brown University, Providence, R.I., made such research much simpler than it otherwise might have been. Anyone who has worked in published sources of early America knows the extent and value of the holdings of the John Carter Brown.

1

Guides

The amount of archival material on the first Patriots is extensive, and Philip M. Hamer's Guide to Archives and Manuscripts in the United States

347

(New Haven, 1961), serves as the best starting place for a search of papers relating to American independence. A number of the more important repositories have their own individual guides. A wealth of this material has been published, but unfortunately no one guide can be used to check published sources against archival sources. The best single aid for this purpose is the annually published Writings on American History (New York, New Haven, Washington, 1904_____), done largely under the editorial guidance of Miss Grace G. Griffin. This aid may be supplemented by William Mathews, ed., American Diaries . . . to the Year 1860 (Los Angeles, 1945), and by two helpful but outdated guides to public documents: A.C. Griffin, "Bibliography of American Historical Societies," and A.R. Hasse, "Materials for a Bibliography of the Public Archives of the Thirteen Original Colonies," in the Annual Report of the American Historical Association for the years 1905 and 1906 respectively. The researcher will find that the sixth volume of Justin Windsor's Narrative and Critical History of America (Boston, 1889), and Charles Evans' American Bibliography (12 vols., New York, 1941-1942) contain near definitive lists of works published during the period of the Revolution and the early nineteenth century. All these guides reveal a remarkable amount of published sources on independence. Two other works are helpful: those who are interested in early assembly records will find a listing of extant records (and reference made to lost records) in William S. Jenkins, ed., A Guide to the Microfilm Collection of Early State Records (Washington, 1950), and, more important, is Thomas R. Adams' soon to be published, Independence: The Growth of an Idea (Printer's proofs, John Carter Brown Library, Brown University). Adams' work is distinguished among bibliographical studies on published

sources, and historians interested in pamphlet literature and independence will do well to begin here. For secondary sources there is The Harvard Guide to American History (Cambridge, Mass., 1954); two brief critical introductions to Revolutionary historiography must serve until a more definitive work is published: Edmund S. Morgan, The American Revolution, A Review of Changing Interpretations (Washington, 1958), and Jack P. Greene, "The Flight from Determinism: A Review of the Recent Literature on the Coming of the American Revolution," South Atlantic Quarterly, 61 (Spring, 1962), 235-259. Last of all, a useful aid is L.A. Harper, "Recent Contributions to American Economic History: American Economic History to 1789," Journal of Economic History, 19 (March, 1959), 1-24.

2

Primary Sources

Public Documents.

Two general collections which contain public documents are important for the study of independence and the Patriots. Peter. Force, ed., American Archives: Consisting of a Collection of Authentick Records, State Papers, Debates, and Letters .... (9 vols., Washington, 1837-1848), contains documents that run into the thousands. Force edited more important parts of the proceedings of Parliament, provincial assemblies and conventions, and included these together with official announcements, newspaper articles, letters, and pamphlets. The first six volumes of W.C. Ford, ed., The Journals of the

349

Continental Congress, 1774-1789, (34 vols., Washington, 1904-1937), are, of course, crucial for the study of independence. A smaller collection that provides convenient reference to major documents from 1765 to 1776 is Henry S. Commager, ed., Documents of American History (7th ed., New York, 1963).

New England: The public papers of New England used in this study are: Nathaniel Bouton, ed., Provincial Papers . . . Documents and Records Relative to the Province of New Hampshire, 1623-1800 (31 vols., Concord, etc., N.H., 1867-1907): particularly volumes 7, 8, and 10; Joseph B. Walker, ed., New Hampshire's Five Provincial Congresses (Concord, N.H., 1905); Journals of the Honourable House of Representatives of Massachusetts Bay (Boston, 1723-1778); Journal of Each Provincial Congress of Massachusetts (Boston, 1838); Papers Relating to Public Events in Massachusetts Preceeding the American Revolution (Philadelphia, 1856); John R. Bartlett, ed., Records of the Colony of Rhode Island and Providence Plantations in New England (10 vols., Providence, 1856-1865), the weaknesses of which are reported by David Lovejoy in his study of Rhode Island (see below: Special Studies, New England); volumes 13, 14 and 15 of The Public Records of the Colony of Connecticut (15 vols., Hartford, 1850-1890) are most relevant for the Revolution.

Middle Colonies: For the Middle Colonies the Journal of the Votes and Proceedings of the General Assembly of the Colony of New-York from 1766 to 1776 . . . (Albany, 1820) contains sufficient information for a study of New York politics in depth; also important is E.B. O'Callaghan and B. Fernow, eds., Documents Relative to the Colonial History of the State of New York (15 vols., Albany, 1853-1887), and E.B. O'Callaghan, ed., Calendar of Historical Manuscripts Relating to the War of the Revolution in New York . . . (2 vols.,

350

Albany, 1866-1868); also used in locating public acts of secondary figures were Henry Onderdonk, ed., Documents and Letters . . . of Queens County, New York . . . (New York, 1846), and Revolutionary Incidents of Suffolk and Kings Counties, New York . . . (New York, 1849); Archives of the State of New Jersey, 1st Series, 10 (Newark, 1886), 18 (Trenton, 1893), 29 (Paterson, 1917), and 31 (Somerville, 1923) were used for the study of that colony; and for Pennsylvania, various volumes in the nine series of Pennsylvania Archives have information of importance for the Revolution; volumes 7 and 8 of the 8th Series (Harrisburg, 1935) contain the votes and proceedings of the Assembly, 1764-1776.

Southern Colonies: volume 11 of the older Archives of Maryland (Baltimore, 1892) proved of use for the delegates to Congress, as did Calendar of Maryland State Papers, The Red Books, no. 4 (Part 1, Annapolis, 1950); the votes and proceedings of the Assembly are in Archives of Maryland, 31-32 (Baltimore, 1946-1947); The Proceedings of the Conventions . . . of Maryland . . . in 1774, 1775, & 1776 (Baltimore, 1836) indicates that the attitudes of the clerks there were similar to those in all the conventions: they kept very skimpy journals; J.P. Kennedy, ed., Journals of the House of Burgesses (4 vols., Williamsburg, 1905-1907), the Colonial Records of North Carolina (10 vols., Raleigh, 1886-1890), A.S. Salley, ed., Journal of the General Assembly of South Carolina . . . 1776 . . . (2 Parts, Columbia, 1906-1909), the Journal of the South Carolina Council of Safety, Collections of the South Carolina Historical Society, 2 (Charleston, 1858), 22-74, constitute the remainder of the public documents consulted for this study.

351

Letters, Papers, and Works.

Members of the Congress: An exceptionally good general collection of letters by Revolutionary leaders exists: E. C. Burnett, ed., Letters of Members of the Continental Congress (8 vols., Washington, 1921-1936). Burnett made a thorough search of the archives and published the most pertinent letters before he wrote his history of the Congress. The volume of letters relating to the First and Second Congresses should, however, be used with some caution since Burnett inserted post independence sources without adequate evaluation. Collections of individuals' papers are abundant and many are indispensable. Foremost among the new editions of papers of Revolutionary leaders is L.H. Butterfield, ed., The Adams Papers, Series 1; Diaries and Autobiography (4 vols., Cambridge, Mass., 1961). John Adams' diaries are the major, unofficial source for Congressional debates. Since the Butterfield edition is not yet complete, it is necessary to supplement it with Charles F. Adams, ed., The Works of John Adams . . . (10 vols., Boston, 1850-1856), Charles F. Adams, ed., Familiar Letters of John Adams and His Wife . . . (Boston, 1875), and the first volume of The Warren-Adams Letters, Collections of the Massachusetts Historical Society, 71-72 (Boston, 1917 and 1925). Henry A. Cushing, ed., The Writings of Samuel Adams (4 vols., New York, 1904-1907) contains valuable public papers as well as personal letters. Josiah Bartlett of New Hampshire left a fair number of letters and papers. The New Hampshire Historical Society at Concord, holds two boxes of Bartlett Papers and a substantial typed manuscript (139 pages) of Bartlett Letters; of limited use are: "The Correspondence of Josiah Bartlett," The Historical Magazine, 6 (March, 1862), 73-78, and Letters by Josiah Bartlett, William Whipple and Others

352

Written Before and During the Revolution (Philadelphia, 1889). Hugh Hastings, ed., The Public Papers of George Clinton (10 vols., New York and Albany, 1899-1914), does not reveal Clinton as well as one would like, while the brief "Letters of Thomas Cushing, from 1767 to 1775," in Collections of the Massachusetts Historical Society, 4th Series, 4 (Boston, 1858), 347-372, are illuminating. The Deane Papers, Connecticut Historical Society Collections, 23 (1930), and The Deane Papers, Collections of the New-York Historical Society for the Year 1886, 19 (New York, 1887), the first of five volumes of Deane papers, constitute prime sources for Congress and New England leadership. Deane made some errors in dating that are not corrected in the Connecticut volume. Of all the first Patriots, John Dickinson deserves greater attention than he has received. Both the historical societies of Pennsylvania and Delaware hold papers of Dickinson, and Paul L. Ford edited some of these: The Writings of John Dickinson, Memoirs of the Historical Society of Pennsylvania, 14 (Philadelphia, 1895). J.H. Powell has done a careful reconstruction of the manuscript of Dickinson's speech against independence: Pennsylvania Magazine of History and Biography, 65 (Oct., 1941), 458-481. Many of the more important writings of Eliphalet Dyer are published in Julian P. Boyd, ed., The Susquehannah Papers (4 vols., Wilkes-Barre, 1930-1933). William Ellery's personal papers and some letters for these years are preserved by the Rhode Island Historical Society at Providence: Channing-Ellery Papers, M-Ch-1 (1765-1777). Benjamin Franklin left an enormous amount of correspondence. For pusposes of this study, volumes 7 and 8 of the Federal Edition of John Bigelow's The Works of Benjamin Franklin (Philadelphia, 1904) and Verner W. Crane, ed., Franklin's Letters to the Press, 1758-1775 (Chapel

353

Hill, N.C., 1950) proved sufficient; Julian P. Boyd presents a carefully
analyzed copy of Franklin's confederation proposals in the appendix to
Anglo-American Union: Joseph Galloway's Plans to Preserve the British Empire,
1774-1778 (Philadelphia, 1941). Elbridge Gerry's important political
correspondence is reproduced in James T. Austin, The Life and Times of Elbridge
Gerry (2 vols., Boston, 1828-1829). Hancock's career can be followed in
Abraham E. Brown, ed., John Hancock, His Book (Boston, 1898), and "Letters
of John Hancock, 1776," Massachusetts Historical Society Proceedings, 60
(Boston, 1927), 98-116; George E. Hastings, The Life and Works of Francis
Hopkinson (Chicago, 1926) contains some Revolutionary writings by one of
America's more prominent early literary figures. Henry P. Johnston, ed.,
The Correspondence and Public Papers of John Jay (4 vols., New York, 1890-1893)
will soon be superseded by another edition of Jay's papers. Another indispensable
collection is Julian P. Boyd, ed., The Papers of Thomas Jefferson (Princeton,
1950   ); it can be supplemented by Edwin M. Betts, Jefferson's Farm Book
(Princeton, 1953). Although James C. Ballagh's edition of The Letters of
Richard Henry Lee (2 vols., New York, 1911-1914), is brief, Ballagh included
seemingly unimportant personal letters that make the collection a useful source
for one of the most powerful figures in Congress. The R.R. Livingston Papers
(1775-1777), Bancroft Collection, New York Public Library, are useful for New
York. Several small collections provide substantial information on alliances in
Congress and local politics: "Correspondence of Honorable Arthur Middleton,"
The South Carolina Historical and Genealogical Magazine, 27 (July, 1926), 107-
155, William T. Read, Life and Correspondence of George Read (Philadelphia,
1870), George H. Ryden, Letters to and from Caesar Rodney, 1756-1784

354

(Philadelphia, 1933), and Leon DeValinger, ed., "Rodney Letters," <u>Delaware</u> <u>History</u>, 1 (July, 1946), 99-110; 3 (Sept., 1948), 105-115. The record kept by Richard Smith is better than that of John Adams for some of the votes in the Congress: <u>Richard Smith Diary,</u> in <u>The American Historical Review,</u> 1 (Jan. and Apr., 1896), 288-310 and 493-516. Volume one of Otis G. Hammond, ed., <u>Letters and Papers of Major-General John Sullivan</u> (3 vols., Concord, N.H., 1930-1939), <u>The Papers of Charles Thomson, Collections of the New York</u> <u>Historical Society Publication Fund Series</u> (New York, 1879), are not as informative as one might expect for the papers of the Congressional clerk for fifteen years. Thomas W. Balch, ed., <u>Willing, Letters and Papers</u> (Philadelphia, 1922) need supplementation from other sources. The three boxes of Ward Manuscripts at the Rhode Island Historical Society, Providence, contain information on William Ellery and Stephen Hopkins as well, and Bernard Knollenberg, ed., <u>Correspondence of Governor Samuel Ward, May 1775-March 1776</u> (Providence, 1952) is admirably done, though Knollenberg over-estimates Ward's property holdings. The volumes of letters covering the years of crisis in John C. Fitzpatrick, ed., <u>The Writings of George Washington</u> (39 vols., Washington, 1931-1944) are a primary source for independence sentiment in Virginia and in the army. Lastly, <u>The Works of James Wilson</u> (3 vols., Philadelphia, 1804) was edited in Wilson's favor by Bird Wilson, and John Rodgers, ed., <u>The Works of John Witherspoon</u> (2nd edition, 4 vols., Philadelphia, 1802) includes mainly those papers of Witherspoon that relate to his politics and ministry.

Other Collections and Papers: Various sources other than those on Congress members contain substantial data on American independence. Those

used for this work are as follows: Part 2, of the Aspinwall Papers, Collections of the Massachusetts Historical Society, 4th Series, 10 (Boston, 1871); The Bowdoin and Temple Papers, Collections of the Massachusetts Historical Society, 6th Series, 9 (Boston, 1897) and 7th Series, 6 (Boston, 1907); The Revolutionary Correspondence of Governor Nicholas Cook, 1775-1781, Proceedings of the American Antiquarian Society, 36 (Boston, 1927), 231-353; Fitch Papers, Connecticut Historical Society Collections, 18 (1920); Harold C. Syrett, ed., The Papers of Alexander Hamilton, 1 (New York, 1961); The Ingersoll Papers, New Haven Historical Society Papers, 9 (1918), 201-472; William T. Hutchinson and William M.E. Kachal, eds., The Papers of James Madison, 1 (Chicago, 1962); Charles H. Hall, Life and Letters of Samuel Holden Parsons (Binghamton, N.Y., 1905); W.H.W. Sabine, ed., Historical Memoirs of William Smith (2 vols., New York, 1956 and 1958), an extremely important source for New York and the Revolution; and Selections from the Letter-Books of Thomas Wharton in The Pennsylvania Magazine of History and Biography, 33-34 (1909 and 1910).

Pamphlets.

Consult Thomas R. Adams, Independence: the Growth of an Idea, for pertinent information about editions, number of copies printed, month advertised, and other facts about the pamphlets cited below pertaining to arguments concerning the Empire.

/Adams, John_7, Thoughts on Government: Applicable to the Present State of Affairs of the American Colonies . . . (Philadelphia, 1776).

/Adams, Samuel_7, An Appeal to the World (Boston, 1769).

Bland, Richard, An Inquiry into the Rights of the British Colonies . . . (Williamsburg, 1766) .

/Braxton, Carter_7, An Address to the Convention of the Colony and Ancient Dominion of Virginia . . . (Philadelphia, 1776).

/Chandler, Thomas Bradbury_7, What Think Ye of the Congress Now? (New York, 1775).

Dickinson, John, A Speech, Delivered in the House of Assembly . . . (Philadelphia, 1764).

_____, A Reply to a Piece Called the Speech of Joseph Galloway . . . (Philadelphia, 1764).

/_____ _7, The Late Regulations Respecting the British Colonies on the Continent of America Considered . . . (Philadelphia, 1765).

/_____ _7, An Address to the Committee of Correspondence in Barbados (Philadelphia, 1766).

/_____ _7 , Letters from a Farmer in Pennsylvania, to the Inhabitants of the British Colonies (Philadelphia, 1768).

/_____ _7, A New Essay on the Constitutional Power of Great-Britain Over the Colonies in America . . . (Philadelphia, 1774)

/Drayton, William Henry_7, A Letter from Freeman of South Carolina, To the Deputies of North-America . . . (Charles-Town, 1774).

/Fitch, Thomas_7, Reasons Why the British Colonies in America Should Not Be Charged With Internal Taxes . . . (New Haven, 1764).

/Franklin, Benjamin _7, The Causes of the Present Distractions in America Explained . . . (New York, 1774).

Galloway, Joseph, A Speech of Joseph Galloway, Esq. . . . . (Philadelphia, 1764).

/_____ _7, A Candid Examination of the Mutual Claims of Great Britain, and the Colonies . . . (New York, 1775).

357

/ Hamilton, Alexander_7 , A Full Vindication of the Measures of the Congress . . .
    (New York, 1774).

Hancock, John, An Oration; Delivered March 5, 1774 . . . to Commemorate the
    Bloody Tragedy of the Fifth of March 1770 . . . (Boston, 1774).

Hewes, Joseph, A Collection of Occurrences and Facts . . . (/ Providence?_7,
    1775).

/ Jefferson, Thomas_7 , A Summary View of the Rights of British America
    (Williamsburg, 1774).

/ Lee, Charles_7 , Strictures on a Pamphlet Entitled, " A Friendly Address to All
    Reasonable Americans" . . . (Philadelphia, 1774); the New London,
    1775, edition with a preface by Silas Deane was consulted for
    use in the present work.

/ Livingston, Philip_7 , The Other Side of the Question: Or, A Defense of
    North-America . . . (New York, 1774).

Otis, James, The Rights of the British Colonies Asserted and Proved . . .
    (Boston, 1764).

/ _____ _7, A Vindication of the British Colonies . . . (Boston, 1765).

/ Paine, Thomas_7 , Common Sense (Philadelphia, 1776).

Witherspoon, John, The Dominion of Providence Over the Passions of Men
    (Philadelphia, 1776).

/ Wilson, James_7 , Consideration on the Nature and Extent of the Legislative
    Authority of the British Parliament . . . (Philadelphia, 1774).

Zubly, John Joachim, The Law of Liberty (Philadelphia, 1775).

Histories by Contemporaries.

The three following historical works are representative of Revolutionary

historical writing. All have been used in the present work: John Drayton, Memoirs of the American Revolution . . . (2 vols., Charleston, 1821), a reliable source on South Carolina, but openly anti-Rutledge and anti-Gadsden; Thomas Hutchinson, History of Massachusetts Bay, From the Year 1750, until June, 1774 (3 vols., London, 1828), one of the finest of all early histories, if Loyalist in point of view; and, Mrs. Mercy Warren, History of the Rise, Progress, and Termination of the American Revolution (3 vols., Boston, 1805) by a close friend of John Adams.

Statistics.

More evidence on colonial trade and commerce for the years following 1763 is available than commonly supposed. Section Z of Historical Statistics of the United States (Washington, 1957) published by the United States Bureau of Census contains a compilation of data for the colonial years. The editors have checked export and import figures against the documents in the Public Records Office in London, and the population figures relating to colonial America are probably as accurate as any of the demographic studies available to historians. Historical Statistics can be used in conjunction with A.H. Cole, Wholesale Commodity Prices in the United States 1700-1861 (Cambridge, Mass., 1938). The Henry Knox returns of Revolutionary military participants is analyzed by C.C. Vermeule, "Number of Soldiers in the Revolution," New Jersey Historical Society Proceedings, New Series, 7 (July, 1922), 223-227, but should be revised consonant with more precise population figures than those used by Vermeule. Lastly, I am indebted to Forrest McDonald, Brown University, for loan of land settlement figures on Connecticut; the approximations stated in Chapter IV of this work are based on his notes from a manuscript volume

entitled "Finance and Currency," 5, Connecticut State Archives, Hartford.
Any errors in estimates, are, of course, my own.

3

Secondary Sources

General Histories.

Although the number of general works that touch on the first Patriots
and independence is large, comparatively few are of use to the scholar.
Several multi-volume works on the Revolution are representative of interpretation and scholarship. First is George Bancroft's History of the United
States (10 vols., Boston, 1834-1875); Bancroft's volumes on the Revolution
stand as among the most thoroughly researched histories, and his influence
is still strong. Henry Belcher, The First American Civil War (2 vols., London,
1911), is as pointedly English Tory as Bancroft's work is American Whig.
A third approach to the Revolution, and one that would have given Bancroft
pause, is Lawrence Henry Gipson's monumental study: The British Empire Before
the American Revolution (9 vols., to date, New York, 1936_____). The final
volumes will deal with the outbreak of the Revolution, and Gipson's The Coming
of the American Revolution 1763-1775 (New York, 1954) probably represents in
summary what will be said in detail. Among the many studies that deal with
the Revolution in two volumes, John C. Miller's The Origins of the American
Revolution (2nd edition, Stanford, 1959) and Triumph of Freedom 1775-1783
(Boston, 1948) are evenly balanced in coverage and interpretation. Lastly, a
good one volume summary of the first years of revolt and the war is John R.
Alden, The American Revolution 1775-1783 (New York, 1954). These works by no
means exhaust the list of general histories available to the researcher.

360

Special Studies.

Intercolonial: Randolph G. Adams, Political Ideas of the American Revolution (3rd ed., New York, 1958), a pioneer work, first published in 1922 has been the subject of considerable revision. Thomas P. Abernethy, Western Lands and the American Revolution (New York, 1937) contains intricate and detailed information. The standard work on the Declaration is, of course, Carl L. Becker, The Declaration of Independence (2nd ed., New York, 1942); Becker, as was his wont, overstated his case for antagonisms to independence. A.C. Bining, British Regulation of the Colonial Iron Industry (Philadelphia, 1933) is marred by the failure to develop particulars of regulation and the iron industry. Carl Bridenbaugh's Cities in Revolt: Urban Life in America, 1743-1776 (New York, 1955) and Mitre and Sceptre: Transatlantic Faiths, Ideas, Personalities and Politics, 1689-1775 (New York, 1962) are more than useful; the former presents a massive amount of information on men and society in colonial cities, and the latter argues the importance of religion as a factor in Anglo-American conflict. The Continental Congress (New York, 1941) by Edmund C. Burnett stands as the standard history of that institution from its inception to its demise. Dora Mae Clark, The Rise of the British Treasury: Colonial Administration in the Eighteen Century (New Haven, 1960) shows the power of the Treasury in policy-making. Oliver M. Dickerson has gone into detail regarding enforcement of commercial regulations in The Navigation Acts and the American Revolution (Philadelphia, 1951), and his careful analysis of the laws, and their operation in the colonies, lays a sound basis for original interpretation. Elisha P. Douglass, Rebels and Democrats (Chapel Hill, 1955), strikes a theme of Patriot conflict on the extent of reform. Jack P. Greene, The Quest for Power: The Lower Houses

of Assembly in the Southern Royal Colonies, 1689-1775 (Chapel Hill, 1963), details the growth of the power of representative bodies. Robert A. East, Business Enterprise in the American Revolutionary Era (New York, 1938) is useful. The details of the politics of independence is handled best by Herbert Friedenwald, The Declaration of Independence (New York, 1904); of all historians who touch on the politics of independence, Friedenwald is the most detailed, accurate, and substantive, and a new work on the Declaration by David Hawke, A Transaction of Freemen (New York, 1965) is an admirable study of ideas and the Declaration. Though the interpretation of Merrill Jensen has often been attacked, his The Articles of Confederation (Madison, 1940), has not been supplanted by a comparable monograph. A few worthwhile details are in Alfred E. Jones, American Members of the Inns of Court (London, 1924). Michael Kraus, Intercolonial Aspects of American Culture on the Eve of Revolution . . . (New York, 1928) is more indicative of the lack of contact among colonials than the extent of cultural intercourse. The colonial flour industry awaits a study equal to the importance of the topic, particularly in regard to the relationships between grower, manufacturers, exporters, and the bakers' guilds; Charles B. Kuhlmann touches the surface of the topic in The Development of the Flour Milling Industry in the United States (New York, 1929). Charles H. McIlwain's The American Revolution: A Constitutional Interpretation (New York, 1923), is the classic study of constitutional theory and rebellion and has bred a host of followers, none of whom are more original than Edmund S. and Helen M. Morgan in their work: The Stamp Act Crisis: Prologue to Revolution (Chapel Hill, 1953). A solid but general work is William H. Nelson, The American Tory (Oxford, 1961). Allan Nevins, The

362

American States during and after the Revolution, 1775-1789 (New York, 1924)
is rich in detail and one of the few works that covers all the colonies from
1775-1776. Chilton Williamson, American Suffrage (Princeton, 1960) summarizes
colonial laws pertaining to the right to vote. Arthur M. Schlesinger, The
Colonial Merchant and the American Revolution (New York, 1917), is the standard
study of the topic. Carl Ubbelohde, The Vice-Admiralty Courts and the American
Revolution (Chapel Hill, 1960) show the importance of this administrative branch
in producing colonial hostility.

New England: Special studies of the three regions are uneven in extent
and value, and New England has received the most attention. Of a general
nature, Alice M. Baldwin, The New England Clergy and the American Revolution
(Durham, N.C., 1928), reveals not only the thought but also the militancy of
the calvinist clergy. For New Hampshire: Charles B. Kinney's Church & State
The Struggle for Separation in New Hampshire 1630-1900 (New York, 1945) and
Richard F. Upton, Revolutionary New Hampshire (Hanover, N.H., 1936) are both
among the best local histories. Robert E. Brown, (Middle-Class Democracy and
the Revolution in Massachusetts, 1691-1780 (Ithaca, 1955) directly contradicts
Robert J. Taylor, Western Massachusetts in the Revolution (Providence, 1954)
on the issue of western aims and motives. James B. Hedges' study of the
Browns of Providence Plantations, Colonial Years (Cambridge, 1952) is a model
for mercantile and economic historians. David S. Lovejoy, Rhode Island Politics
and the American Revolution (Providence, 1958) sheds light on one of the
most vexing of the colonies. Two brief monographs of less stature but of
importance are William D. Miller, The Narragansett Planters, Proceedings
of the American Antiquarian Society, 43 (1933), 49-115, and William Staples,

363

Rhode Island in the Continental Congress (Providence, 1870). Several works
on Connecticut: Edith A. Bailey, Influences Toward Radicalism in Connecticut
1774-1775, Smith College Studies in History, 4 (Northampton, 1920); Julian P.
Boyd, The Susquehannah Company: Connecticut's Experiment in Expansion (New
Haven, 1935); Charles S. Grant, Democracy in the Connecticut Frontier Town of
Kent, (New York, 1961); Isabel S. Mitchell, Roads and Roadmaking in Colonial
Connecticut (New Haven, 1933); and Oscar Zeichner, Connecticut's Years of
Controversy 1750-1776 (Williamsburg, 1949) all make Connecticut one of the
more thoroughly researched of the colonies. Of these, Grant's work raises a
series of new questions about the frontier and politics.

Middle Colonies: Indicative of the nature of society and politics
in the four Middle Colonies is the fact that no one has yet attempted a general
work on the subject. New York history is in a transition period due to
attacks upon Carl L. Becker's The History of Political Parties in the Province
of New York, 1760-1776 (Madison, 1909), and the vacuum created by those
attacks is not filled by Bernard Mason, Organization of the Revolutionary
Movement in New York State, 1775-1777 (Unpublished Ph.D. dissertation,
Columbia University, New York City, New York, 1958). Virginia D. Harrington,
The New York Merchant on the Eve of the Revolution (New York, 1935), and
Mark Irving, Agrarian Conflicts in Colonial New York 1711-1775 (New York, 1940)
contain pertinent information on the nature and structure of New York
society; three lesser works aid in understanding the colony: U.P. Hedrick
A History of Agriculture in the State of New York (Albany, 1933), volume one
of Stephen M. Ostrander, A History of the City of Brooklyn and Kings County
(2 vols, Brooklyn, 1894), and B.F. Thompson, History of Long Island . . .

364

(2 vols., 2nd ed., New York, 1843). For New Jersey: Donald L. Kemmerer, Path to Freedom (Princeton, 1940), and Leonard Lundin, Cockpit of the Revolution (Princeton, 1940) to help clarify rather confusing legal and political details about that colony. Carl and Jessica Bridenbaugh's Rebels and Gentlemen: Philadelphia in the Age of Franklin (New York, 1942) lays the foundation for the study of one of the most important centers of culture and the Revolution. And that study together with Theodore Thayer's Pennsylvania Politics and the Growth of Democracy 1740-1776 (Harrisburg, 1953), and Frederick B. Tolles, Meeting House and Counting House . . . (Chapel Hill, 1948) reveals the sophistocation of society in the Deleware Valley during the late eighteenth century. The colony of Delaware has also been surveyed for the last years: Harold Hancock, The Delaware Loyalists (Wilmington, 1940), and John A. Monroe: Federalist Delaware 1775-1815 (New Brunswick, N.J., 1954).

The Southern Colonies: John R. Alden, The South in the Revolution 1763-1789, volume 3 of A History of the South (1957) is a good survey, and is in intellectual rapport with Carl Bridenbaugh's Myths and Realities; Societies of the Colonial South (Baton Rouge, 1952), important for its precise description of the variety of features of culture in the south. For Maryland, both Charles A. Barker, The Background of the

365

Revolution in Maryland (New Haven, 1940), and Philip A. Crowl,
Maryland During and After the Revolution (Baltimore, 1943) are
useful. Oswald Tilghman, History of Talbot County Maryland 1661-
1861 (2 vols., Baltimore, 1915), contains interesting details and
facts. Charles L. Lingley, The Transition in Virginia from Colony
to Commonwealth (New York, 1910), Charles Sydnor, Gentlemen
Freeholders: Political Practices in Washington's Virginia (Chapel
Hill, 1952), and Robert E. and B. Katherine Brown, Virginia, 1705-1786:
Democracy or Aristocracy? (East Lansing, 1964), provide an interesting
sequence in Virginia historiography. For the lower south, the
following works were found to be most valuable: Charles C. Crittenden,
The Commerce of North Carolina 1763-1789 (New Haven, 1936); E.W.
Sikes, The Transition of North Carolina from Colony to Commonwealth
(Baltimore, 1898); Edward McCrady, The History of The South Carolina
under the Royal Government 1719-1776 (New York, 1899); an illuminating
study is Charleston Business on the Eve of the American Revolution
(Chapel Hill, 1934) by Leila Sellers; Richard Walsh, Charleston's
Sons of Liberty . . . (Columbia, S.C., 1959), evaluates the
artisans' role in one of the largest cities.

366

Biographies.

On the whole, biographical literature on the first Patriots is of surprisingly poor quality, outdated, or non-existent. Historians have, of course, paid more attention to major figures, but even at that, a sound study of Patrick Henry did not appear until 1957. Of a general nature and still of value because it contains information not published elsewhere is George Sanderson, Biography of the Signers of the Declaration of Independence (5 vols., 2nd ed., Nashville, 1831). John Adams seems to encourage caution in his biographers, and both Catherine D. Bowen, John Adams and the American Revolution (Boston, 1950), and Page Smith, John Adams (2 vols., Garden City, N.Y., 1962) are timid in their appraisal of Adams and the outbreak of the Revolution. John C. Miller, Sam Adams: Pioneer in Propaganda (Boston, 1936) details the actions of a central figure of the independence movement. Janet Bassett Johnson's Robert Alexander Maryland Loyalist (New York, 1942) is one of many biographies that does neither the man nor his times justice, while Ellen Hart Smith, Charles Carroll of Carrollton (Cambridge, Mass., 1942) is informative on Maryland society and politics. Ann Hart Clark, Abraham Clark (San Francisco, 1923) is comparable to the biography by Alexander E. Wilder Spaudling, His Excellency George Clinton (New York, 1938) assumes too much about Clinton's early attitudes and career, but certainly ranks above most of the biographical studies of the period. George L. Clark, Silas Deane (New York, 1913), and Charles J. Stillé, Life and Times of John Dickinson (Philadelphia, 1891) are two ellipitical accounts of men of first importance in the early years of the Revolution; both deserve more extensive studies.

367

E.P. Alexander, A Revolutionary Conservative James Duane of New York (New York, 1938) is a judicious appraisal of the man, and contains important facts about land speculation and the New York economy. Edward T. Channing's Life of William Ellery in the Library of American Biography, 6 (Boston, 1836), 87-159, breaks the ground for a more incisive study of a rather shrewd political figure and man of some stature. Franklin has been the subject of a number of biographies; these have been brought together and added to in a political treatment by Verner W. Crane, Benjamin Franklin and a Rising People (Boston, 1954), Crane's second biographical study of the man. Oliver C. Kuntzleman, Joseph Galloway . . . (Philadelphia, 1941), and Herbert S. Allen, John Hancock: Patriot in Purple (New York, 1948) deal adequately with the two men, while W.B. Baxter's The House of Hancock: Business in Boston, 1724-1775 (Cambridge, Mass., 1945) is incisive in its description of the mercantile affairs of Hancock. Francis E. Brown, Joseph Hawley Colonial Radical (New York, 1931), relates the role of a prominent western leader. Robert D. Meade, Patrick Henry Patriot in the Making (Philadelphia and New York, 1957) meets a need of long standing in the literature on the Revolution. Stephen Hopkins (2 vols., Providence, 1884) by William E. Foster is inadequate for the Revolutionary years as is James K. Hosmer, Life of Thomas Hutchinson (Boston, 1896); Frank Monaghan, John Jay (New York, 1935), mainly of use for Jay's later years. Dumas Malone presents intricate details on the author of the Declaration in Jefferson the Virginian, volume one of Jefferson and His Time (Boston, 1948). Edward S. Delaplaine, The Life of Thomas Johnson (New York, 1927) is more extensive in its treatment than most biographies of secondary figures. George C. Croce, William Samuel Johnson (New York, 1937), Lawrence Shaw Mayo,

368

John Langdon of New Hampshire (Concord, N.H., 1937), and John R. Alden, General Charles Lee (Baton Rouge, 1951), an admirable study, all contain information about men who were connected with Congress in various capacities. Julia Delafield, Biographies of Francis Lewis and Morgan Lewis (2 vols., New York, 1877) is a family memoir, while George Dangerfield's Chancellor Robert R. Livingston of New York 1746-1813 (New York, 1960) is detailed on Hudson Valley culture and politics. Theodore S. Sedgwick's Memoir of the Life of William Livingston (New York, 1833) is still useful. Robert Morris' rather non-committal early stance on independence is reflected in the first pages of Clarence L. VerSteeg, Robert Morris Revolutionary Financier (Philadelphia, 1954); Kenneth R. Rossman deals somewhat stiffly with one of the more viable men of the time in Thomas Mifflin and the Politics of the American Revolution (Chapel Hill, 1952). R.T. Paine was more important in Massachusetts politics than writing about him conveys and Ralph Davol's Two Men of Taunton (Taunton, 1912) is woefully inadequate. David J. Mays furnishes a masterful account of Virginia in Edmund Pendleton (2 vols., Cambridge, 1952). Richard Barry renders one of the few excellent treatments of the Patriots in Mr. Rutledge of South Carolina (New York, 1942). Benson J. Lossing, The Life and Times of Philip Schuyler (2 vols., New York, 1860) will soon be superseded by another, more thorough two volume account; Roger S. Broadman's Roger Sherman (Philadelphia, 1938) is superior to Lewis H. Boutell, The Life of Roger Sherman (Chicago, 1896). Charles P. Whittemore, A General of the Revolution: John Sullivan of New Hampshire (New York, 1961), Harley R. Lewis, The Life and Times of Charles Thomson (Philadelphia, 1900), and Glenn Weaver, Jonathan Trumbull, Connecticut's Merchant Magistrate (Hartford, 1956), are all important for the study of independence; Weaver has detailed economic affairs in Connecticut on the advent of

crisis. Other biographies cited in this study are: Curtis P. Nettels, George Washington and American Independence (Boston, 1951), rather vague in its classification of the Patriots; Lawrence Shaw Mayo, John Wentworth (Cambridge, Mass., 1921), one of the few lengthy accounts of a colonial governor, and Charles Page Smith, James Wilson: Founding Father.

Articles.

The following articles were used in this study: Henry M. Baker, "General Nathaniel Folsom," Proceedings of the New Hampshire Historical Society, 4 (1906), 253-267. Roger Champagne, "New York and the Intolerable Acts," New York Historical Society Quarterly, 45 (April, 1961), 195-207 -- a revaluation of radicalism and city politics; A.H. Clapp, "Samuel Huntington," The Congressional Quarterly, 6 (Oct., 1864), 318-327. Trevor H. Colburn, "John Dickinson, Historical Revolutionary," Pennsylvania Magazine of History and Biography, 88 (July, 1959), 271-292; Lawrence H. Gipson, "Connecticut Taxation, 1750-1775," in Essays in Colonial History (New Haven, 1931); Jack P. Greene and Richard M. Jellison, "The Currency Act of 1764 in Imperial-Colonial Relations, 1764-1776," William and Mary Quarterly, 3rd Series, 18 (Oct., 1961), 485-518; George C. Croce, "Eliphalet Dyer: Connecticut Revolutionary," in The Era of the American Revolution, edited by Richard B. Morris (New York, 1939), 290-304; Harold Hancock's articles on loyalists, all in Delaware History: "Thomas Robinson: Delaware's Most Prominent Loyalist," 4 (March, 1950), 1-36; "New Castle County Loyalists," 4 (Sept., 1961), 315-353; "Kent County Loyalists," 6 (March, 1954), 3-34, and (Sept., 1954), 92-139; Ruth M. Keesey, "Loyalism in Bergen County, New Jersey," William and Mary

370

Quarterly, 3rd Series, 18 (Jan., 1961), 558-576; Milton M. Klein, "Democracy and Politics in Colonial New York," New York History, 40 (July, 1959), 221-246, asserts more extensive franchise in New York than does Becker; Arthur Little, "William Whipple, Signer of the Declaration . . .," Proceedings of the New Hampshire Historical Society, 3 (1899), 318-339; Beverly McAnear, "Mr. Robert R. Livingston's Reasons Against a Land Tax," Journal of Political Economy, 48 (Feb.-Dec., 1940), 63-90. Edmund S. Morgan, "Colonial Ideas of Parliamentary Power, 1764-1766," William and Mary Quarterly, 3rd Series, 5 (July, 1948), 311-341; Samuel E. Morison, "Boston Commerce on the Eve of Revolution," Proceedings of the Antiquarian Society, 32 (April, 1922), 24-51; Louis H. Patterson, "John Hart, The New Jersey Signer," New Jersey Historical Society Proceedings, New Series, 10 (Oct., 1925), 375-382; E.I. Renick, "Christopher Gadsden," Publications of the Southern History Association, 2 (July, 1898), 242-255; Richard B. Sheridan, "The British Credit Crisis of 1772 and the American Colonies," Journal of Economic History, 20 (June, 1960), 161-186 -- important for its evaluation of the primary impact of the crisis; Albert Silverman, "William Paca, Signer, Governor, Jurist," Maryland Historical Magazine, 37 (March, 1942), 1-25; St. George L. Sioussant, "The Breakdown of the Royal Management of Lands in the Southern Provinces, 1773-1775," Agricultural History, 3 (April, 1929), 67-98; Warren W. Sweet, "Anglicanism in the American Revolution," Huntington Library Quarterly, 11 (Nov., 1947), 51-70; George R. Taylor, "Wholesale Commodity Prices at Charleston, South Carolina, 1732-1791," Journal of Economic and Business History, 4, 356-377; Francis G. Walett, "The Massachusetts Council, 1766-1774,"

William and Mary Quarterly, 3rd Series, 6 (Oct., 1949), 605-627; James C.
Walett, "James Bowdoin, Patriot Propagandist," New England Quarterly, 23
(Sept., 1950), 320-338; and Robert H. Woody, "Christopher Gadsden and the
Stamp Act," Proceedings of the South Carolina Historical Association (1939),
3-12.

Erich Wasmansdorff

Bernhard Gondorf

Alte deutsche Berufsnamen und ihre Bedeutung

Grundriß der Genealogie

Band 7 der Reihe

Alte deutsche Berufsnamen und ihre Bedeutung

1. Auflage 1934

von

ERICH WASMANSDORFF

2. Auflage 1988

erweitert und überarbeitet von

BERNHARD GONDORF

C. A. STARKE VERLAG · LIMBURG AN DER LAHN

Copyright © 1988 by C. A. Starke Verlag, Limburg an der Lahn

Anschrift des Verlages:
C. A. Starke Verlag, Frankfurter Straße 51/53, D-65549 Limburg / Lahn
Tel. 06431/9615-0; Fax 06431/9615-15
www.starkeverlag.de

ISBN 3-7980-0363

- Bestellnummer 363 -

VORWORT

Den Anlaß zu dem vorliegenden Büchlein gab ein persönliches Erlebnis. Vor Jahren fragte mich ein Bekannter, was ein „Sargédromacher" sei. Er hatte bei seinen Ahnen diese Berufsbezeichnung gefunden, jedoch trotz aller Bemühungen keine Erklärung für das seltsame Wort entdecken können. Schließlich war er — in Ermangelung von etwas besserem — zu der Deutung „Sargmacher", „Tischler" gekommen, die ihn aber keineswegs befriedigte, weil seine übrigen Vorfahren meist Tuchmacher waren, keiner jedoch einem holzverarbeitenden Gewerbe oblag. — Und doch war die Deutung nicht schwer, sie war nur verfehlt durch falsche Betonung und ungewöhnliche Schreibung des Wortes. Es handelte sich nicht um einen „Sargédromacher", sondern um einen „Sargedrómmacher", und „Sargedróm" war „Serge de Rome", ein von den französischen Flüchtlingen (Refugiés) viel hergestelltes wollenes Gewebe.

Dieses kleine Erlebnis, dem sich im Laufe der Zeit viele ähnliche anreihten, veranlaßte mich, einmal auf solche weniger bekannten Berufsbezeichnungen zu achten, und das Ergebnis dieser Sammeltätigkeit findet sich nun in diesem Büchlein.

Man könnte fragen, ob dessen Herausgabe wirklich eine Notwendigkeit war, nachdem vor kurzem das verdienstvolle Werk von Haemmerle „Alphabetisches Verzeichnis der Berufs- und Standesbezeichnungen vom ausgehenden Mittelalter bis zur neueren Zeit" (München) erschien. Aber Haemmerle gibt nur in seltenen Fällen eine Worterklärung, auf die es doch m. E. in der Hauptsache ankommt, und dann legt er das Schwergewicht auf die lateinischen Berufsbezeichnungen. Ich habe aber im Gegensatz dazu gefunden, daß die lateinischen Bezeichnungen viel bekannter sind als die älteren deutschen. Was ein „sartor" ist oder ein „sutor", daß weiß nachgerade jeder Schuljunge. Aber was ein „Fundenhirt", ein „Enke", ein „Litzenbruder" war, ist meist weniger bekannt. Und für diese Fälle soll das vorliegende Büchlein dem Gedächtnis zur Hilfe kommen.

Das Heft ist ausschließlich für die Praxis als kleines Nachschlagewerk des Sippenforschers gedacht. Daher ist von langatmigen etymo-

V

logischen Erörterungen abgesehen worden, und ich habe auch nach Möglichkeit keine Verweisungen vorgenommen, obwohl sich daraus mitunter Wiederholungen ergaben. Der Leitgedanke war, jede gesuchte Berufsbezeichnung sofort ohne langes Herumblättern finden zu lassen und eine knappe Sinndeutung zu geben. Bezeichnungen, die allgemein verständlich und gebräuchlich sind, wurden nur vermerkt, wenn auch noch eine weniger bekannte, abweichende Deutung gegeben werden konnte; eine Erläuterung der landläufigen Bezeichnung fehlt dann aber. Verschiedene Schreibweisen des gleichen Wortes habe ich nicht aufgenommen, vorausgesetzt, daß örtliche Abwandlungen nicht gar zu sehr von der Hauptform abwichen oder von einem sprachlich weniger geschulten Leser nicht vielleicht als neue Wortform empfunden werden könnten. Um jeden den schnellen Gebrauch störenden Ballast zu vermeiden, habe ich darauf verzichtet, die an sich reizvollen und sich vielfach mühelos ergebenden Folgerungen für die Namenforschung zu ziehen; sie hätten den Zweck dieser Schrift nur verwischt.

Daß mein Heftchen bei weitem noch nicht alle deutschen Berufsbezeichnungen erfaßt hat, liegt bei dem unerschöpflichen Reichtum unserer schönen Muttersprache auf der Hand. Sollte daher jemand Worte von besonderer Wichtigkeit oder größerer Häufigkeit vermissen, so bitte ich um deren Bekanntgabe, damit sie gegebenenfalls in einer späteren Auflage berücksichtigt werden können. All denen aber, die schon bei der vorliegenden Arbeit in dieser Weise durch freundliche Hinweise mitgeholfen haben, sei hier herzlich dafür gedankt!

Und noch eine andere Absicht verfolgt diese Schrift. Bei ihrer Abfassung mußte ich leider immer wieder bemerken, daß alte gute deutsche Berufsbezeichnungen dem Volksmunde fremd geworden, vergessen sind, während sich dafür die fremdsprachigen eingebürgert haben. Mitunter erschien es geradezu unabwendlich, das ursprüngliche deutsche Wort durch ein Fremdwort zu deuten. Da möge diese kleine Schrift mit dazu helfen, so manchem Beruf sein ehrwürdiges deutsches Kleid wiederzugeben, das meist sprachlich viel gediegener und schöner ist als der fremde Flitter!

Berlin, im Herbst 1934.   E r i c h   W a s m a n s d o r f f

VORWORT ZUR ZWEITEN AUFLAGE

1935 erschien im C. A. Starke Verlag, damals noch im Görlitzer Stammhaus, ein kleines Heft von Erich Wasmansdorff. Infolge der Zeitläufte konnte es nicht den Interessentenkreis erreichen, den es verdient hätte.

Wer schon einmal auf ihm unbekannte Berufsbezeichnungen gestoßen ist, sei es im Zuge genealogischer Forschung, sei es beim Lesen von Heimatchroniken oder alter Ratsprotokolle und dergleichen, kennt die Schwierigkeiten, die sich bei der Suche nach einer raschen Erklärung des Ausdrucks aufbauen. Hier soll die vorliegende Arbeit weiterhelfen.

Auf Bitten des Verlages habe ich das Verzeichnis erweitert, ohne die Konzeption Wasmansdorffs zu verändern. Natürlich kann die Liste nicht alle Berufe und deren vielfältige Bezeichnungen enthalten. Sie reicht aber in den meisten Fällen aus, um einen unbekannten Ausdruck der deutschen Sprache kurz zu erklären. Im Gegensatz zur ersten Ausgabe wurden diesmal auch verschiedene Schreibweisen berücksichtigt, weil das Heft dem „sprachlich weniger geschulten Leser" (Wasmansdorff) genauso eine Hilfe sein soll, wie dem akademisch ausgebildeten Benutzer, der die einzelnen Schreibweisen leicht lokal zuweisen kann. Wer sich mit der Etymologie einer Berufsbezeichnung befassen möchte, wird in den umfangreichen Wörterbüchern und Idiotika Näheres finden. Zum unmittelbaren Gebrauch beim Studium der Quellen erscheint uns das vorliegende Büchlein ausreichend.

Bernhard Gondorf

Koblenz, Ostern 1988

BEI DER ÜBERARBEITUNG BENUTZTE LITERATUR

Jakob und Wilhelm Grimm:

Deutsches Wörterbuch 16 (= 32) Bände
— Leipzig 1854—1960

Albert Haemmerle:

Alphabetisches Verzeichnis der Berufs- und Standesbezeichnungen vom ausgehenden Mittelalter bis zur neueren Zeit
— München 1933 (reprograf. Nachdruck: Hildesheim 1966)

Wolfgang Ribbe/Eckart Henning:

Taschenbuch für Familiengeschichtsforschung.
Begründet von Friedrich Wecken. 8. Auflage
— Neustadt/Aisch 1975

Wahrig-Brockhaus:

Deutsches Wörterbuch
— Mannheim 1981 ff. (noch nicht vollständig erschienen)

ALTE DEUTSCHE BERUFSNAMEN UND IHRE BEDEUTUNG

A

Abbauer	Pächter mit kleinem Eigenbesitz; Neusiedler; zweiter Sohn, der vom Hofe abbaut
Abdecker, Abstreifer	Schinder, Wasenmeister
Abentürer	Händler mit Luxuswaren; Juwelenhändler
Abnahmemann, Abschiedsmann	Bauer im Ausgedinge, nach Übergabe des Anwesens an seinen Sohn
Acht(s)mann	a) gerichtlicher Taxator b) Wahlherr
Ackerwirt	Bauer, Landwirt
Ältermann	Zunftmeister, Zunftvorgeher
Ältester	(in einigen protestantischen Gemeinden): Pfarrer
Äscherer	Brenner von Holzasche (für Glashütten)
Ätze, Ätzmaler	Eisenätzer, z. B. für Rüstungen
Affengießer	Gießer von Handwasserfässern, Bütten, Taufbecken, Weihrauchgefäßen, auch kleinerer Glocken u. ä.
Agent	Konsul; diplomatischer Vertreter
Agent, öffentlicher	Rechtsgelehrter mit beschränkten Befugnissen, zwischen Notar und Anwalt stehen (in Österreich)
Agtfischer	Bernsteinfischer
Aicher	Eichmeister
Aktuar	Gerichtsschreiber
Allgäuer	Frachtfuhrmann, nach den bekannten Gutfertigern aus dem Allgäu benannt
Allmendherr, -pfleger	Ratsherr, dem die Aufsicht über die Allmende, das Gemeindegut, obliegt
Altarist	Küster, Meßdiener
Altbüßer, -butzer	Flickschuster

1

Altenteiler	Bauer im Ausgedinge, nach Übergabe des Anwesens an seinen Sohn; Nutznießer des Altenteils
Altermann	Vorsteher einer Zunft oder Gilde
Altflicker	Flickschuster; später auch: Altwarenhändler
Altfürer, -geselle	Ältester der Gesellschaft
Altgewander	Flickschneider; auch: Altkleiderhändler
Altlapper, -macher, -placker, -reis, -reusz	Flickschuster
Altsitzer	Bauer im Ausgedinge, nach Übergabe des Anwesens an seinen Sohn; Nutznießr des Altenteils
Altwalker	Althändler, der altes Tuch walkt
Altwender	Flickschneider, auch: Altkleiderhändler
Ambassant, Ambosat	Vertrauensmann der Landsknechte gegenüber ihrem Hauptmann
Amer	Admiral
Amidammacher	Hersteller von Stärkemehl
Ammann	Höherer oder niederer Beamter; Amtmann; Vorsteher; in der Schweiz gelegentlich: Meier
Ammeister	Oberzunftmeister
Amtherr	Ratsherr, der ein öffentliches Amt bekleidete
Amtmann	Landrat; Domänenpächter; Leiter der herrschaftlichen Verwaltung
Amtsgograf, -gohgräfe	Amtsvogt
Amtsrat	Beamter der Amtskammer; gelegentlich auch Titel für verdiente Domänenpächter
Amtsschösser	Steuereinnehmer eines Amtes
Anbauer	Kleinbauer; Pächter; Neusiedler; Kolonist ohne Anteil an der Gemeindeflur
Angstmann	Folterknecht, Henker, Scharfrichter
Anreißer	Kundenwerber, Schlepper
Anspänner	Vollbauer; Gutstagelöhner, dem hauptsächlich die Pflege der Pferde obliegt
Anstößer	Grenznachbar

Antistes	Kirchen- und Schulvorsteher; in reformierten Gemeinden: erster Geistlicher
Anweiser	Anwalt
Anwender	Anlieger, Nachbar
Apengeter	Gießer von Handwassergefäßen, Bütten, Taufbecken, Weihrauchgefäßen, auch kleinere Glocken u. ä.
Arbiter	Schöffe
Armbruster	a) Hersteller der Armbrust b) Armbrustschütze
Arrendator	Pächter
Arröder	Dorfbewohner mit Pachtbesitz und geringeren Rechten an der Allmende
Aschenbrenner	Hersteller der Holzasche (für Glashütten)
Asega	Rechtsprecher; Urteilfinder bei den Friesen
Asenmacher	Rahmenmacher
Auenhäusler	Dorfbewohner mit Haus und Acker, aber geringeren Allmenderechten
Auer, Auermacher	Uhrmacher
Aufdinger	Markthelfer; Auflader; Spediteur; unterer Zollbeamter, der die Aufsicht über die Schiffsverlader führt
Aufschläger	Auflader; Erheber der Akzisen, der indirekten Aufwandsteuern, z. B. der Biersteuer
Aufschwemmer	Flößer
Aufspieler	Spielmann
Aulenbäcker, Auler	Töpfer
Ausbraiter, -breiter	Kupfer-, Kesseltreiber
Ausfaust, Ausknecht	Unterbeamter des Maiers zum Eintreiben der Gefälle
Ausgänger	Ratsherr ohne eigentliche Beschlußbefugnis
Ausgenommener Knecht	Ausgehobener, d. h. pflichtiger Soldat, Kriegsknecht
Ausklinger	Ratsbote; Polizeidiener; Ausrufer
Ausmiener	Versteigerer; Auktionator

3

Ausnehmer	Bauer im Ausgedinge, nach Übergabe des Anwesens an seinen Sohn
Außenbürger	Neu aufgenommener Bürger, der die die gleichen Rechte besitzt wie die innerhalb der Stadt wohnenden Bürger
Austrägler	Bauer im Ausgedinge
Ausweißer	Tüncher; Anstreicher
Auszügler	Bauer im Ausgedinge
Ayrer	Eierhändler

Backmann	Bäcker
Badener, Bader	Inhaber einer Badestube; Barbier; Bartscherer
Badreiber	Masseur; Inhaber einer Badestube
Badstuber, -stüber	Besitzer einer Badestube; Barbier
Bärschneider	Schweinekastrierer
Bailer	Eichmeister
Balbierer	Barbier
Balestermacher	Armbrustmacher
Ballonenmacher	Hersteller von Lederbällen
Bandhauer	Verfertiger von Faßreifen
Bandreißer	Verarbeiter der Weiden zur Herstellung von Faßreifen
Bandschneider	Verfertiger von Faßreifen
Bannwart	Flur-, Weinbergshüter; Gerichtsdiener
Barchentmeister	Siegelmeister, der nach der Prüfung die Tuche mit dem Siegel versah
Barchenweber, Barchet-	Weber des Barchen(t)
Bareler	Böttcher
Baretmacher	Hersteller des Baretts und des Biretts
Bargilde	Freier Grundbesitzer, der von seinem Land Abgaben zu zahlen hatte
Bartenhauer, -heuer	Hersteller der Hellebarden, Beile, Streitäxte
Bartzwicker	Barbier
Bassuner	Posaunist
Bauerngilde	Freier Grundbesitzer, der von seinem Land Abgaben zu zahlen hatte
Bauknecht	Vorknecht; Großknecht
Baukondukteur	Bauaufseher; Landmesser
Baumann	Ackerbürger; Ackermann; Pächter
Baumeister	Gutsverwalter; Vorknecht; Großknecht; Rentmeister; auch: Architekt
Baumgartner	Obstgärtner

Becherer	Verfertiger hölzerner Becher; Drechsler
Beck	Bäcker
Beck(en)drechsel, -schläger	Kesselschmied; Messingtreibarbeiter
Beckenwerker	Handwerker, der Gefäße aus Kupfer oder Messing herstellt
Bedder	Bader, Barbier
Begine	Laienschwester
Behelfer	Hilfslehrer
Beiermann	Anschläger der Glocken, nicht der eigentliche Glöckner
Beindreher	Feindrechsler, der Knochen, Horn und Elfenbein verarbeitet
Beingewender	Verfertiger der Beinschienen
Beischer	Peitschenmacher
Bekenmacher	Böttcher
Bellenmacher	Hersteller von Schellen
Bender	Böttcher; gelegentlich auch: Tüncher
Bennemacher	Verfertiger zweirädriger Korbwagen
Bennenführer	Kutscher des zweirädrigen Korbwagens
Benner	Böttcher; auch: Bennenmacher
Bereiter, Bereuter	a) berittener Ratsdiener b) Aufseher über die Pferde, Zureiter
Bereitknecht	Unterer Forstbeamter
Beritt	Landreiter und Wachtmeister
Berittener Schiffsschlepper	Leinreiter, Schiffzieher zu Pferde
Bermuterer	Pergamentbereiter
Beschaler	Verfertiger der Messerhefte
Beschlagmeister	Fahnenschmied = Hufschmied bei der Kavallerie; gelegentlich auch: Veterinär
Beseher	Unterer Zollbeamter
Beseher der maledey	Beamteter Arzt; Krankenbesichtiger
Besemer	Besenbinder, -händler
Beständer, Bestandmann	Pächter

6

Bestäder, Besteder	a) Spediteur
	b) Bauherr eines Schiffes; Beamter, der das Verdingen der Schiffslasten besorgt; Zollbeamter
Bestätter, Bestetter	Spediteur
Besucher	Kontrolleur; Bruder der Herrnhuter Unität, der den Leuten die „Losung" ins Haus zu bringen hatte
Bettschart	Peitschenmacher
Bettziechenweber	Weber von Bettzeug, dem Ziechen
Beurtmann	Schiffseigentümer, der einer Vereinigung zur Erzielung von Regelmäßigkeit in den Fahrten angehört
Beutler	Verfertiger von Beuteln, Taschen, auch von Handschuhen
Beutner, Bienzeisler	Imker, Bienenzüchter
Biereigen	(Haus-)Brauer
Bierpreu	Braumeister
Bierrufer	Jemand, der den Namen des Brauers, der frisch gebraut hat, und den Bierpreis ausruft
Bierschröter	Bierkutscher
Bierspünder	Bierprüfer
Biesterfreier	Eingewanderter Fremder, der vom Landesherrn wie ein Leibeigener behandelt werden konnte
Bildgießer	Erzgießer
Billetierer	Lotterie-Einnehmer
Binder	Böttcher; auch: Anstreicher
Birmenter	Hersteller von Pergament
Birnengärtner	Obstgärtner
Bisser	Gebiß-, Zaumzeugmacher
Bixnmeister	Kassierer, z. B. einer Zunft; auch: Geschützmeister
Blaicher, Bleicher	a) Leinenbleicher
	b) Tüncher (Bleichmaler)
Blatner	Harnischmacher, Plattner

Blattbinder	Verfertiger der Riet- oder Weberblätter aus Holz für Webstühle
Blattervater	Seuchenhausverwalter
Blattmüller	Flitterschlager; auch: Gold- und Silberplättner
Blatt-, Blättersetzer	Hersteller der Blätter aus Rohr oder Eisendraht für Webstühle
Blechler, Blechner, Blechschmied	Klempner, Spengler
Bleidecker	Bleidach-Decker
Bleidner	Verfertiger, auch Bediener der Bliden (Wurfmaschinen)
Bleiweißholzlein-macher, Bleiweißschneider, Bleyweiß-Steffte-macher	Bleistiftmacher
Bletzer	Altschuhmacher, Flickschuster
Blidenmeister	Geschützmeister, Bediener der Bliden (Wurfmaschinen)
Boddek(er)	Böttcher
Böck	Bäcker
Böker	Böttcher
Bönhase	Unzünftiger Handwerker; umherziehender Lohnhandwerker; Pfuscher
Bogner	Bogenmacher; auch: Bogenschütze
Bokemüller	Zubereiter des Flachses
Bolzdreher	Verfertiger der Armbrustbolzen
Bornfeger	Brunnenreiniger
Borngräber, -macher	Brunnenbauer
Bornmeister	Aufseher über die Brunnenanlagen
Bornzieher	Versorger der Haushaltungen mit Wasser; Wasserträger
Bossierer	Former; Hersteller von Formen aus weichen Materialien, z. B. aus Wachs
Botenmeister	Postmeister

8

Bottelier	Proviantmeister, Ausgeber des Proviants besonders des Alkohols, auf Schiffen
Bracker	Öffentlich angestellter Viehmakler
Brämelmacher	Posamentierer
Brasilholzstößer	Müller von Brasilholz, das als Farbe und als Arzneimittel verwendet wurde
Braueigen	Brauherr, Besitzer einer Braustelle
Breinmüller	Hirsemüller
Breis(l)er	Posamentierer
Brenner	Alkoholbrenner
Brenntlerin	Viehmagd, Sennerin
Bretzenmacher	Spangenmacher
Briechler	Bandkrämer
Briefdreger-, -trager	Hausierer mit Bildern; auch: Briefbote
Briefdrucker	Drucker von Holzschnitten
Briefer	Schrift-, Brief-, Klein-, Initialmaler
Briefkramer	Bilderhändler
Brinksitzer	Kleinbauer, meist am Rande der Dorfflur
Briser	Posamentierer
Britschenmeister	Festordner, Stegreifdichter, Spaßmacher
Brokatmacher	Seidenweber
Brotmacher	Arbeiter in der Zuckerindustrie
Bruch- und Steinschneider	Wundarzt
Bruck(n)er	Steinsetzer, Pflasterer, Brückenbauer
Brüchler	Hosenverfertiger; auch: Hausierer
Brückner	Brückenbauer, -wärter
Brunnenfeger	Reiniger der Ziehbrunnen
Brunnenmeyger	Brunnenbauer
Brunenenpalier, -polier	Brunnenmeister
Bubenmeister	Schullehrer
Buchfeller	Pergamentmacher
Buchführer	Umherziehender Buchhändler
Buchschreiber	Verfertiger von Buchabschriften
Buchstabensetzer	Schriftsetzer
Buchstaber	Weber, der in ein Gespinst Sprüche einwebt

9

Bücheraltreis(s)	Antiquar
Büchsenmeister	a) Geschützmeister
	b) Kassierer, z. B. einer Zunft
Büchsenschäft(l)er, -schifter, -schmied	Büchsen-, Gewehrschmied
Büchsner	Hersteller von schraubbaren Gefäßen, auch von Feuerwaffen
Büdner	a) Kleinbauer
	b) Kaufbudenbesitzer
Bürenweber	Weber von Bettzeug
Bürgermeister binnen der Bank	Amtierender Bürgermeister
Bürgermeister buten der Bank	Abgetretener Bürgermeister
Büthener	Imker, Bienenzüchter
Büttel	Rats-, Fronbote
Büttemacher, Büttenbinder, Büttner	Böttcher
Bund-, Buntfu(e)tterer, -macher	Kürschner
Bungenschlager	Trommler
Butenmann	Gast; Austrägler (Bauer im Ausgedinge)
Buthelor	Nagelschmied
Butterkäffl, -menger	Butterhändler

10

C

Caffamacher	Samtweber
Calcant	Orchesterdiener; Bälgetreter an der Orgel
Carbiner	Musketier
Carpe	Zimmermann
Castner	Rentamtmann, Kastellan
Choradjuvant	Bezahlter Kirchenchorsänger
Chorführer	Tanzmeister
Claiber, Clauber	Estrichmacher, Bodenleger, Lehmverstreicher, Kleber
Clausurmacher	Hersteller von Buchschließen und kleineren Verschlüssen; auch: Gürtler, Nestler
Clavicembelmacher, Clavicordiumbauer	Klavierbauer, -fabrikant
Compir	Pate, Gevatter
Concinierer	Reiniger weißer oder heller Seidenwaren
Consumtionsschreiber	Steuerbeamter
Constabel	Feuerwerker; Bombadierer; Polizist
Conterfehter, -feiter, -fettner	Porträtmaler
Corber	Korbflechter
Corduanmacher	Gerber von Corduanleder; auch: Schuhmacher
Cranatensetzer	Hersteller von Granatschmuck
Credenzer	Kellner
Cridant	Ausrufer
Creutzschmied	Schmied für Degen- und Schwertgriffe
Curtzenwerter	Kürschner

11

D

Dammsetzer	Pflasterer, Straßenbauer
Da(e)ntler	Trödler, Hausierer
Darrer	Besitzer oder Arbeiter einer Malzdarre, eines Röstofens
Daubecker	Armenbäcker
Daubenhauer, -macher	Herstellen von Faßdauben
Decker	Dachdecker
Degener	Degenschmied
Degenrat	Mitglied des Provinzialrates im alten Herzogtum Luxemburg, bestehend aus dem Adel, dem Militär und den Lehensträgern
Demantschneider	Diamantschleifer, -schneider
Deng(e)ler	Sensenschmied, -schleifer
Deuchelbohrer	Hersteller von Holz- und Brunnenröhren
Dickenweber	Weber einer besonderen Tuchart, des Dicken
Diebler, Dübler	Zimmermann, der die Balken mit Dübeln verbindet
Dirredeier	Verfertiger des Tirtei, eines Stoffes, der zu gleichen Teilen aus Wolle und Leinen besteht
Dockenmacher	Hersteller von Puppen
Dolchmacher	Kurzmesserschmied
Doppeler	Würfelschneider, auch: -spieler
Doppengießer	Hersteller von gußeisernem Geschirr
Doppenschneider	Hersteller von Würfeln
Drahtbinder	Umherziehender Topfflicker, Verfertiger von Mäusefallen u. dgl.
Drahtmüller	Besitzer oder Pächter einer Drahtziehmühle, einer Drahtschmiede
Drahtzieher	Drahtschmied
Drapenier, Drapier(er), Draver	Tucher
Dreher, Dreyer	Drechsler
Dreihüfner	Großbauer mit drei Hufen Besitz

12

Dreyerweber	Weber einer besonderen Tuchart, des Dreyen
Dreschgärtner,	Kleinbauer, Pächter, der auf dem Gutshof
Dreschermaß	Dienst beim Dreschen zu leisten hat
Drillichweber	Weber einer besonderen Leinenart, des Drillich
Drost	Adeliger Verwalter einer Vogtei; Vertreter des Landesherrn; eine Art Landrat oder -vogt
Drotsmit	Drahtschmied
Druck(h)enlader	Verlader und Beförderer trockener Kaufmannsgüter
Dübler	Zimmermann, der die Balken mit Dübeln verbindet.
Dütenmacher	Tütenhersteller
Durner	Turmwächter

E

Ebenist	Kunsttischler, der vornehmlich Ebenholz verarbeitet
Ebentürer	Juwelenhändler, Händler mit Luxuswaren
Eberschmied	Bohrerschmied
Edelschmied	Gold- oder Silberschmied
Edelsteinwürker	Edelsteinhändler, Juwelier
Ehegaumer, -goumer	Mitglied des (Kirchen-)Gemeinderates, der die Sittenkontrolle ausübt
Ehehalt	Dienstbote
Ehrbarkeit	Gesamtheit der Gerichts- und Ratsmitglieder
Ehrn	(= Ehrwürden) Anrede für Geistliche
Eicher	Eichmeister
Eiermann, -menger	Eierhändler
Eigenkätner	Kleinbauer, Kötter, Kossät
Einfahrer	Bergbeamter, Steiger
Einleger	Böttcher
Einlieger	a) Mieter b) freier landwirtschaftlicher Arbeiter ohne Grundbesitz, der bei einem Bauern zur Miete wohnt und diesem bestimmte Dienste leistet, im übrigen im Tagelohn arbeitet
Einpfenniger	Vorsteher der Geleitseinnehmer
Einspänner	Vollbauer, Großbauer
Einspänniger, -spenniger	Ratsknecht, -diener; Fuhrhalter, reisiger Söldner, auch: Fußknecht
Einsteher	Ersatzmann für den Heeresdienst
Einungsmeister	(besonders in der Grafschaft Hauenstein:) Vorsteher der „Einung", Innung, Zunft
Einwohner	Pächter, (Unter-)Mieter
Eisengräber	Stempelschneider, Graveur
Eisenhalter	Münzaufseher, -wardein
Eisenhuter	Hersteller von Helmen und Sturmhauben
Eisenmeister	Kerkermeister
Eisenschmelzer	Zerrenner, Waldschmied

Eisenschneider	Graveur
Emmerer	Hersteller von Eimern
Enk(e)	Ackerknecht, Kleinknecht
Entensteller	Jagdgehilfe bei der Wasserjagd
Erbex	An der Markgemeinschaft bevorrechtigt beteiligter Grundherr, erbeigener Großgrundbesitzer; auch: Vorsitzer des Markgerichts
Erchmacher, -meker	Weißgerber
Erdebäcker	Töpfer
Erdtrichsmesser	Feldmesser
Erweißer	Erbsenhändler
Eseler	Kleinhändler, der seine Ware auf einem Esel befördert
Essenkehrer	Kamin-, Schornsteinfeger
Esser	Wagenbauer
Est(er)richer	Fußbodenmacher
Etzmaler	Eisenätzer, z. B. für Rüstungen
Eul(n)er	Töpfer
Ewerführer	Führer eines Ewers oder einer Schute zum Heran- und Fortbringen der Ladung von Seeschiffen

Fadenmacher	Zwirner
Fäßler	Faßbinder, Böttcher
Fahnenschmied	Beschlagmeister, Hufschmied bei der Kavallerie
Fahrender	Umherziehender Spielmann, Gaukler
Fahrensmann	Seemann, Matrose
Faktor	Handlungsbevollmächtigter, Geschäftsführer, Zwischenmeister
Faktotum	Diener, Gehilfe
Fallmeister	Abdecker, Schinder
Faßmaler	Anstreicher, Maler für Bildhauerwerke
Faßschlupfer	Böttcher
Faßzieher	Markthelfer, Auflader
Fastbäcker	Bäcker von Roggenbrot
Fauth	Vogt
Fechner	Pelzhändler, Hersteller von Pelzwerk
Federfechter	Öffentlicher Fechter aus der Bruderschaft des hl. Vitus (Feder)
Federputzer, -schmu(e)cker	Hersteller von Federputz
Federschneider	Posenschaber, Kielfedernschneider
Feger	Straßenkehrer
Feilbeck	Grobbäcker, der Brot bäckt und verkauft, feilhält
Feilenhauer, Feiler	Feilenschmied
Feilschlächter	Schlachter, der Fleisch und Wurst im Laden verkauft.
Feirschlosmaker	Büchsenschmied
Feitler	Hausierer mit Wäsche und Kleidern
Felbaweber	Seidenweber
Feldgeschworener	Einer von meist sieben Dorfgeschworenen, die verwischte oder strittige Grenzen wiederherstellten
Feldmeister	Abdecker

Feldreiter	Gendarm
Feldschieder	Aufsichtsbeamter einer Gemeinde über Feldwege und Eigentumsgrenzen
Feldwaibel	Feldwebel, ein mit der Ordnung eines Fähnleins betrauter Unteroffizier
Felgenhauer, Felger	Verfertiger von Radfelgen; Wagenbauer
Fellhändler, Fellwerkbereiter	Kürschner
Fendrich	Fähnrich
Ferber	Färber
Ferche, Ferge(r)	Fährmann
Ferger	Vermittler zwischen Kleinmeistern und Verleger, z. B. in der Textilindustrie
Feßler	Faßbinder
Festbäcker	Grobbäcker, der kein Weißbrot bäckt
Feuermäuerkehrer	Schornsteinfeger
Feuermaler	Emaillierer
Feuerschloßmacher	Büchsen-, Gewehrschmied
Fiarant	Viktualienhändler, Markthändler mit Lebensmitteln
Fiedler	Geigenspieler
Figurist	Bildhauer
Filler	Abdecker, Schinder
Filter(er), Filzer	Filz-, Hutmacher
Fingerhuter, -hüter	Hersteller von Fingerhüten
Finkler	Finkenfänger, Singvogelhändler
Fischweicher	Händler, der gedörrten Fisch küchenfertig macht
Fischweker	Kleinverkäufer von Dörr-/Stockfisch
Flachsmann	Flachshändler, -schwinger
Flachsmit	Flachschmied
Flader	Kuchenbäcker
Fläminger	Tuchfärber
Flaschner, Flaschenschmied	Verfertiger von Flaschen aus Metall oder Leder; Klempner, Spengler

17

Flecksieder	Kuttler, Kaldaunenkocher, jemand, der Tiereingeweide zubereitet
Fleetenkieker	Sammler von Abfall aus den trockengelegten Kanälen (Fleeten) Hamburgs
Fleischhacker, -hauer, -mann	Fleischer, Fleischverkäufer
Flexer	Flachsarbeiter, Spinner
Flickner	Flickschuster
Flinder(lein)schlager, Flitterer, Flitterschlager	Hersteller von Flittermünzen, Rechenpfennigen u. dgl.
Floßmann	Flößer
Flügelmacher	Klavierbauer
Fluhr, Flurer	Feldhüter, Flurschütz
Fontainizer	Springbrunnenbauer
Forgetzer	Großbäcker
Former	Hersteller von Gußformen
Formschneider	Hersteller von Holzdruckstöcken und von Modeln
Frachter	Fuhrmann, Spediteur
Fragner	Krämer
Fratschler	Trödler; Kleinhändler
Frauenwirtin	Bordellwirtin
Freibauer	Besitzer eines Bauerngutes, das von Frondiensten und Lehensabgaben befreit ist
Freier Knecht	Angeworbener Soldat, Kriegsknecht
Freigärtner	Kleinbauer, Pächter, der von Fron befreit ist
Freiknecht	Abdecker, Schinder
Freimann	Scharfrichter
Freisitzer	Besitzer eines Freigutes, siehe Freibauer
Fretter	Bönhase, Störer
Friedmacher	Steinsetzer, Pflasterer, Brückenbauer
Frischmeister	Meister an der Eisenschmelze
Frohn	Büttel
Fröhner, Frönder	Knecht, herrschaftlicher Beamter
Fruchtschreiber	Gehilfe des Kornmeisters

Fruchttrager	Korn-, Fruchtträger, z. B. an der Schranne
Frumwerker	Tagelöhner; Handwerker, der auf Bestellung arbeitet, dem die Rohstoffe und Betriebsmittel gehören
Fucker(er)	Großkaufmann (wohl abgeleitet vom Handelshaus der Fugger)
Füller	Abdecker, Wasenmeister
Fürsprech	Sachwalter, Rechtsanwalt; auch: Vorsprecher, z. B. einer Zunft
Fütter	Händler mit Viehfutter
Fundenhirt	Waisenvater, Leiter eines Waisenhauses
Fußknecht	Soldat zu Fuß

G

Gadamer, Gademer	Beisitzer; Einwohner, jedoch nicht Bürger einer Stadt; Kaufbudeninhaber
Gadenfrau, -mann	Kleinhändlerin, -händler
Gänder, Gängeler	Hausierer
Gärtner	Kleinbauer, Pächter, Kossät
Gaffelbote	Leichenbitter; im Kölnischen auch: Biedienter einer Gaffel (= Zunft)
Ganser	Geflügelhändler
Ganthauer	Verfertiger von Brunnentrögen
Gantner	Böttcher
Garbrader	Garkoch; Verkäufer gekochten oder gebratenen Fleisches
Garnknecht	Fischer, der mit dem Garn, einem großen Netz, fischt
Gartenkondukteur	Gartenbaudirektor
Garthender Soldat	Bettelsoldat
Gassenschleifer	Umherziehender Scheren- und Messerschleifer
Gassenvogt	Aufseher der Straßenreinigung
Gassenwirt	Schankwirt, der nur Getränke verabreichen darf
Gast	Marinehandwerker; Matrose, der nur bestimmte Verrichtungen erledigen darf
Gastalde	Domänenbeamter, Gutsverwalter, Meier
Gastgeber, -halter	Gastwirt
Gaulichter	Kerzengießer
Gauwemann, Gauwer	Hausierer
Gehuster	Älterer, beim Hof angesessener Knecht
Geischelmacher	Peitschenmacher
Geis(e)ler	Händler, gelegentlich auch Schlachter von Kleinvieh; Verkäufer von Kleinviehfleisch
Geißelträger	Amtsdiener
Gelbgießer	Messing- und Kupferschmied oder -gießer
Geleitseinnehmer	Erheber von Straßen- oder Chausseegeld
Geleitsmann	Vorsteher der Geleitseinnehmer

Gelzenlichter, Gelt- zenleuchter, Gelzer	Viehbeschneider, Kastrierer
Gemeindeammann	Gemeindebeamter, Gerichtsvollzieher, Vollstreckungsbeamter
Gemeindeempfänger	Steuereinnehmer, Rendant einer Gemeinde
Gemeindsmann	Vollbürger; selbständiger Grundbesitzer
Gemeinweibel	Gewählter Gehilfe des Feldwebels, meist zugleich Vertrauensmann der Landsknechte gegenüber ihrem Hauptmann
Generalgewaltiger	Oberster Profoß; oberster Polizeioffizier der Landsknechte und später im Generalstab des Großen Kurfürsten v. Brandenburg
Gepeller	Hersteller von kleinen Gabeln
Gerbensieder	Hefesieder
Gerichtszwölfer	Mitglied der aus 12 Personen bestehenden Gerichts- und Gemeindebehörde
Gerillhändler	Alteisenhändler
Germsieder	Hefesieder
Geschickter	Abgeordneter einer Zunft
Geschlachtwander(er)	Großhändler mit feinen Tuchen
Geschlechter(in)	Patrizier(in)
Geschmeid(e)macher, -gießer	Metallarbeiter, der kleine Arbeiten, besonders in Messing, verfertigt
Geschmeidler	Edelschmied, Goldschmied, Juwelier
Gesindewirt	Besitzer eines Bauerngutes
Geuchler	Gaukler, Schausteller
Gevollmächtigter	Vorsteher, z. B. einer Zunft
Gewänder	Tuchhändler
Gewandführer	Tuchhändler
Gewandschneider, Gewantsnider	Tucher, Tuchgroßhändler
Gewelbherr, Gewölbherr	Großkaufmann
Gezawsigeler	Beamteter Tuchprüfer, der nach der Schau die Stoffe mit dem Siegel versieht
Gigenbuckler	Geigenspieler

21

Giler	Landstreicher
Gilerhalter	Herbergsvater; Wirt der Bettlerherberge
Ginganweber	Schürzenweber
Girschner	Kürschner
Gitterleinmacher	Drahtflechter
Gittermacher	Hersteller von Holzgittern
Gläßner	Glaser
Glätter	Papiermacher, der das Papier mit Achatstein glättet
Glasballier	Glaspolierer
Glasbrenner	Glasmacher
Glasewerter	Glaser
Glasmeister	Besitzer oder Pächter einer Glashütte
Glasmenger, -verleger	Glashändler
Glefener, Glener, Glever, Glevenburger	Berittener Söldner
Gleitsführer	Führer eines Geleitzuges
Gleser	Glaser
Gloeckner	Meßner, Küster; Turmwächter
Glotzenmacher	Hersteller von Holzschuhen, -pantoffeln
Glückshafener, -töpfer	Lotterie-Einnehmer
Glufenmacher	Hersteller von Stecknadeln
Go(e)lschenweber	Weber des „Kölschen" genannten Tuchs
Gogreve, Grohgräfe	Vogt, Gograf; Vollstreckungsgehilfe des Amtmanns
Goldgräber	Abtrittsreiniger
Goldplattner, -schläger	Hersteller von Blattgold
Goldspinner	Hersteller von Gold- und Silberfäden für Posamentierer
Gollerwascher	Reiniger von Lederjacken
Golzer	Gelzer, Viehbeschneider, Kastrierer
Gordeler	Seiler; vielleicht auch: Gürtler
Gortemaker	Grützemüller
Gottesvater	Kirchenvorsteher
Gotzenträger	Händler/Hausierer mit Heiligenbildern
Grabebitter	Leiter der Begräbnisfeierlichkeiten

Grabner	Stempelschneider, Graveur
Gradirer, Grattirer	Radierer
Gräser	Grasmäher; Wiesenwächter
Gräupner	Viktualien-, Getreidehändler
Granat(rosen)schnei- der, -schleifer, -setzer	Hersteller von Granatschmuck
Grapengießer	Verfertiger der „Grapen" genannten dreibei- nigen metallenen Kochtöpfe
Grapper	Salzverlader
Graufärber	Lodenfärber
Grautücher	Verfertiger und Verkäufer grauen Tuches
Greisler	Viktualien-, Getreidehändler
Gremp(l)er	Trödler, Althändler
Greve	Vogt; Obermärker, der bei Markgerichten den Vorsitz führte
Grobbinder	Faßbinder
Grobgrünmacher	Tuchmacher für grüngefärbtes grobes Woll- tuch
Gröp(el)er	Töpfer
Gröpp(n)er	Salzverlader; Verlader von Kaufmannsgut
Gropengießer	siehe Grapengießer
Gropper	Salzverlader; Salzfrachtfuhrmann
Gropschleifer, Grob- schleifer	Rauhschleifer
Großbinder	Küfer; Verfertiger großer Eichenfässer
Großerbe	Besitzer eines größeren Hauses mit vollem Bürgerrecht
Großuhrmacher	Turmuhrmacher
Grüter	Hersteller der Grut, einer Würze für Bier
Grützner	Grützemüller
Gstadlmacher	Verfertiger von Tüten
Gürtelwirker, Gürtler	Gürtel(beschlag)macher, Riemenschläger
Gütler	Besitzer eines kleinen Gutes
Gufener	Nadelmacher
Gulder	Vergolder
Gulichter, Gulister	Kerzengießer

Gumpenmacher	Pumpenmacher
Gutfertiger, Gut- herbestetter	Spediteur
Gutschier	Kutscher
Gwandtschneider	Tucher
Gyseler	Kleinviehhändler

H

Haak	Kleinhändler, Höker
Haararbeiter	Perückenmacher
Haarscherer	Barbier, Friseur
Habermann	Hersteller und Verkäufer von Hafergrütze
Hachmeister	Aufseher über die Jagdhabichte
Hacker, Häker	Kleinbauer, Pächter, Kossät
Häringer	Heringsfischer, -händler
Häuer	Bergmann unter Tage, der Mineralien abbaut
Häuerling	Pächter mit kleinem Eigenbesitz
Häuselfeger	Abtrittreiniger
Häusler, Häusling	Kossät; Besitzer eines Häuschens ohne Acker und Wiese, der meist auch Lohnarbeiter war
Hafenbinder	Umherziehender Topfflicker, besonders von irdenen und gläsernen Gefäßen
Hafner	Töpfer
Haftelmacher	Hersteller von Agraffen, Mantelverschlüssen u. dgl.
Hahnmacher	Hersteller von Zapfhähnen
Hake(n)	Kleinhändler, Höker
Halbhöfner, -spänner	Mittlerer Bauer
Halbwinner	Pächter (zu besonderen Bedingungen)
Hallore	Salzsieder, Arbeiter in der Saline
Halsberger	Schmied, der die Halsberge, einen Teil der Rüstung herstellt
Halter	Viehhirt
Hamenmacher	Hersteller von Pferdegeschirr, besonders des Kummet; Sattler
Hammacher	Sattler
Hammer(er)	Kaltschmied
Hammermeister	Besitzer, Pächter oder Vorsteher eines Eisenhammers
Handdienster	Kleinbauer
Handelsherr	Großkaufmann; Kaufherr
Handelsmann	Kaufmann; nicht: Hausierer

Handlungscommiss	Handelsbedienter
Handmaler	Kunstmaler
Handwerksherr	Ratsreferent für das Handwerk
Hansgraf	Führer und Aufseher der Großkaufleute
Hanteler	Hersteller von Fausthandschuhen
Hantscher	Handschuhmacher
Happenmacher	Sensen- und Sichelschmied
Hardesvogt	Vorsteher einer Harde, einer Unterabteilung eines Amtes
Harfner	Harfenbauer; Harfenspieler
Harmaker	Hersteller von Haardecken
Harnascher, Harnischer	Harnischmacher
Harnischfeger, -polierer	Plattner, Polierer der Harnische
Harpf(f)er	Harfenbauer; Harfenspieler
Harzscharrer	Sammler von Pech und Harz
Hasenneger	Strumpfnäher, -stricker
Haubenmacher, Hauber	Verfertiger der Sturmhauben
Haubenstricker	Hersteller der Ringel-Sturmhauben
Hauder(er)	Lohnfuhrmann
Hausgenoß	Zugehöriger zu einer Hausgemeinschaft; Münzer, Wechsler
Hausknecht	Hausdiener
Hausküper	Speicherverwalter; Lademeister
Hausmaler	Porzellanmaler im Heimbetrieb (im Gegensatz zum Maler in der Fabrik)
Hausmann	Bauer; Platzbesitzer; ländlicher Mieter; Hausverwalter; Türmer
Hauspfleger	Hausmeister, -verwalter
Hausvogt	Vogt in einem Schloß oder kleinen geschlossenen Bezirk; dann: kurfürstlicher Richter in Berlin
Hechelmacher	Hersteller von Flachshecheln
Hef(f)ner	Branntweinbrenner, Essighersteller

Heftelmacher, Heftler	Verfertiger von Heftnadeln, Agraffen
Hegereiter	Forstknecht, Forstschutzbeamter
Heidenswerker	Verfertiger bunter Decken; Teppichsticker
Heidhauer	Arbeiter, der mit der Hacke Heidekraut-Plaggen haut
Heidimker	Bienenzüchter in der Heide
Heiligenpfleger	Verwalter kirchlicher Stiftungen, Kirchenrendant
Heimberger, -bürge, -burge(r)	Ortsvorsteher; Schultheiß, Schöffe, Fronbote; auch: Gemeinderendant
Heimbürge	Leichenbesorger; Totengräber
Heimlichkeitfeger	Abtrittreiniger
Hei(n)zeler	Lohnfuhrmann
Helfer	Eideshelfer; auch: Geselle; auch: Seelsorger, Diakon
Hellefeger	Schornsteinreiniger
Helmer	Helmschmied
Hembder, Hemdspinner	Hemdenmacher
Hemmichspinner	Weber von Hemdleinen
Hemptenmacher	Verfertiger hölzerner Getreidemaße
Henzler	Lohnfuhrmann
Heringer	Heringsfischer, -händler
Herrenschenker	Städtischer Bediensteter, der dem Rat aufzuwarten hatte, den Ehrenwein ausschenkte und Zitationen ausfertigte
Heuerbaas	Stellenvermittler für Seeleute
Heuerling	Tagelöhner; Pächter mit kleinem Eigenbesitz; auch: Söldner
Heuermann	Pächter
Hiepenbäker	Bäcker von Oblatenkuchen
Hierskna(e)uer, -kneuer	Hirsestampfer
Himtenmacher	Hersteller hölzerner Getreidemaße
Hinterfürmacher	Hersteller der bärenmützenähnlichen Frauenkopfbedeckungen

Hintersasse, -sättler, -sieder	Kleinbauer, Kossät, Pächter, der in jedem Fall von dem Herrn dinglich abhängig war, weil er sein Gut nicht zu freien Eigen hatte
Hippenmacher	Sensenschmied
Hirt, der große	Viehhirt
Hirt, der kleine	Pferdehirt
Hocke	Kleinhändler, Höker
Hodeler, Hödel	Lumpenhändler, Produktenhändler
Hölscher	Holzschuhmacher
Höpfner	Hopfenanbauer
Hövtmann	Vertreter einer Bauernschaft; Gerichtssitzer
Hofagent, -faktor	Hofbeamter, dem der Einkauf der Waren für die Hofhaltung obliegt
Hofeigener	Höriger
Hoffrohne	Herrschaftlicher Beamter oder Knecht
Hoffourier, -furier	Unterer Hofbeamter, dem die Überwachung des Ordnungs- und Sicherheitsdienstes obliegt
Hofgänger	Scharwerker; landwirtschaftlicher Hilfsarbeiter
Hofkell(n)er	Gutsverwalter
Hofmann	Tagelöhner
Hofmeister	Verantwortlicher Beamter für die Hofhaltung kleinerer Landesherren; Gutsverwalter; Großknecht
Hofmusikgraf	(im kaiserlichen Österreich:) Kammerherr, der für die Oberleitung der Hofkapelle zuständig war
Hoister	Polizeidiener; Ratsschütze
Holländer	Besitzer einer sog. Holländer-Windmühle; Käsereibesitzer
Hollandgänger	Landwirtschaftlicher Arbeiter, der im Frühjahr in Holland Arbeit sucht
Holzbitschenmacher	Drechsler von Bechern, sog. Bitschen
Holzdreher	Drechsler
Holzer	Holzarbeiter
Holzgraf, grefe, -vogt	Amtsvorsteher für das Forstwesen

Holzknecht	Forstbediensteter
Holzmann	Holz(groß)händler
Holzmenger	Holz(klein)händler
Holzmüller	Besitzer oder Pächter einer Sägemühle
Holzschnitz(l)er	Holzbildhauer
Holzschuher	Hersteller von Holzschuhen und -pantoffeln
Horbmeister	Aufseher über die Straßenreinigung
Hornrichter	Zubereiter des Horns; Kammacher
Hosenstricker	Hersteller von gestrickten Strümpfen, auch von gestrickten Hosen
Hubenschmied	Verfertiger der Sturmhauben
Huber	Häusler; Besitzer einer Hufe Land
Hucker	Krämer
Hudelstricker	Altzeughändler; Lumpenaufkäufer
Hübscherin	Dirne
Hüfner, Hufener	Bauer mit einer Hufe Besitz
Hühnerträger	Geflügelhändler
Hüllenweber	Verfertiger von Frauenkopfbedeckungen
Hümpler	Stümper, Bönhase
Hütmann	Steiger in einem Bergwerk
Humpeler	Hilfsbauhandwerker
Hundt	Vorsteher einer Hontschaft; Schultheiß; später: Fronbote
Hurenwaibel, weibel	Aufseher über die mit der Truppe ziehenden Angehörigen der Landsknechte, der Marketenderinnen usw.
Huter	Hutmacher; Hersteller von Kopfbedeckungen
Hutmacher	Arbeiter in der Zuckerindustrie, der die Zuckerhüte herstellt
Hutmann	Bockhalter
Hutschmucker, -staffierer	Putzmacher; Hersteller von Kopfbedeckungen
Hutwalker	Herrichter des Filzes für Hüte
Hüxter	Kleinhändler; Krämer

I

Illuminist	Initialenmaler für Handschriften, Bücher
Infrau	Einwohnerin
Initialenmaler	Rotmaler, der Handschriften und Bücher mi Initialen ausmalt
Inmann	Einwohner
Inseß	Beisitzer, z. B. in einer Stadt
Inste	Mieter; Einlieger; Insasse; Tagelöhner
Instmann	Gutstagelöhner
Instrumentist	Hersteller von Musikinstrumenten
Ipser	Tüncher, Anstreicher
Ircher	Weißgerber
Italienisch Gutfertiger	Spediteur für Fracht nach Italien

J

Jacobsbruder	Pilger (vor allem nach Santiago de Compo stella)
Jäger	Förster
Jopenhauer	Hersteller von Holztrögen
Jubili(e)rer	Juwelier
Juchtenlederer	Gerber von Ungarisch- oder Juchtenleder
Jungmann	Leichtmatrose

K

Karbatsch	Geldwechsler, Geldverleiher
Kabelschläger	Seiler, Hersteller der „Kabel" genannten Ankertrosse
Kabinettmeister	Abteilungsleiter
Kabuzenbauer	Kohlgärtner
Kacheler, Kächler, Kählinmacher	Töpfer, vor allem für Kacheln und Fliesen
Kämmler	Wollkämmer
Kämpe, Kämpfer	Lohnfechter
Kämpelmacher, Kampelmacher	Kammacher
Kän(d)eler	Hersteller von Röhren und Dachrinnen
Käsebäcker	Milchmeier; Hersteller von Käse
Käskäffl	Käsehändler
Kästner	Tischler, Schreiner
Käuf(e)l	Händler, Makler
Kaffamacher, Kaffhaarmacher	Samtweber, der Kaffhaar = abgeschorene Seide verwendet
Kafiller	Abdecker, Schinder
Kaffl	Händler
Kalamalmacher	Verfertiger von Rohrschreibfedern, Schreibzeugbestecken u. dgl.
Kalchborner	Kalkbrenner
Kalamanymacher	Weber von Kalmany, Kalmank, einem Kammgarngewebe, das dem Lasting oder Halbatlas entspricht
Kalterer	Weingärtner; Arbeiter in der Kelter
Kaltschlächter	Schinder, Abdecker
Kaltschmied	Schmied, der ohne Feuer, nur mit Hammer, Meißel und Feile arbeitet
Kammacher	Hersteller von Kämmen für das Haar, auch der Woll- und Weberkämme
Kammenrichter	Arbeiter, der die Holzblättchen in die Weberkämme einsetzt

Kampelmacher	Kammacher
Kamphäuerling	Pächter adeligen Großgrundbesitzes
Kandelgießer, Kandler	Kannenmacher
Kanefaßweber, Kanevasweber	Weber für Segeltuch und Packleinwand
Kanelgießer	Kannen-, Röhrenmacher
Kantengießer	Kannenmacher
Kappusmann	Weißkohlhändler
Karbender	Radmacher
Karchelzieher	Lastträger mit Handwagen
Karcher	Kärrner, Karrenfuhrmann
Kardätchenmacher, Kardetschen-	Hersteller von Weberkämmen und Weberdisteln
Kardenmacher, Kartenmacher	Kardetschenmacher, Kartensetzer
Karder, Karter	Wollkämmer
Kartenmaler	Holzschneider für Spielkarten und Heiligenbilder
Kasperer	Heilkundiger; heilkundiger Scharfrichter
Kassenpfleger	Schatzmeister, z. B. einer Stadt
Kastenknecht	Klosterbeamter, der die Aufsicht über den „Fruchtkasten" und die Verteilung des Getreides hat
Kastenmeister	Kirchenrendant
Ka(e)stner	Rentmeister; Gehilfe des Amtmanns; auch: Tischler, Schreiner
Katzenritter	Lohnfechter
Kauderer	Makler; Werg- und Flachshändler
Kaufgeselle	Handlungsgehilfe
Kaufhändler	Kaufmann
Kauwarz	Geldverleiher, Wechsler, Wucherer
Kaviller	Abdecker, Schinder
Kawertin, Kawerz(e), Kaworze	Geldverleiher, Wechsler, Wucherer
Kehrichtlader	Straßenreiniger, Kehrichträumer
Kelcher	Verfertiger metallener Becher und Kannen

Kell(n)er	Amtmann, Gutsverwalter, Rentmeister
Kellerlöw	Verwalter des Berliner Ratskellers
Kelterer	Weingärtner; Arbeiter in der Kelter
Kemmetfeger, Kenderkehrer	Schornsteinfeger
Kerselmann	Straßenreiniger
Kesselböter, -bu(e)ter, -lapper	Kesselflicker
Kess(e)ler	Kesselschmied, Kupferschmied
Kesselschläger	Kesselschmied
Kesskaiffer	Käsehändler
Kettleinbieger, Kettlmacher	Hersteller von Geschmeide, Schmuck
Kettler, Kettner	Verfertiger von kleinen Ketten aus Eisendraht
Keuschler	Kleinbauer, Häuser, Kossät
Kezzler	Kesselschmied
Kiechlbäcker, Kiechler	Hersteller von Feingebäck, Küchlein
Kiefer	Küfer
Kiepenkerl	Umherziehender Lebensmittelhändler
Kiepenmann	Botengänger
Kieser	Beamteter Tuchprüfer; vereidigter Schätzer; Taxator
Kilchmeier	Pächter eines Pfarrgutes
Kimmer	Böttcher
Kimmichkehrer	Schornsteinfeger, Kaminkehrer
Kindsmensch	Kindermädchen
Kipp(er)	Münzverfälscher
Kirchendechen	Armenpfleger
Kirchendiener, -knecht	Küster, Meßner
Kirchenvater	(Neben den bekannten Gestalten aus der Kirchengeschichte:) Von der Gemeinde gewählter Beamter, der die kirchlichen wirtschaftlichen Interessen der Gemeinde gegenüber dem Pfarrer zu vertreten und das Kirchenvermögen zu verwalten hat
Kirchner	Küster, Meßner

Kirschner	Kürschner
Kirseymacher	Hersteller von starkem Wollmantelstoff, dem Kirsey
Kistenschreiber	Lohnschreiber
Kistler, Kistner	Schreiner, Tischler
Kitter	Glaser
Klaber	Anstreicher, Estrichmacher
Klämpner	Spengler, Klempner
Klärimacher	Brenner der Kläre, der Knochenasche, die für Gold- und Silberschmelzen, aber auch für die Zuckersiedereien benötigt wurde; vielleicht auch: Stärkefabrikant
Klagansager	Leichenbitter
Klaiber	Klaber (siehe dort); Buchbinder
Klamp(f)erer	Spengler, Klempner
Klauber, Kle(i)ber	Klaber (siehe dort); Buchbinder
Kleibener	Töpfer
Kleidertäuscher	Altkleiderhändler
Kleinbeck	Grobbäcker, der Brot backt und verkauft
Kleinbinder	Faßbinder, der kleine Gefäße herstellt; Böttcher
Kleinböttcher	Bechermacher
Kleinerbe	Besitzer eines Hauses mit minderem Bürgerrecht
Kleinglöckleingießer	Hersteller von Rollen und Schellen
Kleinschmied	Schlosser, Mechaniker
Kleinuhrmacher	Hersteller von Zimmer- und Taschenuhren
Kleremacher	Brenner von Knochenasche (s. Klärimacher)
Kleyderhocker	Altkleiderhändler
Klicher	Kleber, Kleiber, Klaber
Klinger	Hersteller von Degenklingen
Klipper	Klempner
Klopffechter	Schaufechter, Schirmer
Kloterer	Gaukler
Klotzenmacher, Klotzkorkenmacher	Holzschuhmacher

Klüngelkerl	Lumpensammler
Knapphans	Marketender; Kantinenpächter
Knapsack	Hausierer
Knaufelmacher, Knäufler	Knopfmacher
Kneveler	Bierführer
Knochenhauer	Schlachter; Fleischverkäufer
Knopfgießer, -presser	Hersteller gegossener Metallknöpfe; Hersteller gepreßter Metallknöpfe
Knopfsmit	Knopfschmied; vielleicht: Schmied von verzierten Arbeiten (Ggs.: Flachschmied)
Knopfspinner	Hersteller mit Stoff überzogener Knöpfe
Köbler	Kleinbauer
Köllmer	Bauer
Kölschweber	Weber einer besonderen Tuchart, des Gölschen oder Kölschen
Körber	Korbmacher
Körner	Getreidehändler; Einnehmer von Naturalabgaben
Körtzner	Kürschner
Kötter	Bauer, der nur einen kleinen Besitz bewirtschaftet und keinen Anteil an der Allmende hat
Kohlbrenner	Köhler, Hersteller von Holzkohle
Kohlvogt	Öffentlicher Ausrufer
Kolbekerl	Landsknecht oder Söldner, der nur mit dem Streitkolben bewaffnet ist
Kollerwascher	Reiniger der Lederjacken, der Koller
Kolon	Kolonist; Siedler; Bauer
Kompan	Adjutant des Großmeisters vom Deutschen Orden
Kompastmacher	Hersteller von Kompassen und Meßgeräten
Komplethändler	Schnittwarenhändler
Kondukteur	(Ober-)Baurat
Konsorte	Teilhaber des Quartiersmannes (siehe dort)
Konstabler	Büchsenmeister; Feuerwerker; Artillerist; Bombardierer; Polizist

Koppelknecht	Knecht, der Pferde zum Markt führt
Koppenschopper	Hersteller von Holztrögen
Korber	Korbmacher, -flechter
Kordelmacher	Seiler
Korduan(gerber)	Schuhmacher; Verarbeiter des Corduanleders
Korkenmacher	Holzschuhmacher
Kornett	Jüngster Offizier einer Schwadron, der die Standarte trug (Fähnrich)
Kornkäffl, käufler	Kornhändler, Greisler; auch: Getreidewucherer
Kornkapitän	Seefahrender selbständiger Getreidegroßhändler
Kornmann	Getreidehändler
Kornmeister	Einnehmer und Verwalter der Naturalabgaben
Kornschreiber	Gehilfe des Kornmeisters
Kornumstecher	Arbeiter, der für die sachgemäße Behandlung von Getreide zuständig ist
Korssenmeister	Kürschner
Kossät, Kötter, Kotsaß	Kleinbauer; vom Grundherrn angesiedelter Bauer, der ein Haus und etwas Land erhält und auf dem Hof arbeitete
Kotze	a) (männlich) Kleinbauer b) (weiblich) Dirne
Kotzmacher	Hersteller, auch Vorabeiter des groben Lodenstoffs, des Kotze
Kotzmenger	Verkäufer von Wellfleisch
Kotzweber	Weber groben Wollstoffs, des Kotze
Krämer	Kleinhändler
Krämpelmacher	Kardetschenmacher
Krämper	Trödler, Höker
Krätzmüller	Besitzer oder Pächter einer Mühle für Krätze, Gold- und Silberabfall
Kräut(l)er	Gemüsehändler; Händler mit Küchen- und Gewürzkräutern; auch: Apotheker, Botaniker
Krankenvater	Verwalter eines Hospitals
Krebisser, Krebser	Krebsfänger, -händler

Kreidenschneider	Bleistiftmacher
Kreisler	Getreidehändler
Kreisrat	Königlicher Beamter in Ostpreußen, etwa im Range eines Landrats
Kreisrichter	Landrichter
Krempler	Wollkämmer
Kretschmer, Kretschner	Schankwirt
Kreu(t)zschmied	Schmied von Waffengriffen
Kröschner	Händler mit Kleie
Kröslerin	Verfertigerin von Hals- und Busenkrausen
Kromeke, Kromer	Kleinhändler, Trödler, Höker
Krudener	Drogenhändler; Apotheker
Krüger	Gastwirt, Inhaber des „Krugs"
Krüsekerl	Zinngießer, der beschädigte Tranlampen repariert
Krugbäcker	Töpfer, besonders für Mineral- und Branntweinkrüge
Krugelmann	Händler, Hausierer mit Tonwaren
Krukenmacher	Töpfer, vor allem für Tonflaschen, sogenannte Kruken
Ku(e)chler	Feinbäcker, Konditor
Kuderer	Flachs- und Werghändler
Kübler	Böttcher
Küfer	Böttcher; Angestellter in einer Weinkellerei, Weinpfleger
Kümichkehrer	Schornsteinfeger
Kümmer	Küfer
Kürbenzainer, -zeiner	Korbflechter, vor allem von Tragekörben
Kürbler	Hersteller von Schleifsteinen
Küter	(Lohn-)Schlächter
Kufenmacher	eine Art Böttcher, verfertigte u. a. Feuerlöscheimer
Kuhlengräber	Totengräber
Kummeder, Kumuder	Sattler, Hersteller von Pferdegeschirren, besonders des Kummet

Kumpastenmacher	Hersteller von Kompassen und Meßgeräten
Kumper, Kumpgenger	Färbergeselle
Kunkelmacher	Verfertiger der Spinnrocken (Kunkel)
Kunstfärber	Schön- oder Waidfärber
Kunstfechter	Schaufechter, Voltisierer
Kunstmeister	Mechaniker; Orgelbauer
Kunststabler	siehe Konstabler
Kunthormacher	Hersteller von Schreibmöbeln u. dgl. (für Kontore)
Kurdelmacher	Seiler
Kurdewener	Verarbeiter von Corduanleder; Schuhmacher
Kurer	Vereidigter Schätzer, Prüfer, Taxator
Kurischer König	Freibauer eines sieben Dörfer umfassenden Bezirks in Kurland zwischen Goldingen und Hasenpoth
Kurkeler	Holzschuhmacher
Kurschmied	Hufschmied bei der Kavallerie, der zugleich Roßarzt ist; Beschlagmeister
Kurschner, Kursener	Kürschner
Kurzmesserschmied	Dolchmacher
Kutschner	Kleinbauer, Kossät
Kuttelwamper	Verkäufer der Rinderwänste
Kuttler	Kuttelflecksieder

L

Laaber	Käser
Ladener	Verkäufer; Tischler, Schreiner
Ladenmeister	Büchsenmeister oder Tafelherr einer Zunft, der für das Rechnungswesen zuständig war
Lader	Rollkutscher
Läderer	Gerber, Lederbearbeiter
Lädleinmacher	Truhenmacher, Schreiner für Wohn- und Ziermöbel
Lägeler	Hersteller der Legel, kleiner hölzerner Gefäße, auch der Fäßchen
Läufenschmied	Büchsenschmied
Läuter	Glöckner
Lakenkrämer	Tuchhändler
Lakenmacher, -weber	Bettzeugweber
Lakenscherer	Tuchscherer
Lakenwardein	Tuchprüfer
Lampart	Pfandleiher
Landfahrer	Vagabund
Landgebräucher	Landwirt
Landinste	Landwirtschaftlicher Tagelöhner
Landjäger	Gendarm
Landkramer	Hausierer
Landmann	Bauer
Landstörzer	Landstreicher, Vagabund
Langmesserer	Schmied von Blankwaffen
Lapicide	Steinmetz
Lapper	Flickschuster
Lasiterer	Salpetergräber, -sieder
Laßeisenmacher	Hersteller chirurgischer Instrumente, vor allem der Aderlaß-Eisen
Lauenstreicher	Leinwand-Kleinhändler
Lauer	Lohgerber, Rotgerber
Lautenist	Lautenbauer, auch: Lautenspieler

Lebku(e)chler, -küchner, -zelter	Lebkuchenbäcker, Pfefferkuchenbäcker
Lederbereiter, -braiter, -dauer, -thauer, -täuer, Lederer	Gerber, Lederbearbeiter
Lederschmierer	Lederfärber, -vergolder
Legelner	Hersteller der Legel, hölzerner Gefäße
Leggemeister	Schaumeister für Leinengewebe
Lehmentirer	Lehmarbeiter
Lehmer	Töpfer
Lehmklicker	Werkmeister für Fachwerkbauten
Leibgedinger, -züchter	Bauer im Ausgedinge, auf dem Altenteil
Leichenlader	Leichenbitter
Leiendecker	Schieferdachdecker
Leiermann	Drehorgelspieler
Leimenführer	Fuhrmann für das Rohmaterial zu Fachwerkbauten, in der Hauptsache Lehm
Leimenmacher	Töpfer
Leimmacher	Leimsieder
Leinenreider	Leinenweber
Leinhösler	Verfertiger leinerner Strumpfhosen
Leinreiter	Berittener Schiffszieher, Treidler
Leirenzieher	Drahtzieher
Leistenschneider	Hersteller von Schuhmacherleisten
Leitgeb	Schankwirt, Dorfwirt
Lepper	Flickschuster
Lers(e)ner	Hersteller von Lederhosen, auch von Schaftstiefeln
Lesser	Barbier, der zur Ader läßt, schröpft
Lesterer	Landfleischer, Kleinviehschlächter
Lewantstricker	Kleinhändler mit Leinwand
Lewknecht	Aufwärter im Berliner Ratskeller
Licentmeister	Einnehmer der Akzise, der indirekten Steuern
Lichtwark, -werker	Gießer von Talgkerzen
Lichtzieher	Hersteller von Wachskerzen

Ligelner	Böttcher, der vornehmlich Legel, hölzerne Gefäße herstellt
Linguist	Sprachmeister
Linner	Leinenweber
Lionischer Golddrahtzieher	Hersteller unechten Golddrahtes
Lionischer Goldschlager	Rauschgold-, Lohngoldschläger
Lismer	Strumpfstricker
Lite	Zinsbauer
Litzenbruder	Transportvermittler
Loder(er)	Lodenweber
Löber, Lo(e)her, Lo(e)rer	Lohgerber, Rotgerber
Löffler	Hersteller von Löffeln
Löscher	Weißgerber
Löthschlosser	Hersteller gelöteter Vorhängeschlösser
Löwe	Hamburger Ausdruck für Gelegenheitsarbeiter (z. B. Hopfenmarktslöwe)
Lohmüller	Besitzer oder Pächter einer Stampfmühle für Gerberlohe
Lohnarbeiter	Tagelöhner
Lokalist	Ortspfarrer, Geistlicher an einer Filialkirche
Lokalrichter	Ortsrichter; Gerichtsgehilfe auf dem Gebiet der freiwilligen Gerichtsbarkeit
Losbäcker	Feinbäcker, der Weizengebäck herstellt
Losfrau	Landwirtschaftliche Arbeiterin, Tagelöhnerin
Losmädchen	Unverheiratete landwirtschaftliche Arbeiterin; Tagelöhnerin
Losmann	Tagelöhner, der in keinem dauernden Dienstverhältnis steht, sondern unabhängig zur Miete wohnt
Lotter	Gaukler, Taschenspieler
Lou-Goldschmied	Messingarbeiter
Lucernenmacher	Laternenmacher
Luchtenmacher	Laternenmacher; Hersteller von Fensterrahmen

Lüstrierer	Textilarbeiter
Lützenbruder	Lader
Luminist	Kleinmaler, Initialenmaler
Lumpart	Pfandleiher
Luntenmann	Lumpensammler
Lutinist	Lautenbauer; Lautenspieler

M

Ma(e)der, Meder	Mäher, Kornschneider
Mälzer	Brauknecht
Mäntelschneider, Mäntler, Mentler	Mantelmacher
Malschlosser, Malschloßmacher	Verfertiger von Vorhängeschlössern und auch von Vexierschlössern
Malzmüller	Mälzer, Besitzer einer Malzdarre
Manchester(samt)weber	Weber des Baumwollsamt (im Gegensatz zum Caffaweber)
Mandenmacher	Korbflechter
Manger	(Klein-)Händler; auch: Tuchwalker, der das Tuch mit der Mange/Mangel glättet
Markscheider	Vermessungsbeamter im Bergbau
Markschreier	Beamter zur Schlichtung von Grenzstreitigkeiten innerhalb der Gemarkung; Vorsitzer des Ortsgerichts
Marktschreier	Jahrmarktshändler, Storger, Quacksalber
Marxbruder	Öffentlicher Fechter aus des Bruderschaft des hl. Markus
Maskenmacher	Hersteller von Gesichtsmasken, besonders für Fasching, Karneval, auch für Theater
Materialist	Drogist, Gewürz-, Spezereihändler
Mattenmacher, Matzen-	Hersteller von Matten, Matratzen
Maulhirte	Maultiertreiber
Mautner	Zolleinnehmer, Zöllner
Medailleur	Stempelschneider, Graveur für Münzen, Siegel, Medaillen
Meier	(sehr weitgehender Begriff) z. B. Bauer, Pächter, Amtmann
Melber	Mehlhändler
Melcher	Melker, Schweizer
Melreder	Mehlhändler
Menger	siehe Manger

Menkeler	Kleinhändler, besonders für Geflügel
Mentager	(im Elsaß) Besitzer eines Gutes, das kleiner als eine Hufe ist und geringere Fronden hat
Mezler	Kleinhändler, Höker
Mesolanmacher	Weber der halbwollenen Beiderwand, des Mesolan
Messer	Eichbeamter
Messerer	Messerschmied
Messerträger	Händler, auch Hausierer mit Messer- und Schmiedewaren, etwa aus Solingen
Mes(s)ner	Küster, Kirchendiener
Metpreu, Metter	Metfabrikant, -sieder, -brauer
Metz(e)ler, Metzger	Schlachter, Fleischer
Metzner	Müllerknappe, Gehilfe des Müllers
Mietling, Mietmann	Tagelöhner
Miniaturist	Maler kleiner Bilder, z. B. in Büchern
Minierer	Bearbeiter; Schanzengräber beim Festungsbau; Sprengmeister
Modelstecher	Schnitzer von Lebkuchenformen
Modist	Putzmacher
Mörsergießer	Kanonen-, Stückgießer
Moldenhauer, Mollen-	Hersteller hölzerner Mulden, Tröge
Moler	Maler
Mollenpächter	Mühlenpächter
Moluckendreher	Verfertiger von Strohhülsen für Flaschen
Monarch	Landstreicher, Gelegenheitsarbeiter
Moshake	Gemüsehändler
Mostler	Hersteller von Most und Obstsäften
Motter	Kornmesser
Mühlarzt	Mühlenbauer, Zimmermann
Mühlenbereiter	Aufsichtsbeamter über die Mühlen
Mühlenbescheider	Mühlenverwalter
Mühlerbe	Mühlenbesitzer
Müllner	Müller
Mülscher	Müllergeselle
Münzeisenschneider	Graveur für Münzstöcke

Münzer	Münzpräger, Münzmeister
Münzschlosser	Schlosser für das Preßwerk in der Münze
Münzschroter	Münzpräger, -meister
Münzwardein	Münzmeister, der Feingehalt und Gewicht prüfen und garantieren mußte
Mütter	Kornmesser
Muldener, Multeler	Hersteller von Backtrögen (Mulden)
Musikgraveur	Notenstecher
Musterreiter	Reisender
Musterschreiber	Registrator bei der Musterung
Mutter der Sonder-siechen	Vorsteherin des Aussätzigenspitals

N

Nabenschmied	Stellmacher
Naber	Bohrerschmied, Hersteller von Bohrern
Nachbar	Bauer; Dorfgenosse
Nachgänger	Unterer Zollbeamter
Nachgangsschreiber	Gerichtsschreiber am Kriminalgericht
Nachrichter (Nach-Richter)	Scharfrichter
Nachtkönig, Nacht-meister	Abtrittreiniger, Kehrichtlader, der nachts den Unrat wegräumte
Nachtrufer	Nachtwächter
Nadler, Nätler	(Steck-)Nadelmacher
Näbiger	Bohrerschmied, Naber
Näter(in)	Näher(in)
Nagler	Nagelschmied
Neber, Neberschmied	Bohrerschmied
Negociant	Kaufmann
Neher(in)	Näher(in)
Neilschmieder	Nagelschmied
Nepperschmied	Bohrerschmied
Nestler	Schnürsenkelhersteller; Nestelmacher
Nestelbeschlager	Senkler
Netzenschlepper, -träger	Gehilfe bei der Jagd und beim Fischfang
Ney(g)er	Näher
Niederläger, Nieder-lags-Verwandter	Ausländischer Großkaufmann in Wien, bis 1744 mit besonderen kaiserlichen Freiheiten ausgestattet
Noldener, Noldmacher	Nadelmacher
Nonnenmacher	Schweinekastrierer, Verschneider
Nopper	Arbeiter, der das Tuch von Wollknötchen (Noppen) reinigt
Nüscheler	Spangenmacher
Nüschenmacher	Senkler, Nestler
Nüsseler	Nußöl-Presser

Nufeler	Weber einfacher, grober Stoffe
Nuldener	Nadelmacher
Nummernrieder	Berittener Bote, der die auswärts gezogenen Lotterienummern überbrachte

O

Obentürer	Edelsteinhändler; Händler mit Luxuswaren
Oberalter	Mitglied des Hamburger Bürgerausschusses, der aus Kirchengemeinde-Vertretern zusammengesetzt ist
Oberhelfer	Seelsorger; Archidiakon
Ob(m)esser	Obstbauer; auch: Obsthändler
Obristen Perckmeister	Leiter eines Bergwerks
Obst(l)er, Obsthocker, Oebster	Obsthändler
Occlist	Augenarzt
Ochsenschlager	Schlachter, Rindsmetzger
Ochsenweber	Weber von schwerem Tuch
Öffentlicher Agent	Rechtsgelehrter mit beschränkten Befugnissen, zwischen Notar und Anwalt
Ökonomiebaumeister	Baumann
Ölmann, -schla(e)ger, -stampfer	Ölmüller, Ölerzeuger
Of(e)ner	Ofenbauer, -setzer, -heizer; Bäcker
Ofentürer	Edelsteinhändler; Händler mit Luxuswaren
Ohlenmacher	Töpfer
Okulist	Augenarzt
Oldbuter, -kitter	Flickschuster
Oleymann	Ölhändler
Olmacher	Ölmüller
Omenträger	Lastenträger
Operist	Opernsänger
Opfermann	Küster, Meßner, Kirchendiener
Orgeler	Orgelbauer
Orleymacher	Uhrmacher
Ortschmied	Hersteller von Werkzeugen, besonders von Schusterahlen u. dgl.
Ortsschätzer	Gerichtsgehilfe auf dem Gebiet der freiwilligen Gerichtsbarkeit; Ortsrichter

Packer	Ballenbinder; Verlader
Pagamentsherr	Mitglied des Stadtrats, der für das Münzwesen zuständig war
Pagedor	Befehlshaber der friesländischen Reiterei
Palestermacher	Hersteller der Armbrust
Panelenmacher	Verfertiger von Täfelungen
Pannenklöpper	Pfannenschmied
Pantbereiter	Bandweber
Pantinist	Hersteller von Holzschuhen, Pantinen
Papi(e)rer	Papiermacher
Pappenhammer, Pappenheimer	(Nur in Nürnberg gebräuchlicher Ausdruck) Abtritträumer
Paradeiser	Gärtner
Parapluimacher	Hersteller von Regenschirmen
Parasolmacher	Hersteller von Sonnenschirmen
Parche(n)tweber, Parchner	Weber des Barchent
Paretensticker	Biretmacher
Pariserarbeiter	Hersteller unechter Goldwaren; Galanteriearbeiter
Parisgenmacher	Hersteller von Filz-Hausschuhen
Parschalk	Halbfreier Gutsangehöriger
Partikulier	Privatmann; Rentner, Rentier; auch: Schifffahrtsunternehmer mit nur einem Schiff, das er selbst führt.
Paterlemacher, Paternosterer, Paternostermacher	Hersteller von Rosenkränzen
Patinenmacher	Verfertiger von Holzpantoffeln
Patronenzeichner	Zeichner der bei der Weberei verwendeten Musterblätter, der Patronen
Patronierer, Patronist	Briefmaler, der mit Schablonen, sogenannten Patronen, koloriert
Pelzer	Kürschner

Pensionär	(Vor allem in Holland) Stadtsyndikus; auch: Beamter, der regelmäßige Zuwendungen auf dem Gnadenweg erhielt, kein Ruhegehalt, das „Provision" hieß.
Perleinmacher	Hersteller von Rosenkränzen
Permenn(t)er, Permentirer, Permentmacher, Permi(n)ter	Hersteller von Pergament
Petschierer, Petschaftschneider	Graveur, der hauptsächlich Siegel gräbt
Peutler	Hersteller von Lederbeuteln und Taschen
Pfänder	Feldaufseher, Feldhüter; Polizist; Fronbote
Pfänner	Pfannenschmied; auch: Besitzer von Anteilen an einer Saline
Pfahlbürger	Bewohner der Vorstand; Ausbürger; Ausmann
Pfaichmacher, Pfaidler	Hemdennäher, Hemdenhändler
Pfeifenbäcker	Porzellanarbeiter, der hauptsächlich Pfeifenköpfe herstellt
Pfeifenmacher	Hersteller von Flöten und Tabakpfeien aus Ton
Pfeilschifter	Verfertiger der Pfeilschäfte und der Pfeile
Pfennigmeister	Steuereinnehmer einer Stadt; auch: Zahlmeister der Landsknechte
Pferdner	(Voll-)Bauer, der mit Pferdegespannen arbeitet
Pfettenhauer	Hersteller der Dachbalken (Pfetten) und des Dachstuhls
Pfister	Feinbäcker
Pfleger	Amtmann; Meier; Rentmeister; Schatzmeister
Pfortmann	Pförtner
Pfragner	Kleinhändler; Krämer; Trödler
Pfriemenmacher	Werkzeugmacher; Ahlenschmied
Pfundherr	Vorsteher der Pfundkammer, die den Pfundzoll, eine Schiffsabgabe, erhebt.
Physikus	Amtsarzt

Pickeler, Pickleinmacher	Helm-, Haubenschmied
Pieler	Arbeiter in der Zigarrenfabrik
Pilser	Kürschner
Pirmeider, Pirmenter, Pirmiter	Pergamentmacher
Placker	Ausbesserer von Schäden an Fachwerkbauten
Placzbeck	Feinbäcker, Konditor
Planteur	Züchter von Maulbeerbäumen
Plattenschlager	Verfertiger der Plattenharnische
Plattner	Hersteller des Harnischs, besonders des Brustharnischs
Plattschlosser	Fertiger großer Schlösser für Türen und Schränke
Plechhantschuer	Hersteller der Blechhandschuhe für Rüstungen
Plettersetzer	Blattbinder, der die dünnen Holzplättchen für Weberkämme herstellt und einsetzt
Pliesterer	Anstreicher, Tüncher
Pluger	Pflugschmied
Pochschreiber	Rechnungsbeamter eines Bergwerks
Pölter	Kürschner
Pötter	Töpfer
Pogner	Bogenmacher; auch: Bogenschütze
Polierer, Poliermüller	Schleifer
Portenmacher	Posamentierer
Posenschaber	Kielfedernschneider
Possementierer	Posamentierer
Poussierer	Bossierer; Former
Pracher	Bettler
Prachervogt	Städtischer Bettelvogt
Prägschneider	Graveur, Siegel-, Mnzeisenschneider
Prahmknecht	Schifferknecht
Presser	Drucker
Preßwerker	Posamentierer; Schnürriemenmacher
Preuknecht	Mälzer; Arbeiter in einer Brauerei
Prieffkramer	Bilderhändler

Prisilgstoßer	Zerkleinerer des als Farbe und als Arznei verwendeten Brasilholzes
Pritschenmeister, Pritzen-	Festordner, Stegreifdichter, Spaßmacher
Pritstabel	Wasservogt; Aufseher über die Fischerei
Probenreiter	Reisender
Probierer	Scheider; Beamter, der den Feingehalt nachprüft
Profoß	Bei den Landsknechten der Regimentsscharfrichter; Polizei(unter)offizier
Prozeßagent	Rechtskonsulent; nicht akademisch ausgebildeter Rechtsberater
Pruckmacher	Wege- und Brückenbauer
Puchfeller, Puchveler	Pergamentmacher
Püchsenmeister	Schatzmeister, Kassierer, z. B. einer Zunft
Pütjer	Töpfer
Püt(t)ner, Put(t)ner	Böttcher, Büttner, Binder
Püt(z)macher	Brunnengräber
Pulsant	Glöckner
Pumper	Paukenist, Paukenschläger
Puppenmaler	Maler von Heiligenbildern
Putzmacher	Modist

Q

Quartiersmann	Packer, Lagerhalter
Quinterner	Spieler der kleinen, mit nur fünf Seiten bespannten Laute, der Quinterne

R

Rachimburge	Schöffe; Beisitzer des Richters beim Ding-gericht
Racker	Abdecker; Abtrittreiniger
Rademacher, Rade-maker	Stellmacher, Wagner, Radbauer
Radspinner	Flachs-Spinner
Rädermacher, Rädker	Spinnradbauer
Rähmmeister	Appreturmeister; Beaufsichtiger der Rahmen-spanner in der Tuchfabrik
Räßmacher	Verfertiger von Räß, einem leichten Woll-gewebe, das nach der Stadt Arras benannt ist
Raketenmacher	Feuerwerker
Rangschiffer	Schiffseigner, der einer Vereinigung zur Erzie-lung von Regelmäßigkeiten in den Fahrten angehört
Ranzeler	Hersteller von Ranzen, Rucksäcken
Rascher, Rasch-macher	Verfertiger von Räsch/Räß, einem nach der Stadt Arras benannten leichten Wollgewebe
Rastelbinder	Umherziehender Topfflicker, Hersteller von Mäusefallen u. dgl.
Rat kurzen Rockes	Mitglied des Provinzialrates im alten Herzog-tum Luxemburg aus dem Adel, dem Militär und den Lehnsträgern
Rat langen Rockes	Juristisches oder geistliches Mitglied des Pro-vinzialrates im alten Herzogtum Luxemburg
Ratsfreund, -geselle	Schöffe, Ratsmitglied
Ratspensionär	Staatssekretär von Holland und Westfriesland
Ratsschenker	Städtischer Beamter, der dem Rat aufzuwarten, den Ehrenwein zu kredenzen und Zitationen auszufertigen hatte
Ratsverwandter	Mitglied des Stadtrates; auch: früherer Stadt-rat
Rauchfleischmetzger	Selcher
Rauhschleifer	Schleifer grober Werkzeuge

Rauschfärber	Schwarzfärber
Rebmann	Winzer
Rechenmeister	Kämmerer, der für die Finanzen zuständig ist
Rechenpfennigmacher	Flitterschläger
Rechtsagent	Rechtskonsulent; Rechtsberater ohne Anwalts-befugnis
Redmann	Oberster Leiter der „Einungen" in der Graf-schaft Hauenstein; auch: Stadtredner
Redner	Anwalt; Schöffe, Vorsprecher; Stadtredner
Reeper, Reepschläger	Seiler, Taumacher
Reiber	Badeknecht zum Trockenreiben und Massieren
Reichkrämer	(In Schlesien) Handelsleute, die mit Eisen-werk, Blei, aber auch Spezereien usw. handeln
Reid(e)meister	Freier Hammerherr; Hersteller von Osemund-eisen
Reider	Schwertfeger, der die Degengriffe anbringt
Reifer, Reifschläger	Seiler
Reiser	Pilger
Reiser und Gradierer	Zeichner und Radierer
Reisiger	Berittener Söldner zum Schutz eines Reise- oder Kaufmannszuges
Reisser	Zeichner
Reißzeugmacher	Zirkelschmied
Reitender Diener	(in Hamburg) Stadtdiener
Reitmeister	Stadtkämmerer für das Finanzwesen, Rechen-meister
Reitschmied	Hufschmied
Remenschla(e)ger	Gürtler, Gürtelbeschlagmacher, Nestler
Reusse, Reuzze	Flickschuster
Revenirer	Zuckerbäcker
Riemenschneider	Sattler, Gürtler
Riemer	Sattler, Verfertiger von Lederzeug, z. B. von Pferdegeschirr; Riemenmacher
Rietmacher	Hersteller der Rietblätter oder -kämme, die beim Weben die Kette stets in gleichem Ab-stand halten

Riffian	Bordellwirt
Rindschuster, Rind-suter	Gerber
Ringelpanzermacher, Ringer, Ring-harnischer, Rinker	Kettenschmied, Hersteller von Kettenhemden und -panzern
Rinkelmacher, Rinkenschmied	Agraffenmacher
Ringler	Hersteller von Ringen
Rinnenmacher	Verfertiger von Holzrinnen und -trögen
Rippelreier	Tänzer, Seiltänzer
Rockener	Schwarzbrotbäcker
Rockenmacher	Hersteller der Spinnrocken
Röhr(en)meister	Brunnenbauer, -aufseher; Rohrmeister
Röseler	Kalkbrenner
Rösseler	Pflasterer; Boßler; Rößler; Bratspießwender
Rößler, Ro(e)sser	Pferdeknecht; Lohnfuhrmann
Rohrenbohrer, -macher	Hersteller von Holz- und Metallrohren, auch von Zapfen und Zapfhähnen
Rohrrüster, -schmied, Rohrrüstmeister	Hersteller von Gewehrläufen und Büchsenrohren
Rojgast	Rudermatrose
Rollenmacher	Gießer von Schellen und kleinen Glocken
Roller	a) Rollkutscher, Lader, Spediteur
	b) Buchbinder, der mit geschnittenen Metallrollen Ziermuster auf Einbänden usw. anbringt
Rorenschieber	Hausierer in Blechwaren
Roscher	Wollweber, Hersteller des Rosch (siehe Räß)
Rossinger	Pferdeknecht; Lohnfuhrmann
Roßkamm, -täuscher	Pferdehändler
Rotbinder	Böttcher; Faßbinder für kleine Gefäße
Rotdrechsel, Rotschmieddrechsel	Metalldreher, besonders für Kupfer- und Messinggeräte
Rotgerber, -lascher, -löscher	Lohgerber

Rotgießer	Kupferschmied; Glockengießer
Rottmeister	a) Bezirksvorsteher
	b) Führer einer Rotte (im Militär etwa dem Gefreiten vergleichbar)
Royer	Küfer; Bereiter des Weins
Rudersmann	Steuermann
Ruffian	Bordellwirt
Rumormeister	Beamter, der für Ruhe und Ordnung zu sorgen hatte; Feldgendarm; Gehilfe des Hurenweibels (siehe dort)
Rundenmacher	Wächter
Rußbrenner	Hersteller von Ruß zur Farbenherstellung; auch: Rußfärber
Ruße, Russe	Flickschuster
Rußfärber	Schwarzgerber, Hersteller schwarzen Corduanleders; Lederarbeiter
Rußlandfahrer	Sammler, auch Händler von Blutegeln
Rutenbinder	Besenbinder
Ruxengießer	Rotgießer

Säckelmeister	Schatzmeister einer Stadt; Steuereinnehmer, Vermögensverwalter
Säckler	Säckelmeister; auch: Hersteller von Taschen und Beuteln
Säer	Sämann
Sämbler	Samenhändler
Sämer	Frachtfuhrmann mit Saumtieren; Saumtierhalter
Sämischbereiter	Hersteller von Sämischleder
Sänftener	Sänftenträger
Säumer, Saumer	Saumtierhalter; Frachtfuhrmann mit Saumtieren
Sageter	Sägemüller
Saitenmacher	Hersteller von (Darm-)Saiten für Musikinstrumente
Salbürge, Salmann	Treuhänder, Testamentsvollstrecker
Salbenhändler	Salbenverkäufer auf dem Jahrmarkt; auch Apotheker
Salbenmacher	Hersteller von Salben und Balsam
Saltzitzienmacher	Wurstler
Salunenmacher	Hersteller von Salunen, groben Wolldecken, die nach Châlons-sur-Marne benannt sind
Salwirt(h), -würcher, -würker, -wurch(ter)	Waffenschmied, Plattner
Salzaufleger	Unterer Beamter der Salzsteuerverwaltung
Salzer	Salzhändler; auch: Verkäufer von Eingesalztem
Salzfertiger	Salzspediteur
Salzführer, -kärrner	Hausierender Salzhändler
Salzfüller	Zollbeamter, der das Salz zu messen hat
Salzherr	Ratsherr, der die Oberaufsicht über das Salzhaus, das städtische Salzamt hatte; auch: Privateigner einer Saline
Salzlader, -sender	Salzfuhrmann

Salzmann, -werker	Salzsieder, auch: Salzhändler, -fuhrmann
Salzmuter, -mütter	Zollbeamter, der das Salz zu messen hat
Salzstößel	Salzhändler, Salzzerkleinerer
Sander, Sandmann	Händler von (Streu-)Sand
Sandler	Sandalenhersteller, Schuhmacher
Sargenweber, Sarge- drömacher	Verfertiger von feinem Wollgewebe, dem Sarge oder Serge de Rome
Sarwerker, -wetter, -worchter, -würchter	Plattner, Waffenschmied
Sattelhöfer	Besitzer eines Gutes, das mit besonderen Frei- heiten ausgestattet ist
Sattler	Hersteller von Lederwaren, vor allem von Sätteln und Zaumzeug
Sa(e)umer	Frachtfuhrmann mit Saumtieren; Saumtier- halter
Sauter	Schuster
Sayenmacher	Weber eines feinen Wollstoffes, der Saye, die namentlich in Brügge hergestellt wird
Schabkünstler	Schwarzkünstler, Radierer
Schacherer	Hausierer
Schachtelmacher	Hersteller von Futteralen aus Holz, Pappe oder Papier
Schachtschneider	Verfertiger von Stangen, Schaufeln, Mulden
Schaderer	Büttel
Schäffler	Faßbinder
Schäufeler	Hausierender Krämer mit Saumtier
Schaffer	Verwalter; Vorknecht; Zunftvorsteher; Ste- wart auf Kriegsschiffen
Schaffner	Verwalter, Steuereinnehmer; auch: Vertreter eines Richters oder eines Meiers
Schaidmeister	Messerschmied, der zugleich die Scheiden fer- tigt
Schalantsjude	Schacherjude, Trödeljude
Schal(a)uner, Schallaunenmacher	Hersteller der Schalaunen, ärmelloser Mäntel; aber auch Zubereiter von Wolldecken, die nach Châlons-sur-Marne genannt sind

Schalenschneider, -schro(e)der, -schröter	Hersteller von Messergriffen
Schalk	Leibeigener, Unfreier
Schappeler	Verfertiger des Schappel, eines Frauenkopfputzes
Scharnemann	Verkäufer auf einem Markt
Scharmacher	Wagenbauer, Stellmacher
Scharwächter	Nachtwächter; Ratsknecht
Scharwerker	Erbuntertäniger, der mit seiner Familie und seinen Dienstboten auf dem Gut des Landesherrn arbeitete
Schatilger	Schreiner, Tischler
Schatullwirt	Siedler, der seine Abgaben an die Privatschatulle des Landesherrn zu entrichten hatte
Schau(e)r, Schaumeister	Beamteter Tuchprüfer, Schätzer, Visierer, Taxator, Geschaumeister
Schauermann	Schiffslader, Hafenarbeiter
Scheckeler	Verfertiger gesteppter Leibröcke, der Schecken
Scheckensticker	Jacken-, Joppensticker
Scheermeister	Appreturmeister
Scheffler	Faßbinder
Scheibenreißer	Glaser
Scheibenzieher	Drahtzieher
Scheibler	Fuhrmann, der Salz in Blöcken oder Scheiben beförderte
Scheider	Chemiker, Prüfer, der den Feingehalt erprobt, „scheidet"
Scheidler	Hersteller von Messerscheiden
Scheidmesserer	Verfertiger von Taschenmessern
Schelcher	Schiffsführer, Schiffer auf einem von zwei Personen bedienten „Schelch"
Scheler	Schäler der Eichenrinde, die für die Gerblohe verwendet wurde
Schellenschläger	Spielmann, der das Glockenspiel bedient

Schelter	Spielmann, Gaukler, der gewerbsmäßig das „Schelten" gegen säumige Zahler besorgte
Schenker	Schankwirt oder Schankkellner; aber auch: Zunftmeister, der für die wandernden Gesellen seiner Zunft zu sorgen hatte
Schenkjungfer	Amme
Scheppler	Verfertiger der Schappel, eines Frauen-Kopfputzes
Scherer	Tuchscherer
Schermesserer	Hersteller von Scheren
Scheubenzieher	(Messing-)Drahtzieher
Schichtmeister	Führer einer Schicht von Bergleuten; Rechnungsbeamter
Schieder, Schiedmann, Schiedungsverwandter	Aufsichtsbeamter in einer Gemeinde über Feldwege und Eigentumsgrenzen
Schieringer	Aalfischer
Schiffknecht	Matrose, auch: Schiffsführer
Schiffmann	Besitzer und Führer eines Schiffes
Schilder(er), Schildermaker	Maler, Schildmaler
Schinder, Schinner	Abdecker; auch: Straßenräuber
Schindler	Verfertiger der Dachschindeln aus Holz
Schipper	Schiffsführer, Reeder
Schirmeister	Fechtmeister
Schirmer	Umherziehender Fechter, Festmeister
Schirrmacher	Wagenbauer
Schirrmeister	Aufseher über das Fuhrwesen beim Militär oder auf einem Gut; Beamter des Marstalls
S(ch)lachtgewanter	Tuchgroßhändler
Schleiermacher	Sticker, Wirker von Schleiern
Schlepper	Bergmann, der die gewonnenen Mineralien fortschafft
Schleuderer	Schleuderschütze
Schleußerin	Dienst-, Hausangestellte, Beschließerin

Schlichter	Textilarbeiter, der das Tuch glättet und kardet
Schließer	Vorsteher eines Kirchspiels, der — vor allem in Dithmarschen — die Aufsicht über den Kirchenkasten hatte und den Vorsitz beim Dorfgericht führte
Schlotfeger	Kaminkehrer, Schornsteinfeger
Schlüter	Rentmeister, Einnehmer der Gefälle auf Domänen; auch: Hauptpächter
Schnickmann	Eigner oder Führer eines Küstenfahrzeugs, der Schnicke
Schniddeker, Schnit(t)ker, Schnitzler	Tischler, Schreiner; gelegentlich auch: Holzschnitzer
Schnitter	Mäher
Schnorrer	Bettler
Schnu(e)rmacher	Bandwirker, Breisler, Posamentierer
Schoband	Knecht des Abdeckers
Schockenzieher	Drahtzieher an einer Schaukel
Schönefrau	Dirne
Schönfärber	Färber, der bei seiner Arbeit helle Farben verwendet
Schösser	Amtsdiener; Steuereinzieher
Schoffner	Böttcher
Scholarch	Schulpfleger, Schulvorstand
Schopenbrauer	Brauknechte ohne festes Lohnverhältnis; Lohnbraumeister
Schopenhauer	Verfertiger von Holztrögen und hölzernen Schöpfkellen
Schopper	Schiffszimmermann
Schorer, Schorlaker	Hilfsarbeiter der Woll- und Leinenweber, der den Stoff von Knötchen reinigt; regional auch: Straßenfeger
Schotte	Hausierer
Schotteler	Hersteller von Schüsseln und Tiegeln
Schout-bij-nacht	(Ursprünglich:) Führer der Nachhut einer Flotte; Niederländischer Konteradmiral
Schrader	Schneider

61

Schrannegast	Getreidehändler
Schreibemeister	Schreiblehrer
Schreiner	Tischler
Schrepfer	Barbier, Wundarzt, der „schröpft"
Schrobber	Wollbereiter
Schrobelmacher	Verfertiger von Werkzeugen für die Tuchbereitung
Schro(e)der, Schro(e)ter	Arbeiter, der zerkleinert, schrotet; Tuchschneider; Münzschneider; Böttcher; Auflader
Schürer	Kesselheizer
Schüss(e)ler	Hersteller von Schüsseln und Tiegeln
Schüttemeister	Beamter, der die Schütte, die Getreidekammer, beaufsichtigt; auch: Bürgermeister
Schüttmeister	Aufsichtsbamter über die Müllabfuhr
Schulapper, Schuwarte	Schuster
Schuldenbot	Gerichtsvollzieher, Vollstreckungsbeamter
Schuldiener	Anfangs: Schullehrer, später: Pedell
Schwabenweber	Aus Schwaben in Nürnberg eingewanderte Leinenweber
Schwärzfirm	Schwertschleifer
Schwagrin	Viehmagd, Sennerin
Schwager	Postillion
Schwaiger	Viehhirt, Senn, Käser
Schwarzbinder	Hersteller der großen Eichenholzfässer
Schwartzdrahtzieher	Hersteller von Eisendraht
Schwarzgießer	Eisengießer
Schwarzhafner	Verfertiger der sogenannten Passauer Tiegel aus Graphit für die Metallgießerei
Schwarzkünstler	Schabkünstler, Radierer; auch: Magier
Schwefeljunge	Knabe, der mit Schwefelfäden hausiert
Schwegler	Pfeifer, Flötenbläser
Schweiger	Viehhirt, Senn, Käser
Schweineschneider, -stecher	Gelzer, Tierverschneider, Kastrierer
Schweizer	Pächter oder Leiter einer Meierei

Schweizerdegen	Schriftsetzer, der auch das Drucken versteht
	Schwertkämpfer
Schwertfeger	Schwertschleifer; gelegentlich auch: Gladiator,
	Schwertkämpfer
Schwertner, Schwert-schlager	Schwert-, Waffenschmied
Seckelmeister	Kassenverwalter; Stadtrentmeister
Seckler	Seckelmeister; auch: Hersteller von Taschen und Beuteln
Sedelmeier	Verwalter eines Vorwerks, eines vom Herren-haus lokal unabhängigen, fast selbständigen Hofes
Segesenschmidt, Segisser	Sensenschmied
Segner	Führer eines kleinen Frachtschiffes für Faß-ladung auf dem Bodensee; auch: Fischer, der — im Gegensatz zum Kleinfischer — mit Net-zen fischen darf
Seidenmacher	Seidenweber
Seidenmaler, -stücker	Seidensticker, -weber, -wirker
Seidenneger	Seidenstricker
Seidler	Kuttler; auch: Inhaber eines Sattelhofes
Seifenmacher	Seifensieder
Seigermacher, -schmied	Groß-Uhrmacher, z. B. für Kirchtürme
Seigner	Großfischer (siehe Segner)
Seimer	Metsieder
Seitzweber	Weber von Kattun, Zitz
Sekretfäger, -graber	Abtrittreiniger
Selcher	Fleischer, der seine Produkte pökelt, einsalzt oder auch räuchert
Seld(n)er	Kossät, Besitzer eines Häuschens ohne Acker und Wiese, der meist Lohnarbeiter ist.
Seller	Händler, Verkäufer
Selzer	Salzhändler
Semeler, Semmler	Weißbrotbäcker

Senfer	Händler, auch Hersteller von Senf
Senker	Fischer, der das Senknetz verwendet
Senkler	Nestler, Schnürsenkelhersteller
Senn(e)	Bewirtschafter einer Alm, Viehknecht
Sensal	Makler
Sentrin	Sennerin, Viehmagd
Sergenmacher	Hersteller eines mit Leinen oder Seide gemischten feineren Wollgewebes, des Serge de Rome oder kurz Serge
Sesterer	Böttcher, Faßbinder
Seßtaler	Steuermann eines Salzschiffes; Befehlshaber eines Schifszuges
Seuner	Hochseefischer
Sibber, Sieber(er), Siebler, Siebner	Siebmacher
Siebener	Einer der (meist) sieben Feldgeschworenen einer Dorfgemeinschaft, die für die Überwachung der Gemarkungs- und Flurgrenzen zuständig waren; auch: Mitglied eines siebenköpfigen Stadtrates
Siegelgräber	Stempelschneider, Graveur
Siegelmann, Siegler	Beamteter Tuchprüfer, der nach der Schau die Stoffe mit dem Siegel versieht; Visierer; Siegelmeister
Sigillgraber	Stempelschneider, Graveur
Sigrist	Küster, Meßner, Sakristan
Silberbote	Amtsbote, so genannt wegen des silbernen Amtsabzeichens; Postbote
Simmer(macher)	Hersteller des Simmers, eines Meßgefäßes für Getreide; auch: Siebmacher
Sinner	Eichmeister
Sleiffer	Schleifer
Slune	Dirne
Smerde	Wendischer Knecht
Soder	Vereidigter Salzsieder
Söldner, Söllner	Tagelöhner; bezahlter Kriegsknecht

Sohlenmacher	Verfertiger von Holzpantoffeln
Sonnenkrämer	Händler, der seine Waren unter freiem Himmel anbietet
Sonnenuhrmacher	Hersteller von Sonnenuhren, Kompassen und Feinmeßinstrumenten
Spängler, Spengler	Klempner; aber auch: Hersteller von Geschmeide
Spanner	Auflader, Packer
Sparer	Hersteller von Sporen
Spendmeister	Armenpfleger
Spenelmacher, Spener	Stecknadelmacher
Spetter	Auflader, Packer, Spediteur, Markthelfer
Spettreiter	Lohnreiter, Bote
Spezereihändler	Drogist
Spezial	Dekan
Spiegler	Spiegelfabrikant
Spilkendreher	Spinnraddrechsler
Spillmacher	Spindelmacher
Splettstößer	Händler mit Dachschindeln
Splittgerber	Handwerker, der Splitte (Schindeln, Späne) fertigt
Spor(n)er, Sporrer	Sporenmacher
Spragmeister	Sprachlehrer, -meister, Linguist
Sprecher, Sprucher	Fahrender Vortragskünstler, Deklamator; auch: Redner einer Zunft oder Bruderschaft
Springer	Tänzer
Spulenmacher	Verfertiger von Rohrspulen für die Leinenweberei
Spu(o)ler	Textilarbeiter, der das Webgarn auf Spulen zieht
Stabhalter	Vorsitzer eines Gerichts; Ortsvorsteher; (in Württemberg:) Oberamtmann
Stacker	Anstreicher, Kleber, Tüncher
Stadtknecht	Büttel, Bote; auch Stadtschreiber
Staffhauer	Stabholzhauer
Staffirmaler	Tüncher, Weißbinder

Staheler	Armbrustmacher; Aussteller, Händler auf einer Messe
Stahlschütze	Armbrustschütze
Stampfer	Papierhersteller, der das Papier Papier mit dem Hammer glättet
Stationier(er)	Kleinhändler; auch: Apotheker
Statthalter	Stellvertreter; Vogt; Gutsaufseher; Vorknecht
Statzauner	Apotheker
Stauer	Unternehmer, der das Laden und Löschen von Seeschiffen besorgt
Staufer	Böttcher, Becher-, Humpenmacher
Stavener	Landwirt, Bauer
Staynmetz(er)	Steinhauer
Stecher	Radierer, Kupfer- oder Eisenstecher (für Druckwerke)
Steckenknecht	Gehilfe des Profoß
Stefftenmacher	Bleistiftmacher
Stegr(a)iffer	Steigbügelschmied
Steiger	Aufsichtsbeamter im Bergbau
Steinbrech(er)	Arbeiter in einem Steinbruch
Steinbrücker	Pflasterer, Steinsetzer, Brückenbauer
Steindecker	Schiefer-, Ziegeldachdecker
Steindreger	Steinträger
Steiner	Pflasterer, Wegebauer
Steinfischer	Fischer, der Steine zu Bauzwecken aus dem Meer gewinnt; auch: Bernsteinfischer
Steinhändler	Juwelier, Edelsteinhändler
Steinhauer	Steinbrucharbeiter, Steinmetz
Steinschneider	Graveur; Edelsteinschleifer; auch: Arbeiter, der Steinblöcke in Platten zerlegt
Steinsetzer	Pflasterer, Wegebauer
Steinwirker	Steinmetz
Stellenbesitzer	Bauer, Landwirt
Stellmacher	Wagenbauer, Wagner
Sterzer, Stör(t)zer	Landstreicher, Vagabund
Sterzermeister	Bettelvogt einer Stadt

Stetrichter	Richter, der dauernd im Amt ist, der nicht immer neu als Richter berufen wird
Steyger	Steiger, leitender Bergmann
Stieber	Besitzer einer Badestube; Bader; Barbier
Stillständer	Kirchenältester
Stockfrau	Dirne, die beim Büttel wohnt
Stockmeister	Gehilfe des Profoß
Stöcker	Büttel, Ratsknecht
Stöllner	Bergwerksbesitzer, Inhaber des Stollen
Störer, Störarbeiter	Umherziehender Lohnhandwerker, der keiner Zunft angehört; Stümper, Bönhase
Störzer	Landstreicher, Vagabund
Stößer	Händler
Stöver	Besitzer einer Badestube, Bader, Barbier
Storger	Marktschreier, Jahrmarktshändler
Stoßer	Salzhändler, Salzzerkleinerer
Strähler	Wollkämmer
Strählmacher	früher: Kammacher später: Kardetschenmacher
Straßenführer	Fuhrmann
Strident	Ausrufer
Strimpfstricker	Strumpfwirker
Strohschnitter	Wanderarbeiter, der gegen Lohn Häcksel schneidet
Stromer	Landstreicher, Vagabund
Stubenmeister	Vorsteher der Zünfte und Gesellschaften einer Stadt
Stu(c)kator	Stukkateur, Stuckarbeiter
Stu(e)ckhauptmann	Artillerie-Offizier
Stuckknecht	Gehilfe bei der sogenannten französischen Jagd
Stuckreiber	Stukkateur, Stuckmaler
Stüb(n)er	Besitzer einer Badestube, Bader, Barbier
Stückgießer	Geschützgießer, Kanonengießer
Stückknecht	Geschützbediener, Artillerist
Stückweber	Lodenweber

Stülpner	Hersteller von Sturmhauben und Helmen
Stünschenmacher	Böttcher kleiner Gefäße
Stürzner	Klempner
Stuhlgesell	Schöffe, Ratsherr
Stuhlherr	Gerichtsherr, Ratsvorsitzender
Stuhlmacher, englischer	Hersteller englischer Webstühle
Stuhlrichter	Vorsitzer des Femegerichts, Inhaber eines Freistuhls; (in Siebenbürgen:) Richter eines Amtsbezirks
Stuhlschreiber	Gerichtsschreiber; öffentlicher Lohnschreiber
Stu(h)ler	Hersteller von Stühlen
Sudler	Garkoch; Kuttler; Verkäufer warmer Wurst
Sülfmeister	Besitzer einer Pfanne in der Saline
Süßküchler	Konditor
Sulengießer	Arbeiter in einer Saline
Sulzer, Sulzmacher, Sülzer	Salzsieder; Hersteller von Sülze; Wämstler; auch: Gefängniswärter
Supan	Wendischer Gauvorsteher
Swän	Schweinehirt
Sydennäer	Seidenweber, Seidenwirker
Symphoniker	Orchestermusiker; auch: Komponist

T

Tabagist	Schankwirt
Tabakplanteur	Tabakbauer
Tabakspinner	Arbeiter, der die Tabakblätter auf Schnüre aufzieht
Tabulettkrämer, Tafelitter	Hausierer, Trödler
Tändler	Trödler
Tä(u)schler	Hersteller von Taschen und Beuteln
Täucher	Taucher
Tafeldecker	Herrichter der Speisetafel
Tafelmacher	Tischler; Hersteller von Brettspielen
Tafelschneider	Steinschneider von Halbedelsteinen für Dosen und Galanteriewaren
Taferner	Schankwirt
Tagner, Tagwerker	Tagelöhner
Tagneter	Trödler, Althändler
Taillierer	Hausierer
Talemann	Gemeindesprecher, Sprecher
Tallierer	Schnittwarenhändler
Tambour	Trommler
Tandler	Trödler, Altwarenhändler
Tapetenweber	Teppichwirker
Ta(e)schner	Hersteller von Taschen und Beuteln
Tauber	Tubabläser
Taumacher	Seiler
Taverner	Schankwirt
Tegeler	Ziegelbrenner
Teichelbohrer	Hersteller von Holz- und Brunnenröhren
Teigelbäcker	Ziegelformer, -brenner
Tellrer	Schnittwarenhändler
Tendeler	Trödler, Althändler
Teuker	Verfertiger hölzerner Wasserleitungsrohre
Theriakskrämer	Salben- und Balsamhändler; auch: Quacksalber

Thorner	Verfertiger von Haustüren
Tigerer	Kundenwerber (Schlepper, Anreißer) im Pforzheimer Bijouteriehandel
Tischer	Schreiner, Tischler
Tolk	Dolmetscher im Deutschen Orden
Topfstricker	Umherziehender Handwerker, der gesprungene Töpfe und Glasgefäße mit Draht umbindet: Topfflicker
Toppeler	Würfelschneider, auch: Würfelspieler
Torftreter	Preßtorferzeuger
Torzöller	Zollbeamter am Stadttor
Trändler	Händler
Träx(e)l	Drechsler
Tragantkünstler	Arbeiter, der Figuren aus Tragant, aus Zukkermasse bildet
Tragantdockenmacher	Hersteller von Zuckerpuppen
Traguner	Dragoner
Trapier	Großgebietiger des Deutschen Ordens, dem das Bekleidungswesen unterstand
Traubenweber	Weber einer besonderen Tuchart
Treßler	Großgebietiger des Deutschen Ordens, dem das Finanzwesen unterstand
Trippenmacher	Hersteller von Holzschuhen
Trippmacher	Weber von Trippsamt, einem Leinengewebe mit Wollflor
Tromter	Trompeter
Troner	Gauner, Betrüger; Bettler
Tropfhäusler	Kleinstbauer; Besitzer oder Mieter eines Häuschens
Trottmeister	Aufsichtsbeamter für die bei der Weinbereitung notwendigen Arbeiten; Kelleraufseher
Truchseß	Küchenmeister; Oberaufseher über den landesherrlichen Haushalt
Truck(h)enlader	Verlader und Beförderer trockener Kaufmannsgüter
Trumetter, Trumpter	Trompeter

70

Trummenmacher	Hersteller von Trommeln und Pauken
Tschismenmacher	Hersteller der ungarischen hohen Frauenstiefel, meist aus Juchtenleder
Tuchbereider, -braiter, -glätter, -schlichter	Tuchmacher, auch Tuchwalker
Tucher	Tuchweber, Tuchhändler
Tuchermatrose	Matrose eines Fischerbootes, der die Netze schleppt
Tuchknappe	Nichtselbständiger Tuchmacher
Tübler	Zimmermann, der die Balken mit Dübeln verbindet
Tüffelmacher, Tüffenmacher	Hersteller von Pantoffeln
Tüncher	Anstreicher, Weißbinder
Türkischpapiermacher	Hersteller von Buntpapier
Türmer, Turner	Turmwächter
Türwärter	Torwächter; Ratsschreiber; Gehilfe des Stadtschreibers
Tuggermatrose	Matrose eines Fischerbootes, der die Netze schleppt
Tunderkerl	Sammler von Zunderschwamm; Zunderhändler
Turmvater	Eisenmeister, Kerkermeister

U

Uhrblätterstecher	Hersteller von Zifferblättern
Ulenbecker, Ulner	Töpfer
Umbitter	Hochzeitsbitter
Umgelder	Steuereinnehmer, Steuerherr
Umsesse	Nachbar
Ungargerber, Ungarischlederer	Weißgerber, Hersteller von Juchten-, Ungarischleder
Ungelder, Ungeldherr	Steuereinnehmer, Steuerherr, der das Ungeld, eine der späteren Akzise entsprechende Steuer, erhebt und verwaltet; Faßeicher
Unhold	Ausmärker
Unzüchter	Ratsherr, der Polizeivergehen, also „Unzucht" (Unrecht) aburteilte
Unterverkäufler	Makler

V

Venner	Fähnrich; Bannerträger, z. B. eines Stadt-viertels
Verber	Färber
Verganter	Auktionator, Versteigerer
Verheyler	Gelzer, Tierbeschneider, Kastrierer
Verleger	Großhändler, der die von ihm gekauften Pro-dukte durch Heimarbeiter verarbeiten läßt; auch: Bevollmächtigter eines Gewerken, der in der Nähe der Zeche wohnt
Verler	Schweinehändler
Verwandter	Mitglied, Angehöriger, Beisitzer einer Ge-meinschaft
Vexierschlosser	Malschlosser
Vichhandler	Viehhändler
Vierdrahtmacher	Tuchweber, der vierdrähtiges Garn verwendet
Viererweber	Weber einer besonderer Tuchart
Vierhüfner	Großbauer mit vier Hufen Bsitz
Vischer	Fischer
Visierer, Visitator	Beschaumeister, Eichmeister
Viterfechter	Öffentlicher Fechter aus der Bruderschaft des hl. Vitus
Vitztum, Vizedom	Statthalter; erster Beisitzer bei Gerichten; Ver-walter bischöflicher Güter; Rentmeister; auch: Finanzbeamter
Vivandierer	Marketender
Vog(e)ler	Vogelfänger, -händler, -steller, -waidmann
Vogt	Anwalt; Statthalter; Aufseher; Richter; Ge-meindevorsteher
Vollerbe, -höfner, -spänner	Vollbürger, Großbauer
Voltisierer	Kunstfechter
Vordantzer	Vortänzer, etwa auf einer Hochzeit
Vorgeher	Vorsteher einer Zunft

W

Wachsbossierer, -poussierer	Wachsbildner, -former
Wägleinmacher	Wagenbauer; auch: Hersteller von Waagen
Wämstler	Sulzer, Wenster
Wag(e)meister	Wiegemeister, Beamter an einer öffentlichen Waage; auch: Zweiter Bürgermeister
Wagenführer, -mann	Kutscher
Wagenknecht	Gehilfe des städtischen Wiegemeisters
Wagner	Wagenbauer, -schmied
Waibel	Büttel, Ratsgehilfe, Fronbote
Waidfärber, -gießer	Blaufärber, Färber mit Waid
Waidgast	Waidhändler
Waidmann	Jäger
Waidmesser, -schätzer	Beamter der Wollweber, der den Waidverkauf überwachte
Waidmüller	Müller, der Färberwaid bereitet
Waidner	Blaufärber
Waldreiter	Gendarm, dem die Forstaufsicht zusteht
Walker, Wal(k)müller	Tuchwalker
Walkmeister	Hammerschmied
Wandbereiter	Tuchmacher, der das Tuch glättet und kardet
Wandrahmmacher	Hersteller von Rahmen zum Spannen des Tuches
Wand-, Wantscherer, -schneider, -snider, -s(ch)leifer	Tuchhändler, Gewandschneider, Tucher
Wanner	Wannenmacher
War(a)dein	Geschaumeister, Visierer, Schauer, beamteter Prüfer; Münzmeister
Wasenmeister	Schinder, Abdecker
Wasserschout	Vorsteher des Seemannsamtes
Wasserwieger	Wassermüller als Mitglied des Reichswassergerichts in der Wetterau
Wasserzieher	Versorger der Haushaltungen mit Wasser

Watmanger, Waytmenger	Tuchhändler
Wattmann	Tuchgroßhändler, Tuchherr
Wechselherr	Bankherr
Wechselsensal	Geldmakler, Wechsler
Weckwieger	Aufseher der Bäckerzunft; Brotprüfer
Weddeherr	Jüngster Hamburger Senator, dem die Verwaltung der „Walddörfer" oblag
Weddeschreiber	Städtischer Kämmereischreiber
Wedeler, Wedelmacher	Hersteller von Weihewedeln für kirchliche Zwecke; auch: Bürstenbinder
Wegesetzer	Pflasterer, Wegebauer, Steinsetzer
Wehener	Wagenbauer, Wagner
Weidfärber, -gießer	Blaufärber
Weinbleicher	Weinverfälscher, Weinpanscher
Weinführer	Weinwirt, Weinschenk
Weinhecker	Kleinhändler mit Wein; Weinschenk
Weinherr	Weingroßhändler
Weinkaufsmann	Weinmakler, -vermittler; -sachverständiger
Weinknecht	Zapfer; auch: Ungeldherr (siehe dort)
Weinmann	Winzer, Weinwirt
Weinmesser	Weinprüfer; Eichmeister für Weinfässer
Weinrufer	Behördlicher Ausrufer, der die öffentliche Ausschankverkündung vornahm
Weinschenker	Ausschenker selbstgezogenen Weines
Weinschneider	Winzer, Weinlese-Arbeiter
Weinschröter	Weinverlader
Weinsticher	Weinprüfer, -makler
Weinvisierer	Eichbeamter zum Messen der Weinfässer
Weinzierl	Winzer
Weißbinder, -bitner, -büttner	Anstreicher, Tüncher, Stubenmaler; Böttcher, Faßbinder für kleine Gefäße
Weißdreher	Porzellanarbeiter
Weißfrau	Hebamme
Weißkircher, -maler	Weißgerber, Sämischgerber

Weißmacher	Fertiger von Nähpulten und Kästchen aus weißem Holz, z. B. Birke oder Ahorn, für die Wismutmaler
Weißsieder	Arbeiter in der Münze, der die Schrötlinge oder Rohlinge reinigt
Wendenmacher	Hersteller von Winden, Spindeln u. dgl.
Wendschlächter	Schlachter, Knochenhauer
Weneverdinger	Spediteur, Güterbestätter
Wenster	Sülzer, Wämstler, Verkäufer von Wellfleisch, Lohnschlächter
Werber	Werbeoffizier
Werghändler	Flachshändler
Wetzer	Schleifer
Wetzgermacher	Hersteller von Rucksäcken, Felleisen
Weydmann	Jäger
Weyner	Wagenbauer, Wagner
Wiedemutpächter	Pächter eines Pfarrgutes
Wildenhirte	Pferdehirt; Stutenmeister
Wildfang	Eingewanderter Fremder, der vom Landesherrn wie ein Leibeigener behandelt werden durfte
Wildheuer	Grasmäher in den Hochalpen
Wildhirt	Wildhüter, Pferdehirt
Wildkehrer	Feldhüter, der das Wild von den Äckern fernzuhalten hatte
Wildnisbereiter, -bereuter	Unterer Forstbeamter
Wildpretführer	Jagdgehilfe, der für den Abtransport der Jagdbeute verantwortlich war
Wildrufdrechsler, -macher	Hersteller von Blasinstrumenten zum Anlokken des Wildes
Wildschütz	Jäger, auch: Wilderer
Wildwerker	Kürschner
Windener	Hersteller von Winden, Spindeln u. dergl.
Windhitzer	Abrichter der Windhunde; Jäger, der mit Windhunden hetzt

Winkelierer, Winkel-krämer, Winkler	Kaufbudeninhaber, Ladenbesitzer
Wipper	Münzverfälscher
Wirker	Töpfer; auch: Textilarbeiter
Wirt	Bauer, Landwirt; auch: Gastwirt
Wirtschafter	Verwalter, z. B. eines Gutes
Wißler	Anstreicher, Tüncher
Wit(h)ing	Nichtdeutscher Bediensteter des Deutschen Ordens
Witjas	Wendischer Ortsrichter
Witmenger	Holzhändler
Wobber	Weber von grauem Wolltuch
Wollbereiter, -krämp(ler)	Wollkämmer
Wollner	Bereiter der Wolle zum Weben
Wollschläger	Reiniger der Wolle
Worfeler	Toppeler, Würfelmacher, -spieler
Worthalter	Vorsteher der Bürgerschaft oder der Gesellenbruderschaft
Wrö(c)herr	Allmendherr; Mitglied des Feldgerichts; Ältester der Ackergilde
Wurfeler	Toppeler, Würfelschneider, -spieler
Wurst(l)er	Wurstmetzger
Wurzler, Wurzmann	Gewürzkrämer, Händler mit Spezerei

Y

Yngwünner	Steuereinnehmer

Z

Zachweber	Tuch- oder Zeugweber
Zahlmeister	Beamter, der für die Finanzen und die Besoldung zuständig ist
Zainer	Korbflechter; auch: Zainschmied
Zainschmied	Schmied von Stabeisen, Hammerschmied
Zapf(f)enmacher, -ledermacher, Zappenmader	Hersteller von Zapfen und Röhren
Zau(e)r	Tuchmacher
Zaumschläger	Verfertiger von Zaumzeug
Zeichenmeister	Eichmeister, Wardein
Zeidler	Bienenzüchter, Imker
Zeiner	Korbflechter; auch: Stabeisen-, Hammerschmied
Zein(hammer)schmied	Stabeisen-, Hammerschmied
Zeitungssinger	Bänkelsänger
Zeller	Vollbauer, Großbauer
Zender, Zenner	Dorfschultheiß, Dorfrichter; Erheber des Zehnt; Vorsteher einer Hontschaft
Zengener	Zangenschmied
Zerrenner	Arbeiter an der Eisenschmelze
Zerrner	Hammerschmied
Zeuchwirker	Weber von Bettzeug
Zeugschmied	Hersteller, Schmied für Handwerkszeug
Zeugwahrter	Tuchprüfer
Zeugwart	Verwalter des Zeughauses, des Arsenals
Ziechner	Bettlakenweber
Ziegerer	Hersteller von (Ziegen-)Käse
Ziegler	Ziegelstreicher, -brenner
Ziengieser	Zinngießer, Kannengießer
Ziesemeister	Erheber der Akzise, der indirekten Steuer
Zigensmit	Hammer-, Zainschmied
Zimmerchrist	Zimmermann

Zimmerhäuer	Bergmann, der die Auszimmerung der Bergwerkstollen vornimmt
Zimmermaler	Tüncher, Anstreicher, Weißmaler
Zindeler	Verfertiger des Zindel, einer Taftart
Zinkenist, Zinkenblaser, -bleser	Spielmann
Zinner	Zinngießer, Kannengießer, Verzinner
Zinsmeister	Steuereinnehmer, Unterbeamter des Meiers
Zinsnehmer	Wucherer
Zirkelschmied	Feinmechaniker
Zitzweber	Weber von Seitz, einer Art Kattun
Zöwerer	Tuch- oder Zeugweber
Zoller, Zollheber	Zollbeamter, Zöllner
Zollgegenschreiber	Unterer Zollbeamter
Zopfmacher	Hersteller bunter geflochtener Stränge; auch: Perückenmacher
Zuchtmeister	Eisenmeister; Erzieher
Zuckerbacher	Konditor, Zuckerbäcker
Züchner	Weber des Ziechen, der Bettlaken
Zünfter, Zünftiger	Angehöriger einer Zunft
Zundelmacher	Verarbeiter des Zunders, des Zündschwamms
Zunftpfleger	Schatzmeister einer Zunft
Zunftvorgeher	Zunftmeister, Ammann
Zusteller	Kossät, Käthner
Zweihüfner	Bauer mit zwei Hufen Besitz
Zwillichmacher	Weber des Zwillich
Zwirner	Hersteller von Garn